Social Anxiety

by Laura Johnson, MA, MBA, LMFT, LPCC

for dummies®

A Wiley Brand

Social Anxiety For Dummies®

Published by: **John Wiley & Sons, Inc.**, 111 River Street, Hoboken, NJ 07030-5774, www.wiley.com

Copyright © 2025 by John Wiley & Sons, Inc. All rights reserved, including rights for text and data mining and training of artificial technologies or similar technologies.

Media and software compilation copyright © 2025 by John Wiley & Sons, Inc. All rights reserved, including rights for text and data mining and training of artificial technologies or similar technologies.

Published simultaneously in Canada

No part of this publication may be reproduced, stored in a retrieval system or transmitted in any form or by any means, electronic, mechanical, photocopying, recording, scanning or otherwise, except as permitted under Sections 107 or 108 of the 1976 United States Copyright Act, without the prior written permission of the Publisher. Requests to the Publisher for permission should be addressed to the Permissions Department, John Wiley & Sons, Inc., 111 River Street, Hoboken, NJ 07030, (201) 748-6011, fax (201) 748-6008, or online at http://www.wiley.com/go/permissions.

Trademarks: Wiley, For Dummies, the Dummies Man logo, Dummies.com, Making Everything Easier, and related trade dress are trademarks or registered trademarks of John Wiley & Sons, Inc. and may not be used without written permission. All other trademarks are the property of their respective owners. John Wiley & Sons, Inc. is not associated with any product or vendor mentioned in this book.

LIMIT OF LIABILITY/DISCLAIMER OF WARRANTY: THE CONTENTS OF THIS WORK ARE INTENDED TO FURTHER GENERAL SCIENTIFIC RESEARCH, UNDERSTANDING, AND DISCUSSION ONLY AND ARE NOT INTENDED AND SHOULD NOT BE RELIED UPON AS RECOMMENDING OR PROMOTING A SPECIFIC METHOD, DIAGNOSIS, OR TREATMENT BY PHYSICIANS FOR ANY PARTICULAR PATIENT. THE PUBLISHER AND THE AUTHOR MAKE NO REPRESENTATIONS OR WARRANTIES WITH RESPECT TO THE ACCURACY OR COMPLETENESS OF THE CONTENTS OF THIS WORK AND SPECIFICALLY DISCLAIM ALL WARRANTIES, INCLUDING WITHOUT LIMITATION ANY IMPLIED WARRANTIES OF FITNESS FOR A PARTICULAR PURPOSE. IN VIEW OF ONGOING RESEARCH, EQUIPMENT MODIFICATIONS, CHANGES IN GOVERNMENTAL REGULATIONS, AND THE CONSTANT FLOW OF INFORMATION RELATING TO THE USE OF MEDICINES, EQUIPMENT, AND DEVICES, THE READER IS URGED TO REVIEW AND EVALUATE THE INFORMATION PROVIDED IN THE PACKAGE INSERT OR INSTRUCTIONS FOR EACH MEDICINE, EQUIPMENT, OR DEVICE FOR, AMONG OTHER THINGS, ANY CHANGES IN THE INSTRUCTIONS OR INDICATION OF USAGE AND FOR ADDED WARNINGS AND PRECAUTIONS. READERS SHOULD CONSULT WITH A SPECIALIST WHERE APPROPRIATE. NO WARRANTY MAY BE CREATED OR EXTENDED BY ANY PROMOTIONAL STATEMENTS. NEITHER THE PUBLISHER NOR THE AUTHOR SHALL BE LIABLE FOR ANY DAMAGES ARISING HEREFROM.

For general information on our other products and services, please contact our Customer Care Department within the U.S. at 877-762-2974, outside the U.S. at 317-572-3993, or fax 317-572-4002. For technical support, please visit https://hub.wiley.com/community/support/dummies.

Wiley publishes in a variety of print and electronic formats and by print-on-demand. Some material included with standard print versions of this book may not be included in e-books or in print-on-demand. If this book refers to media that is not included in the version you purchased, you may download this material at http://booksupport.wiley.com. For more information about Wiley products, visit www.wiley.com.

Library of Congress Control Number is available from the publisher.

ISBN 978-1-394-23693-0 (pbk); ISBN 978-1-394-23694-7 (ebk); ISBN 978-1-394-23695-4 (ebk)

SKY10096034_011025

Contents at a Glance

Table of Contents

Introduction

What do you have in common with Adele, Julia Roberts, Naomi Osaka, and Warren Buffett? You guessed it. They are some of the most famous people in the world, yet they all have spoken out about having experienced some form of social anxiety. I hope this shows you that you are not alone in having social anxiety. Social anxiety is so common that in any given year, millions of people are diagnosed with it. That doesn't even include the many more people who have a low level of social anxiety that don't show up in the numbers.

Social anxiety affects the way you think and feel about yourself. You may worry that if you show symptoms of anxiety, you could be negatively evaluated, humiliated, or embarrassed and seen as being socially awkward. Social anxiety generally shows up in childhood and the teenage years. For some people, but not everyone, it can lead to lowered self-esteem, social isolation, loneliness, and depression.

If you avoid situations that cause you to feel socially anxious, you'll never learn that you can handle those situations. Your anxiety becomes a vicious cycle. Every time you avoid people and situations that make you feel anxious, the cycle of social anxiety begins again. The good news is that your ability to cope with social anxiety can be improved, and you can even overcome your anxiety if you change your thinking and face your fears.

You no longer need to be scared or self-conscious about having social anxiety or think that there's something wrong with you. I believe people with social anxiety are the kindest and most compassionate people. Tackling social anxiety involves extending your kindness and compassion toward yourself.

About This Book

Congratulations! By picking up this book, you're embarking on a journey of self-improvement. Overcoming social anxiety is challenging. If you are looking for an easy-to-use book to tackle your social anxiety on your own, you're in the right place.

For Dummies books are unique. They are simple-to-use books that mostly avoid technical jargon. In this book, I include a lot of bite-size nuggets of information so that you don't have to wade through stuff that's not relevant to you. I cover many topics about social anxiety and offer tips and ideas on how to help yourself. There's a lot of information and places to write. In this book, you will find information on

>> Understanding the basics of social anxiety, such as how to spot it, where it comes from, the types of social anxiety, and what keeps it alive

>> Pinpointing some of your thinking traps and core beliefs

>> Discovering ways to get motivated to change

>> Using thinking strategies to change your self-talk

>> Doing exposures and staying in a learning mode as you face your fears

>> Applying the strategies for dealing with social anxiety in a general way as well as with special topics like public speaking, dating, in the workplace, and with children

You will also find many case examples that illustrate different types of social anxiety. If you don't see yourself in one of the examples, you may in another one. Just so you know, the people I talk about in the case examples are composites and not actual people. I do not include any identifiable information so privacy and confidentiality are protected. Any resemblance to a person, dead or alive, is purely coincidental.

This book may not be your final destination on your journey to overcoming social anxiety, but I hope it's a good first step.

Foolish Assumptions

In writing this book, I have made some assumptions about you, the reader:

>> You are smart! You are not a dummy. The word "dummy" just means this is a simple-to-use book written in everyday English.

>> Millions of people like you have social anxiety. You are not alone!

>> You'd like to start with a self-help approach. You probably have some social anxiety and you'd like to see if you can tackle it on your own first.

>> You may be a doctor or therapist looking to learn more about social anxiety for your patients.

>> You may be reading this book for some tips to help someone else. It could be your child, another relative, a friend, or a partner.

No matter who you are, this book can help you.

Icons Used in This Book

Throughout this book, icons in the margins highlight certain types of valuable information that call out for your attention. Here are the icons you'll encounter and a brief description of each.

The Tip icon highlights practical advice for putting strategies into action.

The Remember icon is important information to take note of to help you overcome your social anxiety.

The Technical Stuff icon marks interesting but not essential information, so it's fine if you want to skip over it.

WARNING

The Warning icon tells you to watch out for traps that might make your social anxiety worse.

EXPERIMENT

The Experiment icon represents something you can try out in real life to see what happens and what you learn.

CASE
EXAMPLE

The Case Example icon highlights examples of hypothetical people with social anxiety and how they are using the steps in this book.

Beyond the Book

Check out this book's online Cheat Sheet for even more tips on tackling your social anxiety. Just go to www.dummies.com and search for "Social Anxiety For Dummies Cheat Sheet." The Cheat Sheet has a few helpful tips from this book. It's okay to cheat sometimes. (Don't tell anyone I said that!)

Where to Go from Here

I expect that by reading this book, you'll gain a better understanding of social anxiety and be able to complete many self-help techniques on your own. There are many exercises and reflection areas to write so be sure to have a pencil or pen ready. I hope you find this book interesting, simple, and at times, fun to read.

This book is not meant to be read in order from start to finish. Feel free to jump around. Be sure not to miss a couple of critical chapters: Chapter 10, "Changing Your Self Talk," and Chapter 11, "Facing Your Fears." These chapters discuss the heart of tackling social anxiety.

If your social anxiety is severe or you have co-occurring depression or substance abuse, you should also seek out a therapist. In Chapter 15, you'll find suggestions about how to find one.

1

Getting Started with Social Anxiety

Discover what social anxiety is, some of the common fears and beliefs around social anxiety, and how the cycle of social anxiety works.

Explore the core features of social anxiety and what criteria are used to make a formal diagnosis of social anxiety disorder.

Find out where social anxiety comes from and how it develops.

Look at the many ways social anxiety may show up and review examples of common situations that may trigger negative thoughts, uncomfortable feelings, and safety and avoidant behaviors.

Explore the cycle of social anxiety and discover how negative thoughts and core beliefs lead to feelings of social anxiety and unhelpful reactions.

Chapter 1

Understanding Social Anxiety

Welcome to the beginning of your journey of self-discovery! You may be here because everyday social interactions cause you to have feelings of excessive fear, self-consciousness, or embarrassment. You may worry about being judged by others. Your social anxiety may often lead you to feel less than others as well as negatively evaluate yourself. When you are feeling socially anxious, you experience painful emotions, and you likely want to increase your sense of self-worth and feel better about yourself.

This book can help you gain knowledge about social anxiety and provide you with tips and strategies to handle it. In this chapter, you start your journey by discovering what social anxiety is, some of the common fears and beliefs around social anxiety, and how the cycle of social anxiety works. Are you ready? Let's get started.

What Is Social Anxiety?

Social anxiety is more than just shyness. It's an intense, persistent, and irrational fear of social situations that's out of proportion to the actual threat. If you have social anxiety, you may worry that if you show signs of anxiety that others can see, you will be negatively evaluated, humiliated, or embarrassed. You may fear that your actions or symptoms will lead to rejection or offending others. Because of this, you may avoid social situations altogether or participate with dread and fear. You may use any number of subtle safety behaviors, such as staying quiet, minimizing eye contact, or drinking alcohol to get through a social situation, to name just a few.

Social anxiety can cause significant distress and greatly impact how you function in life, affecting your social, work, and family life. You may feel lonely because you avoid opportunities to socialize and don't have many friends. You may perform below your capabilities at work and lose out on promotions. Or you may hold your kids back because you get nervous talking to other parents at your children's sporting events or after-school activities.

Following are common components of social anxiety:

>> Fearing judgment and humiliation

>> Worrying about what others are thinking about you

>> Being self-conscious and not showing emotions

>> Feeling socially awkward

>> Being sensitive to criticism

>> Avoiding people and situations

Signs You May Have Social Anxiety

Social anxiety shows up in many ways. You may feel self-conscious, fear being judged, worry about and avoid social situations, criticize yourself, mind read what others think of you, or jump to the worst-case scenario. Following are common ways social anxiety may show up for you:

>> **Self-talk:** You engage in negative self-talk, such as "I'm socially awkward." "I'm stupid." "No one likes me." "I'm unattractive." "Everyone thinks I am weird." "If everyone doesn't like me, there must be something wrong with me." "If others see signs of my anxiety, they will look down on me."

>> **Behavior:** You avoid social interactions, have difficulty making friends, be alone too often, have trouble making eye contact, speaking in social situations, or try to hide signs of anxiety from others.

>> **Feelings:** You feel anxious, worried, lonely, shame, guilt, fear, embarrassment, and many other negative emotions at times.

>> **Physical:** You react in a physical way by blushing, having a headache, feeling dizzy, trembling, shaking, feeling lightheaded, sweating, having a stomach ache, feeling nauseated, vomiting, or having body aches.

See Chapter 2 for more about the core features of social anxiety.

The ABCs of Social Anxiety

TIP

A simple way to notice and change the pattern of social anxiety is to remember your ABCs. Here's what the ABCs of social anxiety stand for:

>> **Activating event:** The trigger that throws you into a downward spiral and leads to *thinking traps,* or negative thinking patterns (for more on thinking traps, see Chapter 7).

>> **Beliefs:** Your thoughts about yourself and others, including your negative self-talk. These beliefs may be conscious or unconscious.

>> **Consequences:** What happens after the triggering event. The consequences include your negative emotions, behaviors like rumination or avoidance, or physical sensations.

You have the most influence in changing B — your beliefs and self-talk. Chapter 8 explores how to identify your core beliefs, and Chapter 10 discusses how to change your self-talk. In Chapter 11, you discover how facing your fears can help you create new beliefs to help you overcome your social anxiety.

Common Social Anxiety Fears

Many fears are associated with social anxiety. The central fear of social anxiety is the fear of judgment, and some people also experience anxiety about having anxiety. Following are some of the most common fears associated with social anxiety:

>> **Fear of judgment:** You worry excessively about what others are thinking of you and whether you are accepted and fit in. You mind read about what people may be thinking about you before, during, and/or after social situations.

>> **Fear that people will see your anxiety:** You worry that others will see that you are anxious and will look down on you. For example, you may feel self-conscious about blushing, having shaky hands, your voice trembling, or stuttering. You think other people will view you as weak or inferior if you look anxious to them.

>> **Fear of criticism:** You feel especially sensitive when others give you feedback. You may dread getting report cards or performance reviews. You worry about being evaluated as less than or worse than what you think you are or would like to be.

>> **Fear of appearing foolish in front of others:** You worry that you will do something that will make you look foolish. You avoid taking risks and revealing your true self because it could result in embarrassment.

>> **Fear of making mistakes:** You are a perfectionist and think you should never make mistakes. You are often in performance mode and think you will be judged if you make mistakes. You often avoid situations where you feel you won't succeed.

>> **Fear of uncertainty:** You have anxiety around unpredictable situations. You worry that unexpected things could happen in social situations and that you won't know how to handle them or that your mind will go blank.

>> **Fear of feeling anxious:** You worry that you will have uncomfortable sensations in your mind or body that will be intolerable. You may have anxiety sensitivity and avoid situations that trigger anxious feelings.

Common Social Anxiety Beliefs

People with social anxiety often share common beliefs about themselves and others — and about social anxiety in general. Table 1-1 lists many common beliefs. You can find a longer list in Chapter 8.

TABLE 1-1 Common Social Anxiety Beliefs

About Yourself	About Others	About Social Anxiety
I'm boring.	People are critical and judgmental.	Social anxiety is bad or embarrassing.
I'm inferior.		
I'm socially awkward.	Others look down on people with social anxiety.	Feeling social anxiety is intolerable.
I'm uninteresting.	People will notice if I am anxious or have a panic attack and think I'm weak.	Feeling anxious is dangerous.
I don't fit in or belong.		
I'm unattractive or ugly.	Others do not like quiet people.	I must never have social anxiety.

Staying on the Social Anxiety Treadmill

Social anxiety sticks around because you imagine a high perceived threat and have low confidence in coping with that threat. The avoidance and safety behaviors you use interfere with the learning process. You never get to know whether the danger isn't real or not as risky as you think and that you can cope with it.

Following is an outline of the cycle of anxiety and how it can keep you stuck on the social anxiety treadmill. You can read more about the social anxiety cycle in Chapter 5.

>> **Situation:** Something makes you feel uncomfortable or vulnerable.

>> **Core beliefs:** Conscious or unconscious negative beliefs simmer up.

>> **Unbalanced scale:** Fear increases as you overestimate the risks of social interactions while having low confidence in your ability to cope.

>> **Social anxiety mode:** You start to have anxious thoughts, feelings, and bodily sensations. You imagine the worst-case scenario, and you practice safety behaviors, including avoidance.

>> **Repeat:** Your negative core beliefs don't change, and the cycle starts again with another situation.

Protecting Yourself from Social Anxiety

Avoidance and engaging in safety behaviors are common ways you may try to protect yourself from the fear of judgment or experiencing anxiety.

Avoidance

When you avoid situations, you never learn that you can handle them. Avoidance is simply not doing the things that expose you to social risks. You may avoid parties, making phone calls, going to family reunions, going on dates, getting a job, and more. You are missing out on life when you avoid.

Safety behaviors

Safety behaviors are the subtle actions you do to try to reduce anxiety in social situations. Safety behaviors include avoiding eye contact, staying quiet in groups or talking excessively, drinking alcohol, not sharing your feelings or opinions, speaking softly, crossing your arms, over-preparing, and more. See Chapter 6 for more about identifying safety behaviors.

Making a Roadmap for Change

The two most important steps you can take to handle your social anxiety are working on your self-talk and facing your fears.

Changing your self-talk

The first most important step you can take to handle your social anxiety is engaging in effective self-talk. Effective self-talk involves being compassionate, accepting, logical, and motivating. In this book, I call this *CALM thinking*:

>> **Compassionate:** What can you say to yourself that's gentler and kinder?

>> **Accepting:** What part is true and can you accept in a nonjudgmental way?

>> **Logical:** What thinking traps do you notice? What can you say to yourself that's more realistic or helpful?

>> **Motivating:** What can you remind yourself of that can inspire you to change?

TIP

Using the reframing skill can help you move from fearful thinking to CALM thinking. See Chapter 10 for more about the reframing skill and changing your self-talk.

Facing your fears

The second important step you can take to handle your social anxiety is to face your fears by exposing yourself to the situations that cause you anxiety. One of the fundamental principles of doing exposures is being able to get used to having anxiety without escaping it. The second important principle of exposures is being able to learn from them. You may learn that you can tolerate and cope with anxiety better than you expected, or you may learn that your fear did not come true.

Following is an overview of the steps involved in facing your fears:

1. Create a target list of the situations you fear or avoid.

2. Develop a fear ladder for some of the situations you want to work on and rank your fear level for each one.

3. Select something to do from your fear ladder, identify your worry, and make a prediction of what could happen.

4. After the exposure, debrief with yourself on what actually happened and what you learned.

5. Repeat the same exposure or work on a new one.

REMEMBER

Though these steps may feel complicated or overwhelming, you can do them at your own pace and in small chunks. You read more about creating a fear ladder and facing your fears in Chapter 11.

Other ways to tackle social anxiety

In addition to working on changing your self-talk and facing your fears are several often overlooked ways to help you tackle social anxiety: using positive psychology principles, knowing your values, and accepting your anxiety. These topics are covered in more detail in Chapters 12 and 13.

>> **Positive psychology:** Social anxiety is often looked at through a deficit lens, but this book normalizes it and recognizes how common social anxiety is. Positive

psychology focuses on developing your strengths and using them to move toward a meaningful life, which is essential with or without social anxiety. This can help you overcome avoidance and engage in fulfilling social interactions.

>> **Values:** Your values help define who you are and who you want to be. When you are aware of your values, you can use them to guide you. Your values can become motivators to change. You are willing to accept the uncomfortable feelings that come with social anxiety in order to live your values.

>> **Acceptance:** Acceptance means acknowledging the facts despite wishing you did not feel socially anxious. When you are experiencing social anxiety, your first instinct may be to try to push it away. The more you refuse to accept social anxiety, the larger it will grow. Accepting that you are feeling anxiety in social situations does not mean you are giving up.

Motivating Yourself to Tackle Social Anxiety

In Chapter 9, you discover several ways to motivate yourself to tackle social anxiety. Here are a few highlights.

Identify your reasons for changing

This is finding your "why" for changing. You can ask yourself, what is important to you? What are your values? Why do you want to work on tackling your social anxiety? Some reasons could be to have a better marriage, to be a role model for your children, to advance in your career, to make more friends, or to have greater self-esteem, to name just a few.

Stay in a growth mindset

In a growth mindset, you believe your abilities can be developed through hard work and perseverance. Intelligence and talent are important but not the main ingredients. As a result, you develop a love of learning, resilience, and a tolerance for mistakes. Your motto is: "Mistakes are an opportunity to learn."

Identify obstacles to change

Identifying the pros and cons of changing your social anxiety can help you motivate to change. It may surprise you to learn that there are reasons that keep your social anxiety from changing. Bringing these reasons into your awareness can help you tackle your social anxiety.

IN THIS CHAPTER

» **Understanding the features of social anxiety**

» **Seeing that social anxiety is common around the world**

» **Exploring the differences between social anxiety and related problems**

Chapter **2**

Spotting Social Anxiety

S ocial anxiety can be easily confused with other personality traits. You may be wondering what the differences are between social anxiety and shyness, introversion, and avoidant personality. You may also be wondering how social anxiety overlaps with other problems like generalized anxiety, depression, or substance use.

In this chapter, you explore the core features of social anxiety, such as the fear of judgment and humiliation, worrying about what others are thinking about you, and being self-conscious. You also look at what criteria are used to make a formal diagnosis of social anxiety disorder. Finally, you discover just how common social anxiety is — and that you are not alone.

Identifying the Core Features of Social Anxiety

A popular theory as to why humans develop anxiety involves a story about the saber-toothed tiger. In prehistoric days when humans were evolving, there was a productive reason for anxiety. If you encountered a saber-toothed tiger, you were in real danger and you'd better run. The body developed a chemical response system so that when you were stressed, you would escape whatever triggered that stress by exerting physical energy. Once the threat was gone, your body returned to normal, assuming the tiger didn't eat you!

Another theory involves a story that takes place when humans lived in tribes. Back then, human survival was dependent on remaining in a tribe for protection and shared resources. If you were kicked out of the tribe, that could be a death sentence. So people did what they could to gain and keep social approval — and remain in the tribe.

Combining the tiger theory and the tribe theory is the perfect recipe for understanding how social anxiety developed over time. Your brain is designed for survival, so it constantly scans the environment for danger, even in places that may not be dangerous today. Humans also evolved to fear getting kicked out of the tribe, so getting social approval may feel important to survival even though today, we can function more independently.

REMEMBER

When you perceive possible judgment or humiliation as potential dangers, you may experience a fight-flight-freeze response. For example, if you perceive that someone looks at you "the wrong way," and you interpret it as an indication that they do not like you, that look may feel as dangerous to you as being chased by a saber-tooth tiger or getting kicked out of your tribe. And your brain reacts in the same way as it would with the tiger. It can trigger the body's fight-flight-freeze mechanism, often along with uncomfortable and potentially embarrassing physical symptoms like blushing, shaking, sweating, or even worse, vomiting or diarrhea.

If you remain in the social situation (instead of escaping), you may also worry that others will see your anxiety symptoms. This may be the scariest of all. Another challenge is that the fear of having bodily sensations or showing them can become a self-fulfilling prophecy. Naturally, you do what you can to avoid your perceived threats. Avoidance may make you feel safe, but it does not work to ease your social anxiety in the long run.

Fearing judgment and humiliation

Social anxiety is an intense, persistent fear of being watched and judged by others. This fear of judgment and humiliation is the core fear of social anxiety — and all other worries and fears associated with social anxiety stem from it.

If you base your self-worth on the judgment of others, when you make a mistake, say the wrong thing, or commit any other social faux pas, you may feel humiliated and defective in some way. Your social anxiety may also trigger an emotional reaction like shame, which is the feeling of being worthless, flawed, incompetent, unlikable, or unlovable.

TIP

If you look back carefully at your childhood or teen years, your social anxiety may have started after a humiliating experience. It may have been how a parent or peer treated you. It may have been obvious or subtle. In Chapter 3, you explore where your social anxiety may have come from.

Worrying about what others are thinking

It's exhausting to constantly try to interpret what others are thinking about you and avoid negative evaluation by them. However, it may seem to make sense to place a lot of weight on what others think. After all, being part of a group was essential for human survival, and it still is in many ways, even if we can function more independently.

REMEMBER

When you worry too much about what others think, you are chasing social approval. This makes it hard for you to develop a sense of self and your own identity. You become scared to be yourself because you think others will not like you. You think it keeps you safe to hide your true self because you think others would not approve of you if they really knew you. Instead, hiding your true feelings just reinforces your fears and keeps you feeling inferior.

Being self-conscious and not showing emotions

When you feel self-conscious, you may hide your positive and negative emotions and not share much about yourself. You do this so that people won't see your perceived weaknesses and come to a negative conclusion about you. Ironically, the less people know about you, the less comfortable they may feel around you. Hiding your emotions can backfire.

REMEMBER

You may be excessively worried about showing any signs that you have social anxiety. You may worry that people will see you as weak and look down on you — and this can be true in our competitive society. You may think that if people see your anxiety symptoms, they will perceive you as weak. So then they may criticize or take advantage of you because they think they can. It is important to remember that people are not usually focusing on you, and even if they are, they may not notice that you are nervous. But if they do notice and say something about you, such negative evaluation is not dangerous, and you can learn to cope with it.

Feeling social awkward

Social awkwardness refers to feeling uncomfortable and out of place socially. Social situations, especially when meeting new people, can be uncomfortable. There could be some awkward laughing and painful silence. This is to be expected.

REMEMBER

Feeling socially awkward is not necessarily bad. You may just have trouble understanding social norms, have problems with clear communication, or act in a way that's different than other people. With social anxiety, you believe you should never feel socially awkward so social situations become a trigger for you.

If you have social anxiety and define yourself as socially awkward, you probably feel that you are "weird" or uninteresting. You see yourself in endlessly negative ways and think you are unlikable. In the worst case, your inner critic overpowers you and calls you all kinds of bad names, including boring, stupid, loser, and pathetic. The ultimate bad word is the f-word: *freak.* Your inner critic thinks it absolutely knows how little you have to offer to the world, regardless of the facts.

Being sensitive to criticism

Criticism is an inevitable part of life. You may have heard the expression that words can never hurt you. For you, getting feedback can feel excruciating. Just the thought of receiving a performance review at work or a report card at school can send you into a tailspin. You interpret minor comments that mean little to nothing as criticism.

If you often feel criticized to a degree that's not in proportion to the facts, you may be experiencing rejection sensitivity. *Rejection sensitivity* is a type of emotional response in which the pain can feel insurmountable. With rejection sensitivity, you react intensely to rejection, criticism, disapproval, or failure.

Avoiding people and situations

Everyone with social anxiety engages in some form of avoidance behavior. True avoidance involves completely avoiding the social situations that cause you to have anxiety. Most of the time, complete avoidance is neither possible nor practical. When avoidance is not possible, you may use safety behaviors to manage your feelings of anxiety during social or performance situations.

Safety behaviors are actions you take to reduce anxiety but never help you learn that you can handle the anxiety itself. Safety behaviors include avoiding eye contact, having an alcoholic drink "to loosen up," carrying water with you everywhere, or leaving a party early. These actions give you an illusion of control, but they just provide temporary relief.

REMEMBER

Many people with social anxiety are getting out into the world and interacting with people. You may say, "I already do all of that! Why doesn't it ever get any easier?" If you engage in safety behaviors, you are not giving yourself a true exposure to the feared situations. That is why your social anxiety is not improving.

Understanding How Common Social Anxiety Is

Social anxiety is extremely common. You may not believe how many people have it. Social anxiety is the most common anxiety disorder and the third most common mental health disorder in the United States.

>> An estimated 7 percent of U.S. adults over the age of 18 have a formal diagnosis of social anxiety disorder in any given year. That's about 18 million U.S. adults in the typical year.

>> Approximately 13 percent of U.S. adults have a lifetime prevalence of diagnosable social anxiety, which is approximately 34 million adults. And this number doesn't include people with low-level social anxiety.

>> About 9 percent of U.S. adolescents between the ages of 13 and 17 are diagnosed with social anxiety disorder in any given year. This is almost 4 million teenagers in an average year.

>> More than 75 percent of people experience their first symptoms of social anxiety between the ages of 8 and 15. This shows how important it is to get help for your kids so that they do not need to go into adulthood suffering.

Statistics for social anxiety outside the United States vary, and it's hard to estimate. If we extend the lifetime incidence of 13 percent to the worldwide population of 6 billion people over the age of 15, as many as 780 million people around the globe have social anxiety, not including children and young teens!

REMEMBER

These stats represent those who receive a formal diagnosis of social anxiety disorder. Even more people experience extreme shyness and mild to moderate social anxiety that is not diagnosable but cause problems in their lives. Regardless of what the exact numbers are, the data shows that you are not alone with social anxiety.

What Social Anxiety Is and Isn't

Social anxiety is a mental health problem. Its core feature is a fear of judgment and humiliation accompanied by negative thoughts, uncomfortable bodily sensations, and avoidance behaviors. Many similar personality traits and behaviors may be confused with social anxiety, such as shyness, introversion, and performance anxiety. And some disorders have a lot of overlap, such as avoidant personality disorder. In this section, I outline the differences and similarities between social anxiety and various personality traits and disorders.

REMEMBER

Social anxiety exists on a spectrum, as shown in Figure 2-1. Regardless of where you fall, from shy to socially anxious to avoidant personality, there are coping strategies that can help you.

FIGURE 2-1:
The social anxiety spectrum.

Social anxiety versus shyness

Shyness and social anxiety are different, but many people confuse them or use the terms interchangeably. *Shyness* is a common personality trait and is highly regarded in some cultures. It involves feeling reserved or uncomfortable in social situations. If someone is shy, they can still motivate themselves to do things involving other people. Social anxiety, on the other hand, involves more intense feelings of fear and greater avoidance of social situations.

Shyness and social anxiety share characteristics such as negative feelings about oneself, worries about how others view you, and fear of judgment or embarrassment. And everyone, even people who are not shy or socially anxious, can also have these concerns at times. Many shy people are slow to warm up and not overly anxious in social situations. Remember that shyness is not a mental health disorder. Some of the main differences between shyness and social anxiety are whether you have intense fear and anxiety, how these feelings impair your functioning, and how much you avoid situations because of them.

REMEMBER

Although most people with social anxiety experience symptoms of shyness, being shy does not mean you have social anxiety. This may be surprising. According to the *Diagnostic and Statistical Manual of Mental Disorders, Fifth Edition* (DSM-5), only about 12 percent of people who report being shy also meet the diagnostic criteria for social anxiety disorder. (See "Diagnosing Social Anxiety Disorders" later in this chapter for more about the criteria used to diagnose social anxiety.) This breaks the myth that social anxiety and shyness are the same thing.

Social anxiety versus introversion

Introversion and social anxiety are often confused. *Introversion* is a personality style that pertains to where you get your energy. Many introverts are social but need time alone to recharge. Individuals with social anxiety often prefer to spend time with others but experience intense fear in various social situations.

Often, people are surprised when they find out that someone who appears outgoing is actually an introvert. Many introverts can be quite social until they run out of gas. On the other hand, many extroverts with social anxiety may prefer to spend their time with others but are too fearful to do so.

REMEMBER

If you remember that social anxiety started as a means of survival, then someone who is extroverted and has a strong preference for being with other people may be excessively concerned about fitting in and trying very hard to not get kicked out of the tribe.

Table 2-1 lists the differences between shyness, introversion, and social anxiety. Note that shyness is a behavioral style and involves being slow to warm up. Introversion is a normal personality trait and does not include features of social anxiety. In contrast, social anxiety is a mental health concern with negative thoughts and avoidance patterns.

TABLE 2-1 **Common Traits of Shyness, Introversion, and Social Anxiety**

Shyness	Introversion	Social Anxiety
Timid behavioral style	Normal personality trait	Mental health issue
Slow to warm up in social situations	Low stress in social situations	High stress in social situations
A reaction to new people or places	Recharges by being alone	Uses avoidance to deal with anxiety
Feels uncomfortable or awkward around new people	Comfortable with new people	Fears judgment and humiliation

Social anxiety versus performance anxiety

Performance anxiety is sometimes called "stage fright." Performance anxiety is a subset of social anxiety, although many people think they are different. Having a fear of performing in public or being evaluated for your performance is completely normal. Public speaking is the number one fear people report, along with a fear of heights and bugs.

Performance anxiety can come up anytime you have to perform something in a group. This can include giving a presentation, singing, speaking up at meetings, raising your hand to answer a question, or when your work or school performance is being evaluated, such as when taking a test or being evaluated at work. Some people have specific social anxiety that gets worse when they interact with someone in authority.

Athletes, musicians, actors, and company CEOs often get performance anxiety. It's stressful to be the center of attention and have all eyes on you. Performance anxiety becomes a problem when you start to have feelings of fear and worry that significantly interfere with work, school, or hobbies.

Social anxiety versus avoidant personality disorder

Social anxiety and avoidant personality disorder have a lot of overlap. In both conditions, there is a fear of judgment by others. If you have avoidant personality disorder, you follow a broader avoidance pattern, and your life may be more severely impacted than if you only have social anxiety. Avoidant personality disorder often leads to dysfunction in most relationships, whereas those with social anxiety may only struggle with certain social situations and certain relationships.

Avoidant personality is a more extreme version of social anxiety where you have a more pervasive negative self-concept and rejection feels unendurable. You have a profound feeling of shame and a sense of defectiveness about not fitting in. You have chronic feelings of inadequacy and extreme sensitivity to criticism. You would like to get involved with others, but you avoid social interactions due to an intense fear of rejection.

With avoidant personality, you may be able to initiate social interactions, but you may not be able to maintain them over time. You think that the more people get to know you, the more unlikable people will find you to be. So you may end relationships for fear of being rejected. Or you may not start any relationships at all, thinking that they will just end anyway so why bother?

Social anxiety versus low self-esteem

Social anxiety can certainly affect self-esteem. If you are constantly worried about what others think about you, and your negative inner critic beats you up, your self-esteem has certainly been impacted. However, many people with social anxiety have many domains in their lives where they are happy and successful. In that case, you probably have healthy self-esteem despite having social anxiety.

Diagnosing Social Anxiety Disorder

You may have social anxiety but have never received a formal diagnosis of social anxiety disorder. Or you may identify with some features of social anxiety, but the feelings are not debilitating enough to meet the full diagnosis. In this section, I provide an overview of what a diagnosis of social anxiety disorder entails.

TECHNICAL STUFF

Mental health professionals use a thick book called the *Diagnostic and Statistical Manual of Mental Disorders, Fifth Edition* (DSM-5) as their main guide for diagnosing mental health conditions. The DSM-5 defines all the mental disorders that have been currently identified, and these definitions change over time — so it can be controversial. With each update, it gets fatter and fatter. The first DSM, published in 1952, had 102 disorders; the most recent version, published in 2022, has about 300.

Per the DSM-5, to be diagnosed with social anxiety disorder, you must meet the following criteria:

>> You have an intense, persistent, and irrational fear or anxiety about one or more social situations in which you are exposed to possible scrutiny by others.

>> You fear you will act in a way or show anxiety symptoms in which you will be negatively evaluated, humiliated, or embarrassed, which leads to rejection or offending others.

>> Social situations almost always provoke fear or anxiety.

>> You avoid or endure social situations with intense fear or anxiety.

>> The fear or anxiety is out of proportion to the actual threat.

>> The fear, anxiety, or avoidance has been experienced for six or more months.

>> The anxiety or avoidance causes significant distress or greatly impairs your social or occupational functioning or another important life domain.

>> Your anxiety is not due to the effects of a drug or medication or another medical condition.

>> The anxiety and fear cannot be better characterized by a different mental disorder.

>> If another medical condition is present, the anxiety is clearly unrelated or excessive.

TIP

You need to jump through a lot of hurdles for a medical professional to give you a formal diagnosis of social anxiety disorder. In reality, a competent therapist will look at the underlying causes leading to your social fears, how intense your anxiety is, and how you can change your mindset and stop avoiding to help you overcome feelings of social anxiety. That's what this book is all about.

How Social Anxiety Overlaps with Other Disorders

Social anxiety often occurs in tandem with other mental health problems. Social anxiety disorder is more likely to co-occur with another anxiety disorder. It's next most likely to occur with mood disorders, followed by substance abuse disorders. Because social anxiety often comes on at a young age, many of these other mental health issues develop later on, or they are a result of the problems related to having social anxiety. Table 2-2 outlines the core issues of each of the mental health problems discussed in the following sections.

TABLE 2-2   **Mental Health Problems That Overlap with Social Anxiety**

Mental Health Problem	Core Issue
Agoraphobia	Fear of not being able to escape or get help if you panic
Body dysmorphia	Obsessive focus on a perceived flaw in your appearance
Depression	Persistent feelings of sadness
Generalized anxiety	Worry about many things in your everyday life
Obsessive-compulsive disorder	Unwanted irrational thoughts with rituals to reduce discomfort
Panic disorder	Worry about having a panic attack
Social anxiety	Fear of negative evaluation and humiliation
Substance abuse	Excessive use of substances despite harmful consequences

Agoraphobia

Agoraphobia is a form of anxiety where someone has an intense fear of being in places where escape may be difficult or help may not be available. A main concern of people with agoraphobia is what will happen if they have panic-like sensations and there is no one to help. For example, many people with agoraphobia have a fear of having a panic attack in an airplane but do not fear crashing.

If you have agoraphobia, you may avoid social situations when you think you may not be able to escape or get help if you start to have anxiety. You will often go out, but you will use safety behaviors — like sitting near the door — in case you need to leave the situation quickly. Even being home alone can be challenging if you have agoraphobia because you may rely on safety people being nearby who you think can help you if you start to have an anxiety attack.

In contrast, if you have social anxiety, your main concern is what others think of you. If you have both social anxiety and agoraphobia, you may be concerned about what other people will think if they can see that you are anxious. This is often a concern for people with agoraphobia, but usually they don't have social anxiety outside of this concern, so they probably do not have social anxiety as defined in this book.

Body dysmorphia

Your body image is how you think and feel about your body and appearance, such as your height, weight, eye color, hair color, skin color, facial features, and body shape. Sometimes you think a particular aspect of your body is so distasteful that it causes you to worry a lot about what other people think of you. If this happens to you, then you may have both a body image problem and social anxiety. For example, worries about being too short, too tall, or too heavy, or not having big-enough muscles are common with social anxiety. You think people are judging you for a negative bodily attribute, and that is why you don't have friends, you can't get dates, or you aren't excelling at work.

Another condition called *body dysmorphic disorder* (BDD), a form of obsessive-compulsive disorder (OCD), occurs when you can't stop thinking about perceived defects or flaws in your appearance. The supposed flaw could be minor and can't be seen by others, or it may be imaginary and not realistic. For example, you may obsess about whether your hair is symmetrical and so you keep looking at it, re-styling it, or even cutting your hair to try to perfect it. You fear that when people look at you, they will see your defects, so you may avoid going out. If you suffer from BDD, you do a lot of mirror-checking or seek excessive reassurance from others. You feel so embarrassed, ashamed, and anxious that you avoid many social situations. People with BDD often have social anxiety.

Depression

When you are depressed, you feel sad, lonely, scared, or hopeless. These feelings are also normal reactions when something bad happens in your life, such as losing your job, going through a breakup, or grieving the death of someone you love. You are diagnosed with *clinical depression* when you have persistent feelings of sadness, emptiness, and hopelessness and lose interest in things and activities you once enjoyed. Depression can vary from mild, temporary episodes to severe, persistent depression, which is called *major depression*.

Depression affects how you think, feel, and behave and can lead to a variety of problems like lack of motivation and fatigue. With depression, you have trouble performing normal day-to-day activities, and sometimes you feel as if life isn't worth living. You start missing work or school and not participating in your usual social activities. You do not fear social situations; you just don't participate because you don't have the energy.

REMEMBER

Social anxiety and major depression are the most common mental health problems that occur together. When you have both, usually social anxiety comes first, and that results in feelings of depression. Social isolation and not feeling like you fit in can lead to major depression.

If you have social anxiety, you may have trouble making friends and maintaining close relationships. This can lead to feeling down a lot and being socially isolated. Lacking social support is a major contributor to depression. If your depression becomes severe and you have thoughts of hurting yourself, you should seek professional help.

HOW TO GET HELP FOR SEVERE DEPRESSION

If you are having thoughts about harming yourself, it is important to get professional help. If you or someone you know is in immediate distress or is thinking about hurting themselves, call the National Suicide Prevention Lifeline toll-free at 1-800-273-TALK (8255). You also can text the Crisis Text Line (HELLO to 741741) or use the Lifeline Chat on the National Suicide Prevention Lifeline website (https://988lifeline.org). If your thoughts are very dark, you

(continued)

(continued)

should call 911 or go to the nearest emergency room for help today. Otherwise, you can find a caring, licensed therapist to help you relieve your depression. Chapter 15 includes information about how to find a therapist and the different types of therapy available. While cognitive behavior therapy is the treatment of choice for social anxiety, nearly all licensed therapists are trained to help people with depression.

Generalized anxiety

Generalized anxiety is a mental health issue that causes you to worry about many different things constantly, and you have trouble stopping the worry. You may have "what if" thinking and rumination — repetitive thinking about your problems. You may get stuck worrying about your problems and complaining about them but not doing anything to solve them. The worries could be about money, health, family, relationships, work, or other issues, and you commonly catastrophize about what could happen in the future. In addition to feeling worried about many things, you may also feel restlessness, fatigue, irritability, increased muscle tension, and have trouble concentrating and sleeping.

REMEMBER

The difference between generalized anxiety and social anxiety is the subject matter. With social anxiety, your worry is almost exclusively about social situations and what people think of you. However, you could have both generalized anxiety and social anxiety if you have a strong fear of judgment and you also worry about many different things.

Obsessive-compulsive disorder

The other disorder that frequently co-occurs with social anxiety is *obsessive-compulsive disorder* (OCD). OCD involves obsession and compulsions as described here:

>> You experience obsessions, which are irrational and unwanted intrusive thoughts. Obsessions can be about any number of worries.

>> You perform compulsions or rituals, which are time-consuming and repetitive behaviors that you are compelled to do to relieve the distress caused by your obsessions.

>> Your compulsions are often aimed at getting rid of uncertainty, which may or may not appear to be related to the obsessive fear, such as tapping your feet to get rid of a social fear.

If you have OCD and social anxiety, your compulsions could be physical. One example is you may walk over the cracks on your hardwood floors for good luck and confidence at a social gathering, but you may do it repetitively until you feel the relief of it feeling just right. Once you complete your ritual, you are able to go out. As you can see, OCD can involve endless types of obsessions and compulsions, and it's unique to each person.

REMEMBER

Social anxiety may include mental review, but it's typically related to fears that could make a little more sense and more connected with your social fears. For example, you may ruminate on how you came across to others but maybe not as excessively as you would if you had OCD. Social anxiety without OCD doesn't involve time-consuming compulsions. Sometimes, it's hard to tell the difference between OCD and social anxiety, but regardless of what you call it, identifying and working on your symptoms is important.

Panic disorder

A panic attack is a sudden, intense surge of fear that triggers a severe physical reaction. The fear can be unconscious because you may not know what caused it. Panic attacks can be very frightening. When a panic attack happens, you may think you're losing control, having a heart attack, or even dying. If you've had repeated, unexpected panic attacks and spend long periods worrying about having another one, you may have a condition called *panic disorder*.

REMEMBER

With social anxiety, you may also have panic attacks. Certain triggers like giving a speech or going on a date could bring on panicky feelings or even a full-fledged panic attack. However, panic disorder is different than social anxiety. With panic disorder, you fear having another panic attack, and your fear is not just about social situations. If you are not worrying about having panic attacks but you are worrying about being judged, then you probably only have social anxiety.

Substance abuse

Social anxiety and substance abuse often occur together. If you have both, your social anxiety probably came first. According to the Anxiety and Depression Association of America, about 20 percent of people with social anxiety disorder also suffer from alcohol abuse or dependence.

Many people use alcohol and other substances to cope with symptoms of social anxiety. You may use substances to feel more sociable, lessen your concerns about what others think of you, or feel more at ease in social situations. For some people, it may involve having a glass of wine at a party to ease their anxiety. For others, it may involve getting drunk in order to become uninhibited and transform into a social butterfly under the influence.

WARNING

A substance abuse problem can spiral when you are self-medicating with alcohol or drugs to quiet your fears. Unfortunately, the relief is only temporary, and using substances can backfire. When you are drinking or using drugs, you may do things that are embarrassing that you later regret. For example, high doses of marijuana can trigger anxiety and paranoia. Alcohol, marijuana, and other substances can cause higher levels of anxiety when the substances wear off. This is sometimes called "the boomerang effect."

HOW TO GET HELP FOR SUBSTANCE ABUSE

If excessive drinking or using drugs is interfering with your life and becoming a safety issue, you need to get professional help before you can work on your social anxiety. Chapter 15 includes information about how to find a therapist and the different types of therapy available. You may also find help at a local Alcoholics Anonymous (AA), Narcotics Anonymous (NA), or Smart Recovery program. In addition to therapy, your doctor may be able to prescribe medication to help you make the transition off of substances easier.

IN THIS CHAPTER

» Exploring how social anxiety develops

» Understanding the importance of getting your needs met

» Exploring common life themes that develop when needs are unmet

Chapter 3

Exploring Where Social Anxiety Comes From

No one factor causes social anxiety. It can develop from biological and genetic factors, parenting styles, and negative life experiences. You may be able to trace your social anxiety back to a specific negative event that happened. Or maybe you were shy or inhibited as a child, and your social anxiety gradually grew over time. In this chapter, you explore where social anxiety comes from and how it develops.

Understanding How Social Anxiety Develops

One thing that is clear about the origins of social anxiety is that negative life patterns develop when the core emotional needs of children are not met. You likely have *life themes* — thinking and behavioral patterns that started in childhood — underlying your social anxiety, and working on changing these patterns can help you overcome your anxiety. In this section, you explore some ways social anxiety may have developed for you.

Biology and genetics

Some people are born with a tendency to be inhibited. Though the science on the genetics of social anxiety is still developing, you may have specific genes that make you more prone to developing social anxiety. If you have a parent or sibling with social anxiety, you are more likely to develop it, too. You may also have imbalances of certain chemicals in your brain, known as *neurotransmitters,* which can produce an overactive fear response.

Parenting style

If one of your parents had social anxiety, they may have modeled anxious behaviors. That means you watched and learned to inhibit your behavior or avoid people or situations. Or you may have heard your parents talking about their own fear of judgment by neighbors or acquaintances and came to believe that people can be judgmental.

If your parents were overly protective, you may have developed social anxiety because you were not given independence to confront and overcome a fear of social situations. For example, if you were shy and your parents spoke for you or ordered for you at restaurants, you had less experience with common social interactions when you were growing up.

REMEMBER

Not all children are impacted the same way by parents with less-than-effective parenting skills. Even siblings or twins raised by the same parents often do not develop the same problems or characteristics. One sibling may end up with social anxiety while the other doesn't. It's likely that that a combination of issues results in social anxiety disorder, such as unmet childhood needs plus a genetic predisposition and/or triggering life events.

Negative life events

Social anxiety usually develops in childhood or early adolescence. Many people with social anxiety can trace its origins back to their childhood when they faced a negative life event. If you experience teasing, rejection, ridicule, or humiliation at school or in other situations, you are more likely to develop social anxiety. For example, if your parents were critical, you may have internalized negative beliefs about yourself as well as a fear of judgment that contributed to your social anxiety. Your social anxiety may have been triggered if you had a health condition that drew attention to your appearance or your voice, for example. Other events that can be associated with social anxiety include family conflict, trauma, and abuse.

New life experiences

If your family moved around a lot when you were a child, you may have developed social anxiety because you often had to navigate new schools and a new neighborhood with new people. While social anxiety typically starts in childhood or the teen years, you may have experienced your first symptoms during a work situation, such as giving a presentation or starting a new job.

Considering the Role of Emotional Needs

As babies and children, humans are vulnerable and helpless. To develop in a psychologically healthy way, certain basic needs must be met during childhood. When basic needs are unmet, you can develop unhealthy life themes or *schemas* that can cause problems throughout your life if they are not addressed.

TECHNICAL
STUFF

A schema is a pervasive life theme that affects your patterns of thinking and interacting in the world as well as your beliefs about yourself and others. Schema therapy is a form of cognitive behavior therapy that is more depth oriented and based on the idea that you need to have certain core emotional needs met in your childhood. When they are not met appropriately, unhelpful schemas develop and continue into adulthood. Schema therapy was developed in the 1990s by a psychologist named Jeffrey Young, who worked at the prestigious Beck Institute for Cognitive Behavior Therapy, when he discovered that some people needed a deeper form of therapy to heal their schemas and change unhelpful themes.

Maslow's Hierarchy of Needs

Maslow's Hierarchy of Needs is a famous theory about how human needs develop from the most basic to high-level psychological needs. Developed by Abraham Maslow in the 1940s, it has become a classic way to think about human development.

The Hierarchy of Needs is usually drawn as a pyramid, as shown in Figure 3-1. The general idea is that you need to have your basic needs for food, water, shelter, and safety met before your psychological needs can be fulfilled. At the top of the pyramid is the need for self-fulfillment and reaching individual potential. The fulfillment of needs has been correlated with happiness and the development of healthy individuals.

REMEMBER

In real life, the fulfillment of needs is not a straight climb; you'll jump around the pyramid of needs.

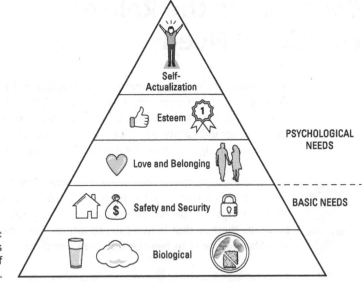

FIGURE 3-1: Maslow's Hierarchy of Needs.

Biological needs

The biological requirements for human survival are at the base of the pyramid. This includes things you need for living such as air, food, drink, warmth, sex, and sleep. These needs must be met for humans to live. If you don't take care of your body, you will feel anxiety. Chapter 14 is all about taking care of yourself.

Safety and security

When safety and security needs are met, you feel safe from danger or harm, and you know that you are taken care of, no matter what. Some basic needs include financial security, a home in a safe neighborhood, healthcare, and safety against accidents and injuries. If you do not have safety and security, you will worry a lot and may possibly develop generalized anxiety disorder.

Love and belonging

At this level, the need for emotional relationships drives human behavior. This level is the need for interpersonal connection and belonging found through family, friendships, romantic relationships, intimacy, being part of a group, and feeling a sense of connection to your community. When the love and belonging need is not fulfilled, you can feel lonely, depressed, and socially isolated. Social anxiety can interfere with making friends, finding love and having a sense of belonging, which is just one reason why working on your social anxiety is so critical.

Esteem

Esteem refers to the need to be accepted and valued by others. You have a need for things like achievement, appreciation, and respect from others. The need to be a unique individual becomes more and more important at this level. When your esteem needs are met, you develop a sense of self-worth and confidence. When they are not fulfilled, it can lead to feelings of inferiority. Having social anxiety can interfere with developing esteem. If you are not exposing yourself to others, then you never learn that you can be accepted and valued.

Self-actualization

The pyramid's peak represents the realization of your full potential, self-fulfillment, and peak experiences. This level includes morality, creativity, spontaneity, acceptance, purpose, meaning, and inner potential. When you are at this level, you are less concerned with the opinions of others and more interested in fulfilling your own potential. No one ever fully stays at this level, but the more self-actualized you are, the more you can focus on your self-development. Working on your social anxiety can help put you on the path to self-actualization.

Core emotional needs

Core emotional needs are universal and all children need them fulfilled to grow up into healthy adults. *Core emotional needs* relate to the psychological needs of love, belonging, and esteem in Maslow's pyramid. The core emotional needs include secure attachment to others; autonomy, competence, and sense of identity; realistic limits and self-control; freedom to express valid needs and emotions; and spontaneity and play (see Figure 3-2). If your core emotional needs were not met during childhood, the ultimate goal is to heal from the past and get your needs met as an adult, which is one form of self-actualization in Maslow's hierarchy.

Secure attachment to others

Secure attachment is the most important need for healthy emotional development in children and adults. A *secure attachment* means having your needs for love, validation, stability, nurturance, protection, safety, and acceptance met. If you had a secure attachment with your parents or a primary caretaker, you developed a sense of trust, safety, and emotional stability.

A lack of a secure attachment can interact with social anxiety in the following ways:

>> You may not have basic bonding skills, which can lead you to feel socially isolated and disconnected.

>> You may feel unacceptable or defective at a deeper level if you did not learn as a child that you were unconditionally loved and accepted.

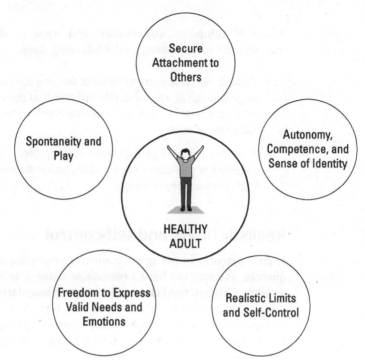

FIGURE 3-2:
Core
emotional
needs.

Autonomy, competence, and sense of identity

Autonomy refers to the ability to make independent choices, exercise personal agency, and develop a sense of self-identity. A parent can prevent a child from developing autonomy, competence, and a sense of identity when they are overprotective. Often, this comes from a parent's anxiety and fears. Maybe they were afraid of something bad happening to you, so they did not allow you to do things on your own or explore your interests and discover your strengths.

Alternatively, you may not have been provided with appropriate guidance and support to face challenges or tasks that were beyond your capacity. Then, you would be left with a sense that you should be able to deal with or master challenges but fail, which would reduce your sense of competence.

A lack of autonomy, competence, and sense of identity can interact with social anxiety in the following ways:

>> If you do not have a strong sense of self, you compare and judge yourself as inferior to other people. You see yourself as less competent, inadequate, uninteresting, or boring compared to others.

>> If you do not have a general sense of competence, you develop low confidence in your ability to handle anxious feelings when they come up.

Realistic limits and self-control

If your parents did not provide adequate discipline and conse-quences, you may not have a reasonable sense of self-control as an adult. Children need clear and consistent boundaries to have a sense of safety, predictability, and structure. Boundaries help you develop self-discipline and learn to respect the rights of oth-ers. It also helps you learn to establish boundaries for yourself.

A lack of limits and self-control can interact with social anxiety in the following ways:

>> You need self-discipline to face your fears. If you give in to social anxiety, you will never learn that you can handle anxiety.

>> If you do not have adequate boundaries with others, then others could walk all over you or bully you. This can cause your social anxiety to go up.

Freedom to express valid needs and emotions

If you were encouraged to express your thoughts, feelings, and ideas, you may have good self-awareness and emotional intel-ligence. When children are supported in communicating their emotions, they develop a deeper understanding of their own inner world. When you feel heard, understood, and validated, you can better navigate your emotions and communicate them to others. You learn expressing emotions is okay instead of keeping them bottled up.

A lack of freedom to express needs and emotions can interact with social anxiety in the following ways:

>> You do not feel comfortable sharing about yourself. You have trouble connecting with others because you can't easily talk about your thoughts and feelings.

>> You feel disconnected from others because you do not feel understood and heard even when the other person is trying to understand.

Spontaneity and play

If your parents encouraged you to play with other kids and they were playful with you, this helped foster your creativity and individuality as well as your ability to form healthy relationships. Through play, children engage in activities that are intrinsically motivating, enjoyable, and imaginative. Play also provides a safe space for children to express and process their emotions.

A lack of spontaneity and play can interact with social anxiety in the following ways:

>> If you are not spontaneous, you may be overcontrolled in social interactions and be less approachable to others.

>> You come across as less joyful or happy, which is less appealing to others in social situations.

>> You lack social skills and need to learn them.

Understanding Common Life Themes with Social Anxiety

When core emotional needs are not met, unhealthy life themes, called schemas, emerge. Think of schemas as your patterns of thinking and interacting in the world as well as your beliefs about yourself and others that started during your childhood and teenage years and continue into adulthood.

REMEMBER

When you are triggered by a situation that causes you to feel social anxiety, a schema that is under the surface can boil up and rise. When a schema bubbles up, the pain can feel intense, and you may not understand why you feel the way you do. Your emotions may feel out of control. Then you might go into one or all three main styles of coping, including being overly compliant or pleasing, avoiding certain situations and using safety behaviors, and/or acting in ways to cover up your anxiety, such as being extra talkative.

Figure 3-3 outlines the schemas in the categories of disconnection and rejection, overvigilance and inhibition, other-directedness, impaired limits, and impaired autonomy and performance. In this section, I highlight six common schemas from this group associated with social anxiety: defectiveness, emotional constriction, emotional deprivation, failure, social isolation, and unrelenting standards. However, there are many more that you can dive into with schema therapy. Table 3-1 outlines twenty schemas that may develop when childhood needs are not met.

Disconnection and Rejection
- Emotional deprivation
- Defectiveness/shame
- Social isolation/alienation
- Mistrust/abuse
- Abandonment/instability

Impaired Autonomy and Performance
- Failure
- Dependence/incompetence
- Vulnerability to harm and illness
- Undeveloped self

ANXIOUS CHILD WITH UNMET NEEDS
- Secure attachment
- Autonomy, connection, and sense of identity
- Realistic limits and self-control
- Freedom to express needs and emotions
- Spontaneity and play

Hypervigilance and Inhibition
- Emotional inhibition
- Unrelenting standards/hypercritical
- Punitiveness
- Negativity/pessimism

Impaired Limits
- Insufficient self-control/self-discipline
- Entitlement/grandiosity

Other Directedness
- Approval/recognition-seeking
- Subjugation
- Punitiveness
- Self-sacrifice

FIGURE 3-3: How unmet needs can lead to unhealthy life themes with social anxiety.

TABLE 3-1

Full List of Schemas

Domain and Life Themes	What It Is
Disconnection and Rejection	
Emotional deprivation	Believing you can't get support and connection from others
Defectiveness/shame	Feeling shame because you think you are unworthy or flawed
Social isolation	Feeling alone and different from other people or like an outcast
Mistrust/abuse	Believing that others will lie or take advantage of you
Abandonment/instability	Fear people will leave you or not be available when you need them
Overvigilance and Inhibition	
Unrelenting standards/being hypercritical	Having a demanding and perfectionistic drive to achieve
Emotional constriction	Inhibiting your emotions, thoughts, and behavior due to shame
Fear of losing control	Inhibiting your emotions, thoughts, and behavior due to fear of losing control
Punitiveness toward self	Believing you should have consequences when you make a mistake
Punitiveness toward others	Thinking others should have consequences when they make a mistake
Negativity/pessimism	Focusing on the negative aspects of life and worrying that things will go wrong
Impaired Autonomy and Performance	
Failure	Thinking you are inadequate compared to others in your accomplishments
Dependence/incompetence	Feeling you are unable to take care of yourself and handle daily responsibilities
Vulnerability to harm and illness	Believing a catastrophe could happen at any moment
Enmeshment/undeveloped self	Having your identity intertwined with someone else

(continued)

TABLE 3-1 *(continued)*

Domain and Life Themes	What It Is
Other-Directedness	
Approval/recognition seeking	Your self-esteem is dependent on what others think of you
Subjugation	Surrendering control to others because you fear consequences
Self-sacrifice	Meeting the needs of others at the expense of your own
Impaired Limits	
Insufficient self-control/self-discipline	Difficulty restraining emotions or impulses
Entitlement/grandiosity	Believing you are better than and more deserving than other people

Defectiveness: Feeling unworthy

Defectiveness may be the most painful of all the schemas when triggered. Defectiveness is a feeling that you are flawed and that if others got to know you, they would realize it and not like or love you. This schema developed if you were abused, neglected, ignored, frequently criticized or punished, or rejected by caretakers. This gave you the message that there was something bad, shameful, or flawed about you.

Some key aspects of the defectiveness schema include:

>> Thinking you are bad, unwanted, inferior, or defective

>> Feeling a sense of shame about your perceived flaws

>> Hypersensitivity to criticism, rejection, and blame

>> Self-consciousness, comparisons, and insecurity around others

CASE EXAMPLE

The following is an example of some common patterns that emerge with social anxiety when the defectiveness schema surfaces:

>> **Situation:** Bill has a defectiveness schema. He's 35 years old and has never been married. He's the director of strategic alliances at a major company. He is looking online at dating apps and hoping to meet someone. He deeply desires to have a wife and children.

>> **Thoughts:** "I will never meet someone. I will be alone forever. Who would want to go out with me? I am ugly and fat. As soon as women see my online photo, I am sure they think about how ugly I am. Most guys my age have been married for a long time by now. Even if I got lucky and went out with an attractive woman, she would just flake on me after the first date anyway."

>> **Reaction:** Bill gives in to the defectiveness schema and thinks and acts as though his thoughts are true. Even though other people think he is handsome and kind, he does not see it. He overcompensates for his shame by overworking because he thinks that the only reason anyone would ever want to be with him is if he can be a financial provider.

>> **Where Bill's social anxiety may have come from:** Bill's mother was critical of Bill and made negative comments about his appearance. His mother did not meet his need for validation.

Emotional constriction: Not showing emotions

With emotional constriction, you believe you must keep your emotions bottled up inside of you or inhibit your thoughts or behaviors. You do this to avoid feelings of shame or embarrassment. Emotional constriction can develop if your parents discourage sharing emotions or spontaneity. Unfortunately, when you do not share your thoughts and feelings or when you inhibit your actions, you can come across as being too serious, rigid, or uptight.

Some major indicators of emotional constriction are:

>> Suppressing your feelings, especially anger or positive emotions such as joy, affection, or warmth

» Difficulty expressing your feelings when you feel vulnerable or communicating about your feelings and needs

» Being overly rational and invalidating your own emotions

CASE EXAMPLE

The following is an example of some common patterns that emerge with social anxiety when the emotional constriction schema is triggered:

Situation: Jim is an introvert with an emotional inhibition schema and social anxiety. His wife wants to have a date night without the kids and go dancing and get romantic afterwards.

Thoughts: "I don't want to go dancing. I get self-conscious because I'm a terrible dancer. I really would prefer to stay home and just hang out with no pressure. I would prefer to make her dinner and watch a movie. I don't know how to tell her what I want. I love her, but she thinks I am cold and boring."

Reaction: When Jim's wife proposes the date night, Jim stiffens up and says, "Whatever you want." His wife gets angry because he is showing no excitement and says he's a party pooper and he always ruins all the fun. Jim feels terrible but holds it in and beats himself up because she is upset and it's his fault.

Where Jim's social anxiety may have come from: Jim's father did not show emotions and he used to say that you have to keep a stiff upper lip and exercise self-restraint. Jim's need to express his emotions and get them validated was not met as a child.

Emotional deprivation: Lacking emotional support

With an emotional deprivation schema, you believe others will not meet your emotional needs. You feel as though you don't matter and that no one will ever care for you. Sometimes, emotional deprivation can feel like a vague sense that something is missing but you can't pinpoint what. This schema develops when a parent or primary caretaker was not attuned with your emotional needs.

The three major forms of deprivation are:

» **Nurturance:** Need for affection, closeness, love, and companionship

» **Empathy:** Need to be listened to and understood

» **Protection:** Need for advice, guidance, and direction

**CASE
EXAMPLE**

The following is an example of some common patterns that emerge with social anxiety when the emotional deprivation schema is triggered:

Situation: Ellen has an emotional deprivation schema and social anxiety. Ellen feels she must suppress her needs for nurturance and empathy because no one will ever meet them. Ellen's coworkers went out to lunch without her. She wanted to go but was afraid to ask.

Thoughts: "I may as well not go because it looks like they are having fun without me. They probably don't care if I go or not."

Reaction: This schema led to a self-fulfilling prophecy. Ellen did not ask to join and did not try to get her current needs met. This reinforced Ellen's cycle of emotional deprivation.

Where Ellen's social anxiety may have come from: Ellen's parents loved her but were so busy with work that they could not meet her needs for nurturance, empathy, and guidance. They did not give her enough time and attention so she did not develop a feeling of being truly loved and cared for.

Failure: Feeling less accomplished than others

With the failure schema, you believe you cannot perform as well as your peers in areas such as career, academics, sports, hobbies, or other areas of achievement. You may believe that you are a failure already or that you will eventually fail. This schema can develop when parents or caretakers ridiculed or criticized your efforts.

Some indicators of the failure schema include:

>> Believing you are less talented, intelligent, or successful than others

>> Not trying hard or pushing really hard to avoid failing

>> Viewing yourself as inadequate or incompetent

CASE EXAMPLE

The following is an example of some common patterns that emerge with social anxiety when the failure schema is triggered:

Situation: Bridget has a failure schema and imposter syndrome. She's in medical school and studying for her license to become a doctor.

Thoughts: "I don't have what it takes to become a doctor. I failed the last exam. Now I have to repeat it. All my friends in medical school already got their residencies. I feel so dumb and like a failure."

Reaction: Bridget spends a lot of time overthinking everything she did wrong on the exam. She compares herself to her medical school friends and decides that she is not good enough. It takes her a long time to get her courage up to re-take the last exam.

Where Bridget's social anxiety may have come from: Bridget's father was a doctor and as a child, he made her feel that she was not smart and that she could never live up to his standards. Briget's need for competence was not met.

Social isolation: Keeping to yourself

Social isolation is the feeling that you are isolated from the rest of the world, different from other people, or not part of any group or community. This schema can result in loneliness and depression because being part of a group and having a sense of belonging is so fundamental to human existence.

One way this schema develops is if your family was different from other families in terms of financial status or because you moved around a lot. It can also develop if there was something different about you, such as your physical appearance, and it caused others to bully or criticize you.

Some indicators of the social isolation schema include:

>> Feeling weird, strange, or different from other people

>> Thinking others see you as socially awkward

>> Feeling like you do not fit in with other people or groups

>> Overestimating how similar others in a group are to each other

CASE EXAMPLE

The following is an example of some common patterns that emerge with social anxiety when the social isolation schema is triggered:

Situation: Ben has a social isolation schema. He works in an office as a support person for the sales team. Sometimes he has to go to trade shows, which usually involve company cocktail parties in the evenings.

Thoughts: "I can't do it! I can't go to another cocktail party. I'll be standing in a corner by myself, looking awkward. I have nothing in common with the sales staff. I am so different, and they would not want to talk to me anyway. I feel like maybe my colleagues are talking behind my back."

Reaction: Ben decides to stay in his hotel room by himself and have a few alcoholic drinks from the mini-bar. He forgets his worries and passes out. The next day, he wonders if anyone noticed that he did not go to the party after the trade show ended.

Where Ben's social anxiety may have come from: Ben's family moved to a new town when he was ten. The other families were wealthier and lived in bigger houses. He experienced some bullying for this reason. His parents did not provide the guidance he needed to handle the transition.

Unrelenting standards: Being demanding

With unrelenting standards, you think that what you do is not good enough, so you must try harder and harder. You have very high internal standards that you think you must meet or you could be criticized either by your own inner critic or by other people. You often feel stress and pressure and have difficulty slowing down and relaxing. This schema can develop if your parents were never satisfied with your performance or their love was conditional on your accomplishments.

Unrelenting standards can show up in a few ways:

>> Perfectionism, being extremely detail-oriented, and underestimating your performance

>> Setting rigid rules in many areas of life about how you or others should be

>> Concern about time and efficiency so you can accomplish more

CASE EXAMPLE

The following is an example of some common patterns that emerge with social anxiety when the unrelenting standards schema is triggered:

Situation: Diana has an unrelenting standards schema with social anxiety and perfectionism. She's an engineer and she fears making mistakes at work. She's working on a big project and is having trouble deciding what direction to go in the next phase of her work.

Thoughts: "I need to come up with the perfect way to develop this software. If it's not right, everyone will think I am incompetent, and I'll get a bad job review. If I make any mistakes, people will think I don't know what I am doing, and they'll look down on me."

Reaction: Diana overcompensates by working overtime. She takes a long time researching alternatives and examining detailed specs of different ways to code. She asks her boss for reassurance that she is going in the right direction. She meets with a bunch of coworkers to talk things through, but she thinks they don't know as much as she does so maybe she wasted some time.

Where Diana's social anxiety may have come from: Diana's dad expected her to get straight As in school. If she got a B, she felt ashamed that she let him down. Instead of playing with friends after school, she was doing homework. She missed out on opportunities to explore her need for play because she was always working to make her dad feel proud.

Chapter **4**

Looking at the Types of Social Anxiety

Social anxiety can show up in many ways. It may show up during certain situations that cause you to feel anxiety, such as participating in social activities, using social media, and initiating and maintaining relationships. It may also show up within your thoughts and beliefs about yourself (I am awkward), about other people (people are judgmental), about social performance (I must be outgoing), and about having social anxiety itself (social anxiety is bad).

In this chapter, I outline the many ways social anxiety may show up and provide examples of common situations that may trigger negative thoughts, uncomfortable feelings, and safety and avoidant behaviors. You may only relate to a couple of situations if your social anxiety is more specific, such as with public speaking. Or you may have moderate to severe social anxiety and are triggered on a day-to-day basis by many types of social anxiety.

Identifying Common Situations That Trigger Social Anxiety

Because social anxiety can show up in many ways, it is helpful to divide the various types into eight broad categories, as shown in Figure 4-1. Categorizing social anxiety like this can help you feel more confident because you can see that your social anxiety is not endless. If your social anxiety falls into just one or two categories, it may feel more manageable to tackle. If your social anxiety falls into many categories, don't worry. That just means your social anxiety is more generalized, but many of the strategies you can use to manage one type of social anxiety can apply to other types, too.

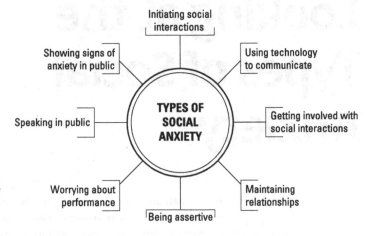

FIGURE 4-1: Types of social anxiety.

In the following sections, I present examples of common situations that trigger social anxiety and offer tips on how to handle them.

Initiating Social Interactions

Initiating social interactions is a common form of social anxiety. It can be stressful to introduce yourself to someone, start small talk, maintain eye contact, or leave a conversation.

Introducing yourself or being introduced to someone else

Situation: You are with a close friend and will meet some of their friends for dinner.

Thoughts	Feelings	Behaviors
"I will sound dumb." "I won't know the right things to say."	You feel awkward and insecure. You feel your hands trembling a little.	You avoid introducing yourself and stay quiet. You wait for someone else to make introductions. You worry that they can see your hands trembling.

TIP

>> Start with one person and say hello. You don't need to dazzle anyone.

>> Instead of "I will sound dumb," consider telling yourself, "No one really cares what I say. I can just be myself."

>> Remember, you are not the center of attention; they do not notice your hands.

Initiating small talk or starting a conversation

Situation: You are starting a new class and sitting next to someone you don't know.

Thoughts	Feelings	Behaviors
"They'll think it's weird that I am trying to talk to them."	You feel uncomfortable and embarrassed. You feel stiffness in your shoulders.	You stay quiet and regret missing the opportunity to make a new friend.

TIP

>> Other people are probably feeling uncomfortable, too. They'd probably welcome someone talking to them.

>> It's easier to make friends on the first day of class before people buddy up.

Making or maintaining eye contact

Situation: You are talking to a coworker who is an up-and-comer at your company.

Thoughts	Feelings	Behaviors
"This person is a rock star. Why would they even want to talk to me? I have nothing to offer."	You feel inferior and ashamed. You feel some physical symptoms in your body.	You look down or away when your coworker is talking to you. You hope to get out of the conversation as soon as you can.

TIP

>> You're on the same team with others at work. Everyone needs your support to succeed.

>> Don't put others on a pedestal. Others do not walk on water. You have just as much value as they do.

Joining a group conversation already in progress

Situation: You are at work and a couple of coworkers are having some coffee in the break room. You are getting your morning coffee.

Thoughts	Feelings	Behaviors
"They are so close-knit. I feel uncomfortable trying to join them." "I don't think I am welcome."	You feel lonely and excluded. You feel stiffness in your body.	You walk over to them, but your body language is stiff. You quickly fill up your coffee mug, softly say hello to one of them, and go back to your desk.

TIP

>> Ask yourself if there is any real reason why other people would not want to talk to you.

>> Try to relax your body language and look friendly.

Sustaining conversations once the interaction has begun

Situation: You are at a party talking to an acquaintance you don't know well.

Thoughts	Feelings	Behaviors
"Oh no, there's an awkward silence. I ran out of things to say. They must think I am awkward."	You feel nervous and worried, scared, and your body wants to flee from this situation.	You start looking around instead of focusing on the person you are talking to.

TIP

» It takes two to tango. It is not your full responsibility to figure out what to say next.

» If you look around because you are nervous, others may think you lost interest.

Moving on from a social interaction when it's nearing its end

Situation: You are chatting with a small group of people at a party. You are ready to move on but worried about offending them if you leave.

Thoughts	Feelings	Behaviors
"I ran out of things to say. I want to end this conversation but don't know how." "They will think I don't like them if I leave."	You feel anxious and guilty. You feel your face turning red.	You stay in the group but slowly start moving away because you think they are noticing your red face. You awkwardly say, "I am going to refill my drink," and run to the bathroom.

TIP

» It's natural for someone to leave a group at some point.

» No one will care if you leave. They are busy with each other right now.

Using Technology to Communicate

Technology has introduced many more ways to communicate than just interacting in person. You may get stressed out by using technology to communicate. When you can't see someone's reaction, you assume things that may or may not be true. The situations that often cause social anxiety include calling someone or answering the phone, using social media, and texting and emailing others.

Making posts on social media

Situation: You see a post on social media made by a friend who is at the beach with a group of people.

Thoughts	Feelings	Behaviors
"Everyone else is having so much fun except me." "My life is so boring compared to them."	You feel hurt and isolated. You feel like crying because you feel so sad.	You eat some ice cream to make yourself feel better.

TIP

>> You are only seeing the external face others are presenting online and you do not know how they are feeling inside.

>> They may not even be that social, and this image may be taken out of context.

Texting someone

Situation: You texted someone you recently met and added a smiley face emoji, the one with the tongue sticking out.

Thoughts	Feelings	Behaviors
"Oh no, I just hit send. I shouldn't have attached that emoji. It seemed funny at the moment, but it is really weird."	You feel anxious and your heart rate increases.	You start to overthink it. You wonder if you should send an email apologizing for sending that emoji.

TIP

>> They will probably either find it funny or think nothing of it.

>> Even if they think it's weird, they probably won't think about it too long.

Calling someone or answering your phone

Situation: Your boss is calling you on your cell phone.

Thoughts	Feelings	Behaviors
"I wonder why my boss is calling me. Maybe I did something wrong." "I'll let it go to voice mail until I can work up the courage to listen and call them back."	You feel alarmed and nervous. You feel trebling in your body.	You let the call go to voice mail. Then you listen to the message, and it turns out not to be a big deal. But you do not call back. You message your boss instead.

TIP

>> Having live, personal interactions are important for developing relationships.

>> Try to answer the call the first time.

>> If they called you instead of messaging, it is polite to call back in person.

Writing an email

Situation: You are writing an email to your project team about a problem that needs to be solved this week.

Thoughts	Feelings	Behaviors
"I just found a typo. I had better check the email again, or they will think I am not good at writing." "I better make sure I write clearly so they understand the plan, or they will think I am not a good project leader."	You feel worried and indecisive. You feel your jaw clenching.	You check your email at least five times. You hesitate to hit send, and you spend a couple of hours rethinking what you wrote. You rewrite it and check it again.

TIP

» You never notice nor care when others make mistakes. If you do notice, you assume they were in a hurry to get the email out.

» It's a waste of time to keep rereading. They'll get the gist of what you are trying to say.

Getting Involved with Social Events

Getting involved with social events may create the most social anxiety in you. Situations that are purely social in nature can be hard because you don't know what to expect and you could be thrown off guard. This is certainly the area where most people with social anxiety get stuck. Typical situations include attending or planning a party, hosting an event, having someone over for dinner, or even participating in your own wedding. Many times, just thinking about a social event causes anticipatory anxiety, and you may end up not going.

Attending a party or social gathering

Situation: You are invited to a friend's engagement party. Her family, extended family, and others you don't know will be there.

Thoughts	Feelings	Behaviors
"I'm not going to know anyone. I'll feel all alone if no one talks to me." "I should go because this party is so important to my friend, but what if I have a panic attack?"	You feel panicky and worried. You feel many panicky symptoms in your body.	You end up staying home. You see photos on social media the next day. You feel guilty for not going.

TIP

» It is always better to push yourself to go out and tackle your fears.

>> No one notices when someone is panicking, but if they do, they will want to help you.

Inviting someone to dinner

Situation: You just met someone at school, and you seemed to hit it off in class. You decide you would like to invite them to go pick up dinner at a local eatery.

Thoughts	Feelings	Behaviors
"They will never want to be my friend. They are too cool for me."	You feel intimidated and depressed. You feel your body slumping down.	You get up the nerve to ask, but instead of being specific, you say, "Maybe we can go out one day." They say "Sure," and you leave it at that.

TIP

>> It's great you worked up the courage to ask, but don't hesitate. Suggest a time and place.

>> You can always follow up. Set up a date the next time you see each other.

Hosting a party or event

Situation: It's your birthday and you'd like to celebrate with a party with a group of friends and acquaintances.

Thoughts	Feelings	Behaviors
"I am no good at planning a party. It is just too stressful to figure it out." "If the party is not fun, no one will like me, and I will be embarrassed."	You feel apprehensive and nervous. Your body shakes because you fear asking too many people to come.	Instead of having a party, you invite two friends over who you know like you and will not care if you do things perfectly or not.

TIP

>> It may be okay to limit the size of the gathering this time, but be sure to challenge yourself in the future.

>> If you keep avoiding, you will never learn that you are likable and do not need to be perfect.

Planning a guest list

Situation: You are planning your wedding and working on the guest list.

Thoughts	Feelings	Behaviors
"Maybe no one will come to my wedding." "If they accept my invitation, it's just because they feel obligated to come."	You feel unlikable and ashamed. You feel your eyes getting watery.	You don't want to think about it anymore, so you stop working on the guest list and do something else. The avoidance makes you feel relieved, but it maintains your social anxiety cycle.

TIP

» Either you, your fiancé, or your families know everyone on the guest list. They all feel some connection with you.

» Not everyone attends every event they are invited to. You can expect some people to decline.

Having a friend over for dinner

Situation: You invited a friend over to your home for dinner. You are waiting for your friend to arrive, and then you'll order pizza.

Thoughts	Feelings	Behaviors
"Is my friend going to show up? What if they stand me up?" "What will we talk about?"	You feel nervous, anxious, and worried. You feel your body getting stiff.	You make sure your house is perfectly clean. You keep checking your phone to see if your friend sent you a message that they're canceling.

TIP

» Have confidence. Your friend accepted your invitation and will show up.

» If your friend has to cancel at the last minute, there will be a good reason.

» Don't catastrophize about worst-case scenarios.

Participating in your wedding ceremony

Situation: The big day is approaching and you feel yourself getting cold feet.

Thoughts	Feelings	Behaviors
"Everyone will be looking at me. I will be the center of attention."	You feel uncomfortable and worried and start to sweat just thinking about it.	You think about calling off the wedding. You call your mom in a panic to discuss your fears.

TIP

» While you think cold feet is about doubts about getting married, it often comes from social anxiety about the day of the wedding.

» Being the center of attention is hard, but think about how great the honeymoon will be!

Maintaining Relationships

Social anxiety is common when you have to maintain relationships. It's a lot of work to maintain relationships for anyone — let alone if you have social anxiety. The worry of what people think of you and fear of rejection can come up.

Asking to go on date with a potential romantic partner

Situation: You see someone you like and want to ask them out on a date.

Thoughts	Feelings	Behaviors
"They're really cute. I wish I had the nerve to ask them out."	You feel inferior and not good enough.	You don't ask.

TIP

>> It is normal to face rejection when dating. You need to be able to tolerate getting rejected to eventually have a partner.

>> There is no such thing as someone being too good for anyone. If someone thinks they are too good for you, that is about them, not you.

Initiating activities with friends

Situation: There's a new movie coming out that you'd really like to see, but you don't want to go alone. You'd like to ask a few people to come along.

Thoughts	Feelings	Behaviors
"Maybe they'll say no because they think I am too boring to hang out with."	You feel sad and lonely. Your hands tremble as you text them.	You decide to ask, but you tell them it's just a movie and no pressure to hang out afterward.

TIP

>> They are your friends and you've done things with them before.

>> If you give them an out and they take it, you may feel even worse later.

Meeting the friends of your friends

Situation: In a couple of weeks, your good friend is having a party at their home. Many of their friends and acquaintances will be there. You only know one or two of them, and you do not even know them all that well.

Thoughts	Feelings	Behaviors
"I don't want to go. I won't know what to say." "They will see how awkward I am and talk behind my back later on."	You feel ashamed, inferior, on edge, and untrusting.	You think about this for hours every day, anticipating what could happen. You can't refocus your attention, and the worry feels uncontrollable.

TIP

>> Anticipatory anxiety can be worse than the anxiety you may feel in the moment.

>> Find ways to redirect your attention back to the current moment or find things to do when you are worrying in advance.

Telling a story or making a comment in a group

Situation: It's Monday morning at work. Everyone is talking about what they did over the weekend and you want to tell them what you did.

Thoughts	Feelings	Behaviors
"They all had such a fun time over the weekend. They did such interesting things. My weekend was so boring."	You feel alienated, sad, and boring.	You listen but do not participate.

TIP

>> You can always find at least one small thing to say. Even if it is not super exciting, at least you will be connecting with your coworkers in a small way.

>> Don't compare so much. Comparing only makes you feel worse.

Running into people you know or acquaintances in public

Situation: You are at the mall and you see a parent from your child's school.

Thoughts	Feelings	Behaviors
"I'll freeze if they approach me. They'll see how nervous I am and look down on me."	Your heart starts racing, and you feel nervous.	You keep your head down and pretend you don't see them.

TIP

>> A simple hello would be sufficient.

>> They are probably more interested in shopping than worrying about you.

Being Assertive

Being assertive can be a challenge with social anxiety for several reasons. One reason is that you have to deal with the fear of judgment. You may have all kinds of worries tied up in what people will think of you if you act assertively. The other is you may equate being assertive with being aggressive. This is a common misconception. Assertiveness exists on a continuum from passive to aggressive. Assertiveness is in the middle of the continuum where you are neither passive nor aggressive. Being assertive means balancing your needs and the needs of others. Sometimes, you may feel yourself getting unbalanced and moving too far to one side or the other. No one is perfect, and many people have problems with being assertive. When you notice your assertiveness is getting unbalanced, notice it and ask yourself how you can get closer to the middle.

Expressing an idea or opinion during a discussion or meeting

Situation: You have a great idea for how to improve your department's efficiency.

Thoughts	Feelings	Behaviors
"They will think my idea is stupid." "If they don't like it, I will make a fool of myself in front of the entire department."	You feel stupid. You feel like your heart is dropping in your body.	When they call on you, you do not mention your idea.

TIP

>> You have done your research and you are prepared. It is time for you to shine by sharing your ideas.

>> Instead of calling yourself stupid, be kind and nonjudgmental with yourself.

Experiencing conflict and anger with another person

Situation: Your best friend is mad at you because you said you would hang out with them and their friends, but you canceled at the last minute because your social anxiety got in the way.

Thoughts	Feelings	Behaviors
"I should have gone. I feel so guilty for copping out." "My friend is tired of me bailing, and I don't know what excuse I can make this time."	You feel guilty and embarrassed. You are upset because you ended up alone and you disappointed your friend again. You feel like crying.	You avoid talking to your friend the next day to avoid conflict.

TIP

>> It is better to face conflict than avoid it. If you avoid your friend the next day, they will only take it as evidence that you are not taking responsibility.

>> Maybe you can explain how your social anxiety got in the way so your friend does not think you do not like them.

Reporting dissatisfaction or returning an item

Situation: You bought a size too small for your child and you need to exchange it.

Thoughts	Feelings	Behaviors
"The customer service clerk thinks I am a bother." "They look busy and will think that I am demanding too much." "I don't want to be a nuisance."	You feel self-conscious and nervous. You feel your face getting red.	Instead of making an exchange, you return the item and don't say too much. You leave the store and tell your child to go shopping for a replacement item.

TIP

>> You are entitled to an exchange. You are not imposing or being too demanding.

>> It's the customer service clerk's job to help you.

Worrying about Performance

Performance anxiety is a subset of social anxiety. People are often surprised when they find out that actors, singers, business people, and others in the spotlight also struggle with social anxiety. Because social anxiety is the fear of judgment, it makes sense that many people, even outgoing people, can have social anxiety.

Performing for an audience

Situation: You are playing soccer on the college team.

Thoughts	Feelings	Behaviors
"If I make a mistake, I will disappoint the team." "The team will think I am a bad player and kick me off the team."	You feel nervous and worried. You notice that you start to sweat.	You hold back and don't give it your all because you are scared of making a mistake. You worry others can see you sweating.

TIP

» You are a great player or you would not be on the team.

» Everyone is sweating because they are playing soccer. No one will notice you are sweating.

» Stop catastrophizing. Think about more likely outcomes.

Teaching a class or training people

Situation: You are a trainer in the human resources department. You are preparing a training session for the company's employees.

Thoughts	Feelings	Behaviors
"What if my training is not good enough?" "I feel like an imposter, and others will see it, too."	You feel insecure and your chest feels tight.	You overprepare to make sure everything is perfect, but in doing so, you exhaust yourself and can't give your full energy to the training.

TIP

>> Imposter syndrome is real, but you are a high-performing employee and may be looking through dark-colored lenses.

>> Are you aware of the 80/20 rule? Eighty percent of the outcome comes from 20 percent of the input. So overworking may not produce that much more.

Talking to authority figures

Situation: You need to talk to your boss's boss about a problem you encountered.

Thoughts	Feelings	Behaviors
"My boss's boss is more powerful than me. They will think I am a peon and dismiss me."	You feel worried and lack confidence. Your throat feels tight.	You are meek and submissive when you speak.

TIP

>> Authority figures were once in your shoes.

>> Most authority figures like to talk to their employees and hear new ideas.

Eating or drinking in front of others

Situation: You are having dinner with a group of friends, some of whom you do not know well.

Thoughts	Feelings	Behaviors
"They are going to judge me for what I am eating." "They will think I am overweight because I eat too much."	You feel self-conscious.	You don't eat much at dinner because you think they are looking at what you eat. But you are starving when you get home and gorge yourself with snacks.

TIP

» Everyone tends to eat a little too much, so it's doubtful they will be thinking about what you're eating.

» It is unhealthy to deny yourself and then overeat by yourself.

Networking at a professional event

Situation: You are at an offsite retreat with a couple hundred people from your company. Your boss is encouraging you to network.

Thoughts	Feelings	Behaviors
"I need to push myself, or my boss will give me a bad performance review." "My boss told me repeatedly to get out there, but I keep failing."	You feel overwhelmed and your hands tremble at times.	You nervously get a drink of alcohol. You hold onto your glass to keep your hands busy. You talk to a few people you know but you do not meet anyone new.

TIP

» Try to identify a few people you'd like to meet and think of a few things you may have in common to help ease your anxiety.

» Go with a buddy who can introduce you to new people.

Using a public restroom

Situation: You need to go to the bathroom to urinate, but there is someone in the stall next to you.

Thoughts	Feelings	Behaviors
"It will take a long time for me to urinate, and they will notice and think something is wrong with me."	You feel embarrassed and inadequate.	You leave and hold your urine until you get home.

TIP

» Be patient and don't pressure yourself.

» Realize that the other person doesn't see you or notice you.

Speaking in Public

Public speaking is one of the most common phobias. Even most people without social anxiety have some fear of speaking in public. It can be scary to have all eyes on you. In addition to standing up and giving formal presentations or speeches, social anxiety can pop up when speaking in smaller groups.

Giving a presentation to a large group

Situation: You are an engineer and your boss wants you to present your project at the division meeting.

Thoughts	Feelings	Behaviors
"I'm going to stumble over my words." "I'll freeze when they ask me questions." "I may have a panic attack." "Everyone will know I'm anxious."	You feel scared and nervous. At times, you feel like things are not real, which is called *derealization*, and you worry you might panic.	Every day you have intrusive images of panicking. You practice your presentation again and again.

TIP

>> Focus on one or a few people in the audience. It will make the audience seem more manageable and less intimidating.

>> You know your stuff, so even if you are a little nervous, remind yourself that you can handle anxiety.

>> Consider letting people know that you are nervous. Doing so removes the power from the fear that they'll know you are nervous.

Introducing yourself in a group meeting

Situation: You are at your weekly staff meeting. A new employee is at the meeting and your boss asks everyone to introduce themselves and their projects.

Thoughts	Feelings	Behaviors
"I just can't talk. I don't know why." "It will be so embarrassing if they notice I am nervous."	You clam up and feel your throat getting tight.	You keep your comments short. You say your name and your department's name, but you skip talking about your projects.

TIP

» Listen to what others are saying to get a sense of what's expected.

» If possible, write some notes on a piece of paper so you feel more prepared when it's your turn.

Answering or asking questions in a class or meeting

Situation: You are in your math class. Your professor asks the class to raise their hand if they know the answer. You did all your homework the night before.

Thoughts	Feelings	Behaviors
"I want to raise my hand. I know the answer, but what if I say it wrong?"	You feel intimidated, and your hands get sweaty.	You raise your hand tentatively, hoping your professor will not call on you or, if they do, that no one will notice your sweaty hands.

TIP

» Good job for raising your hand, but raise it a little higher.

» Ask yourself what you would do if you were confident or what you'd tell your best friend to do, then do that.

Showing Signs of Anxiety in Public

Many people worry about what others will think of them if they know they are nervous. It comes back to if someone sees you are nervous, they could think you are weak or that something is wrong with you.

Blushing

Situation: You are in class and you are called on to answer a question.

Thoughts	Feelings	Behaviors
"Everyone will notice I am blushing and think I am nervous."	You are terrified and feel your face turning red.	You freeze and can't say anything.

TIP

>> Not "everyone" is noticing you are blushing. The spotlight is not on you.

>> If some people notice your face is a little red and judging you, it says more about them than you.

Sweating

Situation: Your friends invited you to go out to eat at an Indian restaurant.

Thoughts	Feelings	Behaviors
"Oh no, what if I start sweating from the spicy food and they notice?" "They are going to ask me why I am not eating more, and I won't know what to say. It will be awkward."	You feel embarrassed and worried.	You go, but you only eat chicken tikka kebobs and skip all the spicy curry and vindaloo dishes that everyone else is sharing.

TIP

>> Recognize that you are asking yourself a hypothetical question when a sentence starts with "what if?"

>> At least try a small taste and see what happens. If you try it, you may discover that you can handle it if you sweat a little.

Chapter 5

Feeling Stuck with Social Anxiety

ocial anxiety exists when you overestimate the threat and underestimate your ability to cope. For you, the threat of being judged by others and feeling humiliated or embarrassed may be something you think you can't handle. So you avoid situations where these risks could happen, and you never learn how to handle your worries. In this chapter, you explore the cycle of social anxiety and what makes you feel stuck. You discover how negative thoughts and core beliefs lead to feelings of social anxiety and unhelpful reactions.

How Social Anxiety Works

Social anxiety sticks around because you aren't able to kick your negative thoughts and self-defeating behaviors. If you have negative thoughts about yourself and what people think of you, and then you engage in self-defeating behaviors, you will stay stuck on the social anxiety treadmill. You won't learn that you can handle anxiety, so you will never get off the treadmill. It's like the old saying about doing the same thing over and over again and expecting different results. You may feel some initial relief by avoiding the situation or using safety behaviors, but the next time you try to engage in the situation, you may have even more social anxiety.

Table 5-1 presents some examples of how negative thoughts and behaviors keep socially anxious people stuck.

TABLE 5-1   ## How Social Anxiety Sticks Around

Perceived Danger or Risk	Behavior (Inability to Cope)	Result
"I'll come across as awkward, and they'll think I am weird."	You stay home instead of going to the party and miss out on fun.	Social anxiety
"My voice will tremble, and I'll embarrass myself."	You stay quiet in meetings even though you know your stuff.	Social anxiety
"If I make a mistake, people will think I am stupid."	You rewrite all your emails multiple times before sending them to make sure they are perfect.	Social anxiety

TIP

One way to visualize how social anxiety develops and is kept alive is to imagine a scale that weighs danger on one side and confidence on the other. With social anxiety, you tend to have the belief — conscious or unconscious — that social interactions and negative evaluations are dangerous. You also tend to have low confidence in your ability to cope with the perceived danger. If you can either reduce your perception of danger or increase your belief that you can cope, then your scale will become more balanced in facing your fears.

Understanding the Cycle of Social Anxiety

Figure 5-1 illustrates how the cycle of anxiety can keep you stuck on the social anxiety treadmill. The cycle involves the following phases:

1. **A triggering situation occurs.**

   The anxiety cycle starts with a situation that makes you feel uncomfortable or vulnerable. For many people, the same trigger may not cause any concern.

2. **Negative core beliefs appear.**

   If you have social anxiety, then unconscious negative core beliefs simmer up without you even noticing.

3. **The scale becomes unbalanced.**

   The unbalanced social anxiety scale is activated. Your fear increases because you overestimate the danger and risks of social interactions while having low confidence in your ability to cope.

4. **You experience symptoms of social anxiety.**

   You are in a full-on social anxiety emergency. You experience anxious thoughts, images, feelings, and bodily sensations. Avoidance and other safety behaviors interfere with the learning process, so you never get to know that the danger is not as risky as you think and that you can cope with it.

5. **The cycle repeats.**

   Your negative core beliefs never change, and the cycle starts again when another situation triggers you.

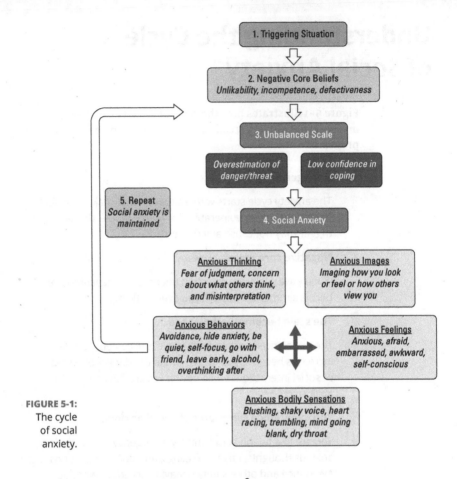

FIGURE 5-1:
The cycle
of social
anxiety.

Factors Perpetuating Social Anxiety

The factors that prolong social anxiety are what keep you stuck with it. These factors are what need to change for you to overcome social anxiety. Even small changes can go a long way in alleviating social anxiety.

Negative thoughts

We all have automatic thoughts that pop up without us realizing them. Sometimes, we may notice that a demanding or harsh critical voice shows up in our heads and we experience negative self-talk. Common negative thinking patterns associated with social anxiety — also called *cognitive distortions* or what I call *thinking traps* because it's a less judgmental term — come in many forms. Here are a few examples:

>> **Mind reading:** "They think I look awkward."

>> **Catastrophizing:** "What if I say something stupid and I end up alone?"

>> **Labeling:** "I am such a loser."

>> **Shining the spotlight:** "They can see I am nervous."

>> **Shoulds:** "I shouldn't have anxiety."

REMEMBER

Thinking traps are negative patterns of thinking that are repeated again and again. I cover thinking traps in detail in Chapter 7.

Negative core beliefs

Core beliefs are beliefs you hold about yourself, others, the world, and the future. These beliefs can be held in the form of thoughts or images. Often core beliefs are unconscious. Core beliefs are like unwritten laws about how people should be or how the world should work. They act as filters that guide your perceptions and expectations. Core beliefs usually start to develop in childhood and can be hard to change. Some common core beliefs with social anxiety include the following:

About Myself	About Others	About the World/Future
I'm unlikable.	People are critical.	The future is hopeless.
I'm undesirable.	People will reject me.	The world is dangerous.

Negative self-image

You probably have high standards about how people should behave in social situations. You think everyone else is confident and outgoing except you. If you have a negative evaluation of your social skills, you will be very fearful of other people judging you.

Self-focused attention

Self-focused attention occurs when you pay too much attention to how you come across to others. It's the thinking trap of *shining the spotlight*. Similar to feeling self-conscious, when you experience this thinking trap, you focus inward and think about your bodily sensations, your thoughts and feelings, and how you think you are performing. You are not really focused on the conversation, so you miss what is going on and come away with a biased interpretation. Worse, focusing inward can make you seem disinterested in the other person.

Avoidance

When you avoid situations, you never learn that you can handle them. Avoidance is simply not doing the activities that expose you to social risks. You might avoid parties, making phone calls, going to family reunions, going on dates, getting a job, and much more. You miss out on life when you avoid.

Safety behaviors

Employing safety behaviors is a subtle form of avoidance. *Safety behaviors* are avoidance behaviors you take when you are engaging in social situations to try to control how you come across to others. Sometimes, they backfire and cause the exact opposite result than what you intended. Safety behaviors include avoiding eye contact, staying quiet in groups, talking excessively, drinking alcohol, not sharing your feelings or opinions, speaking softly, crossing your arms, over-preparing, and more.

Experiencing the Stages of Social Anxiety

REMEMBER

Social anxiety is not just about the actual trigger. It often starts well before you talk to someone or attend an event. Feelings of social anxiety occur in three stages: anticipating anxiety before an event, participating in the event, and overthinking after the event.

Anticipating anxiety before an event

You probably feel nervous before engaging in a social situation. For example, before you go to a meeting, a party, or on a date, you may think about who will be at an event and what you will say. You may start thinking about past failures, engaging in negative self-talk, and catastrophizing about what could go wrong. This could even cause you to skip going out and stay home alone.

Participating in the event

When you think of social anxiety, you usually think about what happens when you are actually in a social situation. During social interaction, this involves monitoring how you think you look, how you think you sound, and how you feel. You can be self-critical and judge yourself in the moment. You engage in safety behaviors like staying quiet, speaking in a low voice, and avoiding eye contact. You are not truly present in the moment when you are worrying. All of this can make the exact opposite impression than you want.

Overthinking after the event

After a social event or interaction, you overthink everything you said, what others said, and what they may have thought of you, and you beat yourself up for what you think went wrong. This is a way of checking your performance and thinking about what you could have done differently. You think this is helpful because it will help you improve in the future. However, in reality, such overthinking can backfire. You become biased and interpret things that happened through a negative mental filter. Overthinking can also lead to more anxiety in the future, as well as depression.

Following is an example of the stages of social anxiety. Suppose that John is giving a presentation to his team. These are some of his thoughts before, during, and after the event:

Anticipating (Before)	Giving the Presentation (During)	Overthinking (After)
"I bet Susan will ask me a question and I won't know the answer."	"I am perspiring and they can see I am nervous."	"I got so nervous that I forgot to talk about the business projections."
"If my presentation is not good, I will get fired." "I better work overtime on this presentation and practice it again and again."	"I feel really awkward." "My voice is shaky." "They think what I am saying is stupid."	"I rushed through my presentation. I should have been more calm." "I sounded really nervous and now they are probably wondering how I even got this job in the first place."

What could John do instead?

Before — Be Calm: John could focus on evaluating his thoughts in a helpful, realistic way. He could use the CALM thinking skills introduced in Chapter 10, which mean being compassionate to yourself, being accepting of reality, being logical by coming up with more realistic and helpful self-talk, and being motivated by finding reasons to help you tackle your social anxiety. He could also calm down by relaxing his body with progressive muscle relaxation described in Chapter 14.

During — Be Present: In the moment, it would be helpful for John to notice what is happening externally, rather than looking internally. Instead of focusing on what he is thinking and feeling in the moment, he could pay attention to delivering the presentation, communicating information to his audience, and listening to the questions so that he can answer confidently.

After — Be Positive: He could focus on what went well and limit the time he spends dwelling on the situation. John could focus his mind on other productive activities like listening to music or even paying his bills!

Identifying Unhelpful Coping Behaviors

Social anxiety sticks around because you may be engaging in unhelpful coping behaviors —consciously or unconsciously — that keep it alive. These unhelpful coping behaviors need to change if you want to tackle social anxiety. You may not need to change every behavior 100 percent, but some change will be needed to convince yourself that you are stronger you're your social anxiety.

Avoiding

Avoiding is the Godfather of social anxiety. If I had to name the number one issue that maintains anxiety, it's when you avoid. You miss out on life when you avoid, so this could be the worst thing you do to try to cope with social anxiety.

CASE EXAMPLE

Sally had so much anticipatory anxiety that she talked herself out of going on dates and often canceled. Rob was looking for a job, but he got nervous about job interviews so he procrastinated in his job search. Chapter 11 is all about confronting your fears by not avoiding.

TIP

Instead of avoiding, start approaching. Take baby steps because small changes all add up.

Overcompensating

Overcompensating is when you do the opposite of what you feel or believe. You overcompensate when you engage in behaviors to mask your discomfort and perceived flaws.

CASE EXAMPLE

Jane wanted to make a good impression at a party, so she talked too much when she met new people, hoping they would think she was friendly and not notice how nervous she was. Mitch told boisterous jokes to make people laugh, hoping they would like him.

TIP

Try to be yourself. That's the only way you will learn that others will accept you.

Overpreparing

When you are nervous about your performance, you may over-prepare. Some of these behaviors can be helpful when needed, but it can also be stressful to think you must be perfect or perform at such a high level or if you do the behaviors in excess.

CASE EXAMPLE

Helen thought she did not deserve her job and that people would notice she was an imposter, so she worked overtime almost every evening. Steve was worried he was not attractive, so he bought new clothes before every date.

TIP

Be okay with good enough. Don't overdo it.

Self-monitoring

Self-monitoring occurs when you place too much focus on what is going on inside you and miss what is going on in the moment.

CASE EXAMPLE

When Linda was talking to her teacher, all she could think about was how hot her face felt and that her teacher must be noticing it and seeing that she was nervous. When her teacher asked her a question, she did not even know what they had asked and she had to ask them to repeat the question. Then she got even more nervous and started to mumble her words.

TIP

Focus on the present and what is going on outside of yourself.

Giving in

Giving in means surrendering to your negative core beliefs. If you define yourself as socially anxious, you feel you are stuck in this make-believe character. You don't try. You think you can't change anyway.

CASE EXAMPLE

Rudolf saw himself as shy, quiet, and reserved. He was anxious because he thought these traits were negative. He also felt that if he acted differently, his friends would be shocked and notice. That would make him even more anxious, so he continued to be quiet and reserved with his friends.

TIP

Recognize that you are not seeing reality when you give into a negative core belief.

Distracting

Distraction can be a positive or a negative. It is positive when you can refocus on the here and now while acknowledging your thoughts and feelings. Distracting becomes a negative when you have to think about or do something else to avoid your feelings because you they are so intolerable. Distraction can be great in an emergency when you are too overwhelmed to handle your feelings in the moment. However, when you use distraction to avoid feelings too frequently, it becomes an avoidance tool. You never learn that you can handle your emotions.

CASE EXAMPLE

When Raley came home from parties, they had to listen to loud music to drown out their rumination. Instead of using tools to learn how to handle their overthinking, they avoided their thoughts and feelings instead.

TIP

Don't use distraction to avoid your feelings or you will never learn that you can handle feeling anxious.

Excessive checking

Excessive checking is when you are compelled to repeatedly check things, often checking the same thing many times. It can become a compulsive behavior. You are looking for something specific to relieve your anxiety. When you finally find it, you feel temporarily better.

CASE EXAMPLE

Rosie was self-conscious about the size of her nose, and she thought other people notice it. She spent a lot of time looking at her nose in the mirror, measuring it, and comparing it to the average nose size. When she found data that showed her nose was in the average range, she felt better but then something would bother her and she would check again. Rosie often avoided social situations because she thought her nose was too big.

TIP

Try to limit checking. It might be okay to check once or twice, but beyond that, it's becoming a ritual.

Seeking reassurance

Reassurance seeking is when you ask others what they think, hoping they will tell you that things are okay. You get temporary relief, but you can never really take it in or learn to handle your feelings of anxiety on your own.

CASE EXAMPLE

Cindy had a lot of anxiety about her weight and what she looked like. Before going out to dinner parties with her husband, she would try different outfits and ask him how she looked. When he'd answer and tell her that she looks great, she'd feel okay for a little while, and they'd make it out the door just in time. However, she'd repeat the reassurance-seeking cycle the next time they went out. It was frustrating for her husband. He did not know how to stop it because she'd get angry if he did not answer.

TIP

Instead of asking others for reassurance, try to answer your own questions.

Ruminating

Rumination is what cows do when they swallow, unswallow, chew, regurgitate, and reswallow. For a human with social anxiety, it refers to replaying social events in your head again and again in many different scenarios after it has already happened.

CASE EXAMPLE

Mark always spent hours after going out with his friends thinking about what happened, what he did wrong, and what they probably thought of him. He did this so much that he became severely depressed.

TIP

Break the cycle of ruminating by focusing on something else. This will be hard so you will have to turn your mind repeatedly until it gets easier.

Using substances

You may drink alcohol or use drugs to help you stay calm during an event. Or maybe you use alcohol or other substances to help quell your mind before or after the event and turn off the negative inner critic.

CASE EXAMPLE

Bette always went straight to the bar before socializing with anyone at parties. She also drank afterward to calm her nerves. As a result, she developed an alcohol problem.

TIP

Limit how much you drink to one or two drinks. Try not to use substances before or after to quell anxiety. Find healthy substitutes.

REMEMBER

Social anxiety can feel like a house on fire. You may not know exactly what caused it, but the way to put out the fire is to keep working to spray water on what is keeping you stuck.

2

Understanding the Social Anxiety Cycle

Explore the many situations that may cause you to feel social anxiety, and discover three exercises you can do to help you identify the situations that make you anxious, the common negative thoughts you may have when you start to feel anxious, and any underlying fears.

Identify the safety behaviors you may engage in and how they may be causing your social anxiety to stick around.

Discover what thinking traps are, how to identify your thinking traps, how to handle thinking traps when they come up, and what happens when you get stuck in a thinking trap.

Look at the basics of core beliefs and how to identify the core beliefs you hold about yourself, others, the world, your social performance, and your social anxiety.

Chapter **6**

Assessing Your Social Anxiety

Many situations may cause you to feel social anxiety. Participating in social activities, using social media, and initiating and maintaining relationships are just a few common circumstances that may bring about these feelings. In this chapter, I discuss three exercises you can do to help you identify the situations that make you anxious, the common negative thoughts you may have when you start to feel anxious, and any underlying fears. Next, I help you identify the safety behaviors you may engage in and how they may be causing your social anxiety to stick around. You will use this information later to work on changing your self-talk and developing experiments to confront your anxiety. I then discuss the importance of monitoring your social anxiety as the first step in changing it. At the end of the chapter, I discuss three self-reporting tools available for free online that you can use to measure the impact of social anxiety in your daily life.

Identifying Situations That Make You Anxious

The first step in assessing your social anxiety is to identify the situations that make you feel anxious. Table 6-1 lists several examples of the many ways people experience social anxiety. Which ones apply to you, and how severe is your social anxiety in these situations?

Using the following scale, rate how much social anxiety you feel in the situations listed in Table 6-1:

10	Panic level
8–9	Very high social anxiety
7–8	High social anxiety
5–6	Moderate social anxiety
3–4	Mild social anxiety
0–2	Little to no social anxiety

TIP

Keep your ratings handy. Later in Chapter 11, you will use them to create a fear ladder (a list of situations you need to confront to overcome social anxiety).

TABLE 6-1   **Situations That May Cause Social Anxiety**

Situation	Rating
Initiating social interactions	
Introducing yourself or being introduced to someone else	
Initiating small talk or starting a conversion	
Making or maintaining conversations	
Joining a group conversation already in progress	
Sustaining conversations once the interaction has begun	
Moving on from a social interaction when it's nearing its end	
Do you have other specific fears in this category? If so, list them here and rate them:	

Situation	Rating
Using technology to communicate	
Posting pictures of yourself or allowing others to post pictures of you on social media	
Making posts on social media	
Texting someone	
Calling someone or answering your phone	
Writing an email	
Do you have other specific fears in this category? If so, list them here and rate them:	
Getting involved with social events	
Attending a party or social gathering	
Inviting someone to dinner	
Hosting a party or event	
Planning a guest list	
Having a friend over for dinner	
Do you have other specific fears in this category? If so, list them here and rate them:	
Maintaining relationships	
Asking to go on a date with a potential romantic partner	
Initiating activities with friends	
Meeting the friends of your friends	
Telling a story or making a comment in a group	
Running into people you know or acquaintances in public	

(continued)

TABLE 6-1 *(continued)*

Situation	Rating
Do you have other specific fears in this category? If so, list them here and rate them:	
Being assertive	
Expressing an idea or opinion during a discussion or meeting	
Experiencing conflict or anger with another person	
Reporting dissatisfaction or returning an item you purchased	
Do you have other specific fears in this category? If so, list them here and rate them:	
Worrying about performance	
Performing for an audience, such as acting, singing, dancing, or playing a sport	
Teaching a class or training people	
Talking to authority figures	
Eating, drinking, or writing in front of others	
Networking at a professional event	
Using a public restroom	
Do you have other specific fears in this category? If so, list them here and rate them:	
Speaking in public	
Giving a speech or presentation to a large group	
Introducing yourself in a group meeting	
Answering or asking questions in a class or meeting	

Situation	Rating
Do you have other specific fears in this category? If so, list them here and rate them:	
Showing signs of anxiety in public	
Blushing	
Trembling	
Sweating	
Shaky voice	
Do you have other specific fears in this category? If so, list them here and rate them:	
Other things you fear that you have not yet mentioned	

Identifying Your Negative Thoughts

The next step in assessing your social anxiety is to identify the common negative thoughts you have when you start to feel anxious. Using the following scale, review and rate the thoughts listed in Table 6-2:

3	Exactly what I think
2	Very similar to what I think
1	Sort of what I think
0	Not at all what I think

TIP

If the thought listed in Table 6-2 seems like you, but the words are not exactly how you would describe it, it's fine to rephrase the statement to better reflect how you feel. Try to divide up your ratings between 0, 1, 2, and 3 so that not everything comes out high or low (but it's okay if they do). You will use the results from this list in Chapter 8 and in Chapter 10 when you explore your negative core beliefs and work to change your mindset.

TABLE 6-2   **Common Negative Thoughts**

Negative Thought	Rating
Thoughts about yourself	
I'm awkward	
I'm not interesting	
I don't fit in or belong	
I'm strange	
I can't change	
Something's wrong with me	
I'm a loser	
I'm an imposter	
I can never think of anything to say or the right thing to say	
I'm weird or odd	
I'm inferior	
I'm weak	
I'm foolish	
I'll be alone forever	
I'm nervous	
I'm stupid	
I'll lose control	
I'm boring	
I'm unattractive or ugly	

Negative Thought	Rating
I'm hopeless	
I'm bad	
I'm worthless	
Thoughts about other people	
Others will look down on me if they know I have social anxiety	
People are judgmental	
Others are uncomfortable around me	
People pay a lot of attention to me or watch me	
People will notice if I am anxious or have a panic attack	
People are untrustworthy	
Others do not like quiet people	
People do not want to be around me	
People are just being nice if they hang out with me or say something positive about me	
People are critical	
Thoughts about social performance	
I must be outgoing	
I should be friendly	
I can't make a mistake	
I must never have social anxiety	
Thoughts about social anxiety	
Social anxiety is bad or embarrassing	
Social anxiety is uncontrollable	
Feeling social anxiety is intolerable	
Panic attacks are dangerous	
Other thoughts and beliefs	

(continued)

Identifying Your Underlying Fears

In this section, you take a look at the common fears associated with social anxiety. If one or more of these fears apply to you, take a few minutes to reflect on the questions and then use the space provided to write down a few thoughts about how this fear applies to you.

REMEMBER

Social anxiety is unique to each individual, so if your specific fears do not match the fears listed here, use the space provided to write down your specific fears.

Fear of judgment

Do you worry excessively about what others are thinking of you? Are you worried that you may not be accepted or fit in? Do you mind-read about what people may be thinking before, during, and/or after social situations? What are some of your worries about being judged?

_____

_____

_____

Fear that people will notice your anxiety

Do you worry that others will see that you are anxious and will look down on you in some way? Do you think other people will view you as weak, inferior, or in some other negative way if you look anxious to them? Are there ways that you think they can tell you are anxious? What's the worst thing about people noticing that you are anxious?

Fear of criticism

Do you feel especially sensitive when others give you feedback? Do you dread getting report cards or performance reviews? If you are criticized, what do you think that means about you?

_____

_____

_____

Fear of appearing foolish

Do you worry that you will do something that will make you look foolish in front of others? What do you worry you might do?

_____

_____

Fear of making mistakes

Are you worried about making mistakes? If you made a mistake, what bad thing do you predict would happen?

_____

_____

_____

Fear of uncertainty

Do you worry that unexpected things could happen in social situations and that you won't know how to handle them or your mind will go blank? How do you deal with uncertainty?

_____

_____

_____

Fear of feeling anxious

Are you worried that you will have uncomfortable sensations in your mind or body that will be intolerable to you? What feelings would be uncomfortable for you to experience?

_____

_____

_____

Assessing Your Social Anxiety with a Formal Survey

Many self-report tools are available for free online if you'd like to get a formal measurement of your social anxiety, including the Liebowitz Social Anxiety Scale-Self-Report, the Social Phobia Inventory, and the External and Internal Shame Scale.

WARNING

These tools are for your information and should not be considered a formal assessment. Only a licensed therapist can make a formal diagnosis.

Liebowitz Social Anxiety Scale — Self-Report (LSAS-SR)

A popular tool used for assessing social anxiety is the Liebowitz Social Anxiety Scale — Self-Report (LSAS-SR). The LSAS-SR is a 24-question survey that assesses two aspects of social anxiety: fear and avoidance. Specifically, it asks about your fear of social and performance situations and how much you avoid them.

The LSAS was developed in 1987 by Dr. Michael Liebowitz, a psychiatrist and researcher at Columbia University and the New York State Psychiatric Institute. The LSAS-SR is a good starting point to gauge the severity of your social anxiety. You can take the LSAS-SR on the National Social Anxiety Center website at https://nationalsocialanxietycenter.com/liebowitz-sa-scale.

Social Phobia Inventory (SPIN)

The Social Phobia Inventory (SPIN) is a self-rated instrument consisting of 17 questions that assess fear, avoidance, and physiological discomfort in social or performance situations. It was developed at Duke University. This tool enables you to assess your social anxiety symptoms over the past week to understand social anxiety's impact on your daily functioning. You can take the inventory at https://psychology-tools.com/test/spin.

External and Internal Shame Scale (EISS)

Shame is central to social anxiety. The External and Internal Shame Scale (EISS) has eight questions to assess shame. *External shame* involves a distressing awareness that others view you negatively. *Internal shame* comes from inside of you and involves self-criticism and negative self-evaluation. You can complete the scale at https://nationalsocialanxietycenter.com/selfscoring-shame-scale.

Identifying Your Safety Behaviors

Safety behaviors are actions you do that you think make you safe. Many times they do, but performing safety behaviors rather than addressing the underlying cause of your anxiety leads to social anxiety sticking around. Generally, safety behaviors performed by someone with social anxiety are used to avoid disapproval from others or reduce the likelihood of getting judged or criticized by others. Sometimes, safety behaviors may seem like helpful coping behaviors, or maybe they seem harmless and you don't see why you should change them.

The problem is that safety behaviors can become maladaptive over time by maintaining anxiety and fear around situations that are not threatening. In Chapter 2, I discussed how it made sense for our ancestors to fear things like saber-toothed tigers, as they were a real threat to our safety. Today, you do not have to fear getting eaten alive by a tiger, but you may still react as if you do if you have social anxiety.

Table 6-3 lists common safety behaviors performed by people with social anxiety. Use the following scale to rate how often you do each safety behavior:

3	All the time or very often
2	About half the time
1	Every now and then
0	Don't do this at all

REMEMBER

You may not be aware of all the subtle ways you may be engaging in these behaviors since many safety behaviors are not as clear-cut as avoidance.

TABLE 6-3   **Common Safety Behaviors**

Behavior	Rating
Avoiding eye contact	
Staying quiet or speaking very little	
Talking too much	
Drinking alcohol or using drugs	
Not sharing your feelings or opinions	
Speaking softly	
Holding your arms stiffly at your side or crossing your arms	
Focusing inward on how you are feeling	
Staying home	
Making excuses	
Being overly entertaining	
Trying to use the exact right words	
Standing far from others to avoid being approached	
Leaving social events early	
Making your appearance just right before socializing	
Not eating during social events	
Rehearsing or planning what to say	
Using your phone or other things appear busy or to be unapproachable	
Exaggerating to look better	
Seeking reassurance or approval	
Doing what others want or giving into peer pressure	
Carrying water or food to reduce anxiety	
Giving into superstitious beliefs	
Saying no to invitations	

There are countless types of safety behaviors and they are specific to each person. Following are some questions to ask yourself that can help you identify your safety behaviors. Write your responses in the space provided.

>> What are the ways you engage in unhelpful coping behaviors to protect yourself from social anxiety?

_____

_____

>> When you can't avoid a situation, what do you do to make yourself feel less anxious?

_____

_____

>> Are there things you do to avoid attention?

_____

_____

>> What do you do to come across better to others?

_____

_____

Monitoring Your Social Anxiety

It is important to monitor your social anxiety if you want to change it. A social anxiety log includes what situations trigger you, how intense your social anxiety feels, what thoughts and beliefs come up, and what you do such as safety behaviors and avoidance. Ideally, you will keep a log every day for at least one week. You may see patterns that repeat themselves, which is great because then you'll know what to work on. A sample social anxiety log is shown in Table 6-4.

REMEMBER

If avoidance is one of your common safety behaviors, you may think you have nothing to log. Often people say, "Nothing came up." It could mean that you are detached from your feelings and don't even realize when you are anxious. This response could also be because you are using it as an excuse to not keep a log or because you are not engaging socially because you are avoiding. If you avoid, then of course you have nothing to log!

TABLE 6-4 ## Social Anxiety Log

Situation (triggering event)	Intensity of feelings (Rate 1–10)	What automatic thoughts, images, or beliefs came up?	What did you do when these thoughts and feelings came up?

TIP

Over time, it is helpful to return to your log when something causes you to feel intense anxiety because it might be something you did not track earlier.

Chapter **7**

Identifying Your Thinking Traps

Thinking traps are negative patterns of thinking that people with social anxiety can fall into, consciously or unconsciously, and repeat again and again. If this sounds familiar, you aren't alone — everyone has thinking traps, even people without social anxiety. But when you can identify your thinking traps and talk back to them in a helpful and realistic way, you'll be ahead of the game.

In this chapter, you discover what thinking traps are, how to identify your thinking traps, how to handle thinking traps when they come up, and what happens when you get stuck in a thinking trap. After reading this chapter, you'll have greater insight into your thoughts and beliefs and their effects on your emotions and behaviors. You'll also know what to do when you get caught in a thinking trap.

Understanding Thinking Traps

A *thinking trap* is an unhelpful pattern of thoughts that causes you to have unpleasant emotions and to see the world more negatively than it really is. When your mind gets stuck in a negative way of thinking that doesn't make sense or isn't based on facts, you're probably in a thinking trap. When you're in a thinking trap, you attach meaning that may not be realistic or helpful. You may not even be aware of your thinking traps, and you probably fall into the same traps again and again.

TECHNICAL
STUFF

In the field of psychology, thinking traps are referred to as *cognitive distortions*. If you read about cognitive distortions online or in another book, just know that they're the same as thinking traps.

REMEMBER

Whenever you fall into a thinking trap, you are doing two things:

>> Overestimating the risk of threat and danger or how bad the consequences could be

>> Underestimating your ability to cope with or tolerate the situation

Thinking traps affect your mood and how you behave. With social anxiety, your most common reaction when you fall into a thinking trap is to avoid people or events. The problem is, if you avoid these things, you never learn that what you think is true isn't really true or, if it is true, that you can handle it.

Thinking traps are often unconscious and happen outside of your awareness. Something may happen to you, and before you know it, you feel like you're traveling a hundred miles per hour on a 55-mile-per-hour road. You feel like you can't hit the brakes because you feel like you've already spiraled out of control.

When you're in a thinking trap, you engage in *automatic self-talk* (things you say to yourself that you don't even realize you're saying). The good news is that if you can notice your thinking patterns and make your automatic self-talk more conscious, you can tackle your social anxiety more effectively.

REMEMBER

Social anxiety is ultimately a fear of judgment and that you will do something embarrassing. You fear criticism and rejection, leading to feelings of inadequacy, humiliation, and shame. If you have a negative thought, it leads to negative interpretations and negative feelings. You can't stop feeling like people think poorly of you. On the other hand, if you have a positive thought and interpret the situation positively, you tend to feel good — you can let go of or better manage your fear of judgment.

TIP

Feelings are typically one word, such as sad, embarrassed, or ashamed. Anything that's more than one word is usually a thought, for example, "People think poorly of me" or "People are judging me." Thoughts and feelings are related, so if you can practice more balanced and realistic thoughts, you tend to feel better.

Sometimes, you'll insist that what you're thinking — your thinking trap — is true, and you have proof. For example, suppose that you got a B on your final presentation and you had hoped to earn an A. Your professor told you that you needed to speak a bit more loudly and not read from your notes, but you know that you felt nervous during the presentation. So you think, "My professor could see that I was nervous and is looking down on me. All my classmates think I'm socially awkward. They're probably talking about me behind my back." Now, getting a B on your presentation is certainly not evidence that any of those thoughts are true. All those thoughts show is that you're really good at imagining what people are thinking about you. It would be *more* helpful to tell yourself this: "Getting a B shows I did well overall in the class. My professor's feedback is an opportunity to learn and grow."

REMEMBER

What you think influences what you do and how you feel. With social anxiety, negative thoughts can lead to negative feelings and unhelpful behaviors. This is why becoming aware of your social anxiety cycle is so important in helping you tackle your anxiety.

Knowing Your ABCs

When you're experiencing social anxiety, you may have intense emotions like fear, dread, nervousness, and more. You may feel like a deer in the headlights and freeze in the moment. Then afterward, you probably overthink what happened and relive the situation, which only makes you feel more anxiety — maybe even more anxiety than when the situation was happening.

You may also feel like you can't name your thoughts when it comes to social anxiety. In fact, you may even say you didn't have any thoughts at all because the social anxiety came on so quickly that you weren't even thinking. This is when knowing your ABCs (see Figure 7-1) can help you to name your thoughts and then change them. Identifying and modifying your thoughts can give you a sense of control. You can begin to see your patterns, and you may even be able to learn to use better self-talk in the moment if you know what triggers you. With thinking traps related to social anxiety, you can use the ABC format to understand how your thoughts lead to social anxiety.

Here's what ABC stands for:

>> **Activating agent:** The trigger. This is what initially throws you into a downward spiral. The triggering event may even be something minor, like how someone looked at you. Or it can be big, like giving a presentation in front of a hundred people.

>> **Beliefs:** These are your thoughts about the activating event. This is where you fall into a thinking trap. If you can recognize what you're thinking and what thinking trap you're falling into, you can correct the errors in your thinking.

>> **Consequences:** What happened after the event. The consequences include your emotions, behaviors, physical sensations, and thoughts about what happened. Consequences can also include how you behave afterward. You may act in a way that confirms your social anxiety, which can lead to self-fulfilling prophesies.

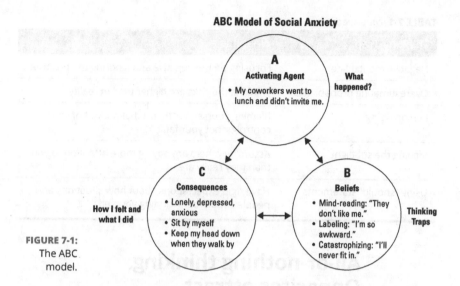

FIGURE 7-1: The ABC model.

Looking at the Types of Thinking Traps

Thinking traps come in many shapes and sizes (see Table 7-1). In this section, I define how each is unique.

TABLE 7-1 ### Types of Thinking Traps

Thinking Trap	What It Is
All-or-nothing thinking	Thinking in opposites or absolutes
Catastrophizing	Thinking of the worst case with a downward spiral
Emotional reasoning	Using your feelings as evidence of the truth
Fortune-telling	Predicting that things will turn out badly
Jumping to conclusions	Making assumptions and ignoring the facts
Labeling	Using a negative word to describe yourself or another person
Mind reading	Assuming you know what others are thinking

(continued)

TABLE 7-1 *(continued)*

Thinking Trap	What It Is
Negative mental filter	Focusing on the negative and ignoring the positives
Overestimating probabilities	Thinking the risks are higher than in reality
Personalizing	Blaming yourself for things that are out of your control or not your fault
Shining the spotlight	Assuming others are paying more attention to you than they really are
Using "should" statements	Have rigid expectations about how situations and people should be, including yourself

All-or-nothing thinking: Opposites attract

If this is your thinking trap, you see the world as "black or white" or "right or wrong." You see people in dichotomies or opposites. Instead of realizing that qualities exist on a continuum, you only see the extremes. You have trouble thinking in shades of gray. You make social comparisons. If you think you're better than someone else, you feel good. But most of the time, you rate yourself lower than other people and perhaps as the absolute lowest. In addition to anxiety, this thinking trap can lead to envy, jealousy, or depression because you're thinking unrealistically and making social comparisons.

Think of a continuum as a scale from 1 to 100, with 1 being someone who is completely avoidant to the point of being homebound and 100 being an extreme extrovert who parties all the time and needs to be with people nonstop. Most people are somewhere in the middle, and you probably are, too. This same idea can apply to any issue you find yourself dealing with.

For example, you may think you need to be perfect. If you aren't perfect, you think of yourself as a failure. If this thinking were a scale with failure on one side and perfection on the other, you would see yourself as a total failure. But no one is perfect, and no one is a complete failure. Instead, you're doing your best and maybe getting to "good enough" is enough.

You may be in an all-or-nothing thinking trap if you regularly have thoughts like the following:

>> I am a total failure at public speaking because I get nervous.

>> I wasn't nominated as the best employee of the year, so I'm a bad employee.

>> I didn't perform perfectly at my job interview, so there's no way I'll get the job.

TIP

If you find yourself in the all-or-nothing thinking trap, here are some things you can do instead:

>> Think flexibly. Think about a continuum from best to worst and the possibilities in between. You're very unlikely to be the best or the worst. Stop assigning the worst label to yourself.

>> Be balanced. Notice when your thoughts are at the worst end of the continuum, and use positive self-talk to bring yourself to at least the middle.

>> Notice black-and-white thinking. A situation is rarely all good or all bad. Instead, try to see shades of gray.

Catastrophizing: Making a mountain out of a molehill

Catastrophizing is when you anticipate that the worst-case scenario will happen. With the catastrophizing trap, you start with one negative thought, and before you know it, your thoughts spiral out of control. You blow things out of proportion, or, as the old saying goes, you make a mountain out of a molehill. You may imagine that if you raise your hand at work to ask a question, you will say something stupid. Then everyone will talk behind your back. Then it will get back to your boss. Then, you will get a bad performance review. Then you will be fired and lose your home.

Spotting the catastrophizing trap:

>> If I fail my test, I will never graduate, I will be poor, and people will look down on me forever.

>> I tripped on the steps at the museum. My friends joked that I was clumsy. They will never go out with me again in public; they will tell my other friends, and I will be alone.

>> If I give a poor presentation at work, my coworkers will laugh behind my back, and I will be fired.

TIP

When you find yourself falling into the catastrophizing trap, here are some things you can do:

>> Catch your catastrophic thinking before it goes into a downward spiral. Stop at the first level of your thinking process.

>> Notice when you have a worry and accept the worry for what it is. Do not make an entire movie out of your initial worry.

>> Imagine yourself coping. Catastrophizing often comes from feeling that you could not handle it if something bad happened. Instead, ask yourself, "What is the worst that could happen?" and then ask, "What would you do if that happened?"

Emotional reasoning: I feel it, so it is true

Emotional reasoning means that you believe how you feel is reality. You use your feelings to draw conclusions. You feel awkward, therefore you are, and others can see it. You take your emotions as truth. You draw false conclusions about the world based on how you feel.

Spotting the trap of emotional reasoning:

>> I feel sad, so that means no one likes me.

>> I feel anxious, so that means people could see that I was sweating.

>> I feel embarrassed, so that means people think what I said was stupid.

>> I'm nervous and lack confidence, so I can't socialize.

TIP

Here are a few ideas to get out of the emotional reasoning trap:

>> Recognize and name your emotions. Ask yourself if you are basing your thoughts on facts or emotions. Stop using your emotions as a thermometer of reality.

>> Separate your emotions from your conclusions. Ask yourself if how you feel is actually creating your conclusion.

>> Think the opposite. If you replaced the negative emotion with a positive emotion and positive outcome, would that mean the positive thing was true? For example, I feel happy, so that means everyone likes me.

Fortune-telling: Becoming a psychic

With fortune-telling, you are anticipating that things will turn out badly. You are convinced that your conclusion is an established fact, and you use it to make predictions. With fortune-telling, your belief that you are socially awkward becomes true because you avoid and do not gain skills to interact confidently in social settings. Your predictions become a self-fulfilling prophecy.

Fortune-telling can also include the hindsight bias. This means that you should have been able to see that bad things were going to happen. In retrospect, you should have been able to predict that bad thing, and you beat yourself up because you should have known. Hindsight bias leads to a lot of overthinking after an event. You even think that if you keep reliving it in your head, you could have changed the past in some illogical way.

Spotting the fortune-telling and hindsight bias traps:

>> The party will be dreadful and I will make a fool of myself, so I will leave early.

>> I knew I was going to say something dumb to that girl, so I should have kept my mouth shut.

>> I am going to be bored at the movies, so I will tell my friends I can't go.

TIP

To get out of the fortune-telling trap, try these ideas:

>> Stay present. Don't let your imagination go wild with thoughts about what might happen.

>> Take risks. Try going to the party. Try talking to a coworker or classmate. Be open-minded and see what happens.

>> Don't beat yourself up about the past. There is no way you could have predicted what happened. Hindsight is 20/20.

Jumping to conclusions: Just the facts, please

You are jumping to conclusions when you make an assumption that isn't supported by facts. You assume you know what is happening based on your unrealistic interpretations. When you jump to conclusions, speed is the enemy and you are thinking too quickly.

You may also overgeneralize. If something happens to you once, then you think it will happen again and again. You jump to the conclusion that whatever negative thing happened once will be a pattern.

Spotting the trap of jumping to conclusions:

>> My coworkers laughed when I was at lunch with them the other day. I think they were laughing at me because I was quiet.

>> The audience looked bored during my rehearsal so all audiences will find me boring.

>> I screwed up at the meeting. I can't do anything right.

TIP

When you find yourself jumping to conclusions or overgeneralizing, try this instead:

>> Stick to the facts. Look at the evidence. Try to observe and describe what actually happened before making any assumptions.

>> Flip it around. Think of the good things that have happened and start to expect more good things.

>> Slow down. Think of different possibilities before forming an opinion.

>> Don't look at one instance as proof that the same thing will happen again. If you do end up eventually seeing a pattern, then that is a signal to improve but not to get stuck in negative thinking.

Labeling: Calling someone (or yourself) names

This may be one of the most dangerous thinking traps. You label yourself or someone else negatively with a defective character trait. You become your own worst enemy. When you label yourself, it can become a self-fulfilling prophecy because then you feel hopeless about changing and do not try.

You know you are labeling when your self-talk starts with "I am" followed by a one-word insult. Labeling reflects some of your deeply held beliefs about yourself. You may also label others when this has become a habit. With the labeling trap, you are judgmental toward yourself and possibly others. When you label, you are making a global generalization about yourself or others.

Spotting the labeling trap:

>> I am boring.

>> I am unattractive.

>> They are a misfit.

TIP

Here are some tips on how to stop labeling and name-calling:

>> Challenge your thoughts. Try to confront your name-calling by asking yourself if you would say this to a friend or loved one.

>> Use encouraging words. Instead of telling yourself you are dumb, for example, you can say, "I feel dumb sometimes, but that does not make it true."

>> Be compassionate toward others. Try to look at other possible reasons why someone did what they did.

>> Try to describe behaviors instead of labeling yourself or others. Instead of saying, "I am lazy," you can say, "I did not spend enough time studying for my test."

>> Look at your values. Do you think it's okay to call someone stupid for a momentary misstep? If the answer is no, consider your values and reconsider giving yourself or someone else a harsh label. Chapter 13 talks about values.

Mind reading: Guessing what people think

When you are mind reading, you assume you know what other people are thinking or feeling. You look for evidence to support your mind-reading thoughts. You assume others are thinking negatively of you. You come to these conclusions without bothering to check them out. On the flip side, you may also expect people to read your mind. You get angry and frustrated when you think they should know what you are thinking.

Spotting the mind-reading trap:

>> No one responded when I posted on social media because they thought what I said was dumb.

>> The Starbucks cashier thinks I am awkward because I did not say much when she took my order.

>> My coworkers think I am stupid because I had a grammar error in my email.

>> The audience members think I am nervous because my voice trembled during my speech.

TIP

If you find yourself in the mind-reading trap, here are some steps to help you.

>> Name it. Remind yourself that you mind reading. Be aware you are doing this. Notice what you are thinking others are thinking.

>> Think about other possibilities. Maybe your interpretation of what others are thinking is not true. Don't dwell on this, but you may think about the other things they may be thinking and admit you could be wrong.

>> Come up with some new self-talk. Tell yourself, "I really do not know what other people are thinking. It is not helpful to mind read. I need to let this go."

>> Ask yourself whether you actually expressed your thoughts and needs to the other person, or are you expecting them to already know how you feel.

Negative mental filter: Wearing dark sunglasses

The negative mental filter trap refers to the tendency to focus on specific negative details, often taken out of context, and ignore other important parts of an experience. It is also called selective attention. You pick out one detail and dwell on it, then think the entire situation is negative.

To help understand selective attention, imagine your brain as a circle with a small hole in the shape of a triangle. Negative information can enter your brain because it comes in the form of triangles. But positive information comes in the form of squares and doesn't fit into the triangle, so they bounce off.

Discounting the positive is a variation of the negative mental filter. You ignore your positive qualities and your strengths. Instead, you only focus on what is wrong with you. This thinking trap is also called *magnification* and *minimization*. You magnify the good things about other people and minimize the good things about yourself.

With minimization, it is hard for you to accept compliments because you do not believe anyone could see the positive in you. But when you sense any critical comments, you take those in as if they are true.

Spotting the trap of the negative mental filter:

>> My boss said I need to improve my interpersonal skills. All I can think about is how I am failing at work.

>> My friend complimented my new haircut, but they were just saying that and they do not really mean it. They were just being nice.

>> I got an A on my English test, but I missed a few questions and did not study enough so I just got lucky. The professor was being generous when grading the tests.

>> I am terrible at small talk, so at my son's basketball games, I will sit far away from the other parents and look at my phone. That way, they will think I am busy and not know that I am anxious.

TIP

If you are discounting what is good about you, try these strategies:

>> Focus on the big picture. Ask yourself how important each detail is. See how all the details add up and try to make a realistic assessment.

>> Identify your strengths. Look at what you are doing well. Write a list of all your positive qualities. At first, this may be hard. If you can't think of anything, ask a friend or family member to help you.

>> Notice when positive information is coming at you in the shape of squares and turn them into triangles so your brain can accept the positives. On the other hand, when negative information comes to you in the form of triangles, turn them into squares so they bounce off.

>> Accept compliments. Do not tell people that their compliment is not true. If someone says, "You have a nice smile,"

don't respond by saying, "Thank you, but I do not like my teeth," or "You are just saying that; my smile is really not that nice." If you are not ready to believe the compliments, a start is to just say thank you and leave it at that.

>> Start a "positive data log" to keep track of information you get that doesn't fit the negative filter and that supports healthy new beliefs about yourself. If someone thanks you for helping them, make a note that someone said you were helpful. If someone responds positively to an email you sent, make a note that you communicated effectively.

Overestimating probabilities: Making bad bets

Overestimating probabilities goes along with catastrophizing. It is when you overestimate the likelihood that something bad will happen. When you are overestimating probabilities, you make an assumption with 100 percent certainty that your feared outcome will happen. Realistically, the chances are much lower that what you fear will actually happen. And many times your bets are so bad that they have little to no chance of coming through.

Spotting the trap of overestimating probabilities:

>> I will get fired if people know I have social anxiety.

>> My coworker passed by without saying hi so that means they don't like me.

>> I will have a panic attack and throw up if I go to the party this weekend.

TIP

You can practice getting out of the trap of overestimating probabilities:

>> What are the odds? Ask yourself what is the actual likelihood that what you are thinking is true or what you are fearing will happen. Better yet, ask yourself what are the odds that you actually said or did something so dumb that anyone noticed or cared.

>> Identify two to three possible outcomes or alternate explanations. Then, divide 100 points and allocate the appropriate number to each possibility. Hopefully, you will notice a couple of things. One is that there are multiple possibilities. And two is that your worst outcome will not get all 100 points. Even if you allocate 70 or 80 points to your greatest fear, it is still not 100!

Personalizing: It's all my fault

Personalizing is when you feel responsible for things you can't control. You think that whatever happened was your fault or shows you are inadequate. When you personalize, you focus on the internal causes of a problem and ignore external reasons why it happened.

Spotting the personalizing trap:

>> If I hire the wrong person, it's my fault and a bad reflection on me. My manager will think I am a weak leader.

>> My child was sent home from school because he hit another kid. It is my fault because I did not raise him better, and others will think I am a bad mom.

>> My dog ran across the street and barked at someone. It's my fault because I could not control him. Now, my neighbors won't talk to me.

TIP

If you find yourself in the personalizing trap, consider these ideas.

>> Don't blame yourself. You can't control everything. Think about why it's not your fault.

>> Ask yourself if anyone or anything else contributed to this situation or if you are solely responsible. Be realistic about how much you actually could have controlled.

Shining the spotlight: All eyes are on me

When you are in the trap of shining the spotlight, you think others are focused on what you are saying or doing. Because you think of yourself as extremely shy or socially anxious, you think everyone can see it and this makes you feel defective.

Shining the spotlight often happens alongside mind reading. When you think people are paying attention to you, even if they aren't, then you think you know what they are thinking about you. In reality, people usually think of themselves or are lost in their own thoughts.

Spotting the spotlight effect:

>> The person I am speaking with can see I am sweating. They will know I am nervous and think less of me.

>> When I pee in the public bathroom, and it takes a long time to come out, people will think there is something wrong with me, and that will be embarrassing.

>> When I walked into the store, the cashier looked at me strangely when I went to pay. She must know I am anxious.

TIP

If you find yourself in the spotlight trap, consider these ideas:

>> Stop being self-centered. It's not about you. Most people are thinking about themselves and are not focused on you.

>> Focus outward. It is easier to manage social anxiety when you are focused outward instead of inward. Stay engaged in conversations by listening to others instead of thinking about yourself.

Using "should" statements: Playing by the rules

When you are in the should statement trap, you have rules or expectations about how things or people should be, including yourself. You think you should or must do things a certain way or be a certain way. You use shoulds and musts to motivate yourself, but it just makes you feel shame and guilt. You end up feeling apathetic and unmotivated, and then you avoid it. It just confirms your negative feelings about your ability to interact with people in a positive way. You might also use shoulds and musts with other people and become judgmental about them.

Spotting the should statements trap:

>> I must always pronounce my words clearly.

>> I should be likable with every person I meet.

>> I should fill awkward silences when talking with people.

>> I shouldn't feel anxious.

TIP

To stop using should and must statements, here are a few ideas:

>> Be compassionate. Because you can become judgmental when you are "shoulding," try to think kind thoughts about yourself and others.

>> Change your language. When you notice you are making a statement using words like *should* and *must,* change it to "it would be nice if . . ." or "I could do . . . ."

>> Validate your emotions. When you notice yourself making a statement about how you should feel, actually change it to how you are feeling. "I shouldn't feel anxious" could be replaced with "I am nervous."

Noticing Thinking Traps

The following sections illustrate two examples of how social anxiety thinking traps may show up in different situations.

Thinking traps at work

CASE EXAMPLE

Noelle was a successful architect with performance anxiety. Her main worry was that deep down she was secretly incompetent and that one day people at work would see it. You'd never know she had some illogical and unhelpful ways of thinking because she hid her fears well. Noelle saw others in her office as being more successful than her. She imagined her boss thought that her work was terrible. In meetings, she often did not speak up. While she was one of the most creative architects in her office and the clients loved working with her, she suffered from performance anxiety and imposter syndrome. She was often nervous that if people really knew how she felt inside, she would be exposed as a fake.

A few of Noelle's thinking traps are:

>> **All-or-nothing thinking:** "I am terrible at my job."

Noelle saw herself in absolutes and thought she was terrible rather than realizing there is a continuum from great to not so great. She certainly was not terrible at her job. If she could see herself on the continuum from 0 to 100, she would certainly not be on either end. But realistically she was above 50, and after she used the mental reframing skill, she eventually put herself at 80.

>> **Mind reading:** "My boss thinks poorly of my work."

She imagined her boss was thinking her work was terrible. She dreaded performance reviews but she always received outstanding ratings. During meeting with her boss, she was often sweating and thought her boss could see it.

>> **Fortune-telling:** "I will never amount to anything."

Noelle saw others in her office as more successful than her. She predicted that she would never be as good as them at her job and she would never be as successful. This made her feel like an imposter because she was doing well in her job.

Thinking traps with dating

CASE EXAMPLE

Billie had social anxiety and was scared to ask girls on a date. He had many strengths that would appeal to girls, but he could not see them. He felt nervous anytime he was in the presence of pretty girls, which caused his throat to clench up, making it difficult to talk, and he would break out in a sweat in his armpits. When he was around his male friends or girls he was not interested in, he did not have any social anxiety. But around girls he liked, he thought they would think he was socially inept and unattractive.

A few of Billie's thinking traps are:

» **Disqualifying the positive:** "I am too short, and that means no girl will ever like me."

Billie disqualified all the strengths he did have, such as a friendly disposition when he was not anxious and many hobbies and interests like being a varsity soccer player. He did not think girls would be impressed by him, so he avoided asking them out.

» **Emotional reasoning:** "I feel like a freak, so I must really be one."

Billie made assumptions about himself based on his feelings. He concluded that pretty girls looked down on him based on how he felt about himself. He exaggerated his negative qualities in his mind and thought girls only saw him through the same dark glasses.

» **Shining the spotlight:** "Girls can see I am sweating and think I am awkward."

In reality, although Billie did sweat, it was not enough that anyone would notice. When Billie was near a pretty girl, his attention went inward and he noticed all his feelings and bodily sensations. But even if he did sweat a lot, it did not matter because no one was looking at his armpits!

Understanding What Happens When You Get Stuck in a Thinking Trap

In the previous two examples, you can see the thinking traps Noelle and Billie often fell into. Instead of lingering in a thinking trap, ask yourself, "Is it helpful to think this way?" Most of the time, the answer is no. Why put yourself down or exaggerate reality when that will only make you feel worse? Thinking traps can also create a self-fulfilling prophecy and sabotage your success. In Noelle's case, she did not speak up in meetings because of her self-doubt. This led to her boss noticing and commenting on it during her performance review. In Billie's case, he was scared to talk to pretty girls so he didn't approach them, which reinforced in his mind that he was inadequate.

WARNING

When you have unrealistic standards and get stuck in a thinking trap, the following can happen:

>> Your attention focuses inward. You hyperfocus on how you are feeling and your bodily sensations. You are focusing on your words and what you are saying or not saying.

>> You believe you have no control over your feelings or how you act. If you stutter and sweat, you feel you have no control over it.

>> You overestimate that bad things will happen, such as people thinking poorly of you.

>> You think your social skills are inadequate and you can't cope in social situations. You dread the situations because you think you will be a failure.

Then the consequences of this thinking are that you avoid social situations, you use safety behaviors when you do participate, and you overthink everything that happened at the event afterward. This leads to continued social apprehension in the future.

REMEMBER

All of this thinking perpetuates the cycle of your social anxiety. You want to review and identify your thinking traps and use the tips to confront them rather than letting them control you.

IN THIS CHAPTER

» Exploring what core beliefs are

» Identifying your own core beliefs

» Using the downward arrow
technique to delve deeper into
your core beliefs

» Knowing the difference between
schemas and core beliefs

Chapter **8**

Pinpointing Your Core Beliefs

C ore beliefs are deeply held thoughts about yourself, others, and the world. They are learned in childhood and are hard to change. Your core beliefs may be positive or negative. Negative core beliefs usually fall into three main categories: unlovability, helplessness, and worthlessness. If you have unhelpful or unrealistic core beliefs, you may have a higher level of social anxiety because these beliefs can lead to you feeling that people don't like you, that there's something with you, or that you can't cope with anxiety.

This chapter focuses on identifying the core beliefs that can keep you trapped in the social anxiety cycle. You look at the basics of core beliefs and how to identify the core beliefs you hold about yourself, others, the world, your social performance, and your social anxiety. You also look at the differences and similarities between core beliefs and schemas, which are your patterns of thinking that started during your childhood and teenage years and continue into adulthood.

WARNING

Changing your core beliefs is difficult because you can't just think yourself out of them. Engaging in exposures where you face your fears and learn through experience can be a useful tool to ultimately change your core beliefs. See Chapter 11 for more about doing exposures.

Understanding Core Beliefs

Think of core beliefs as glasses through which you view situations and experiences. You either view them through a clear lens or a dark lens. You may hold both positive core beliefs and negative core beliefs.

You probably have realistic and helpful beliefs most of the time. However, when something happens that you interpret through a negative lens, negative core beliefs that are unrealistic and unhelpful may become activated. Some characteristics of negative core beliefs include the following:

>> They are learned, usually in childhood, during a traumatic or stressful period. With social anxiety, for example, your core beliefs may have been learned through parental modeling or overprotection, bullying, or some other stressful event.

>> They are firmly embedded in your thinking and shape your reality. For example, with social anxiety, your core beliefs drive your thinking traps and perpetuate the cycle of social anxiety.

>> They feel so fundamental that you never question them. For example, if you think you are unlikable, then you assume it's true and don't question it, but this thought shapes all other thoughts, feelings, and behaviors.

>> They may not be true even if the negative beliefs feel true. For example, you may feel awkward, but it may not be true that anyone sees it.

>> They can become a self-fulling prophecy when information that contradicts your negative core beliefs is ignored. For

example, you may get information that others are not judging you, so you continue to act as if they are, and this belief — along with social anxiety — continues.

>> They are rigid, long-standing, and hard to change (but it is possible). For example, you may have thought you were unlovable from a young age, so it would be hard to break this belief.

REMEMBER

It's important not to move too quickly when working to change your core beliefs because they are the most challenging to change. A great deal of change can happen by looking at your automatic thoughts and underlying assumptions (your rules about what can lead to something else often showing up as if/then self-talk). Even if you struggle with changing core beliefs, you can still successfully tackle social anxiety. When you learn to reframe negative self-talk, it's often unnecessary to address core beliefs. Once you stop avoidance and safety behaviors, you will experience a great deal more positive social feedback, which shifts your core beliefs without any direct effort.

Table 8-1 outlines an example of how negative and positive core beliefs affect your reactions. When a core belief is positive, you will generally have helpful reactions. When a core belief is negative, your automatic thoughts, feelings, and behaviors can be unrealistic and unhelpful, and you will have greater social anxiety.

CASE EXAMPLE

Situation: Your social anxiety is triggered by a poor performance review at work that included feedback not only from your boss but your coworkers as well.

TABLE 8-1   **Negative versus Positive Core Beliefs**

Person	Core Belief	Reactions
A	I'm inadequate.	**Thoughts:** Others are judging me. My boss and coworker think I can't do this job. No one likes me. I can't handle feeling this way. I may as well quit this job.
		Feelings: Sad, depressed, worried, anxious, self-conscious.
		Behaviors: Doesn't try any harder. Avoids the boss and coworker.

(continued)

TABLE 8-1 *(continued)*

Person	Core Belief	Reactions
B	I'm capable and smart.	**Thoughts:** I messed up on a few aspects of my job this year because I had too many balls in the air. People respect me most of the time. Maybe I am overreacting.
		Feelings: Disappointed but energized for the new year.
		Behaviors: Works harder. Focuses. Networks with people effectively.

Categorizing Negative Core Beliefs

The idea that people hold core beliefs that guide their thoughts, feelings, and behaviors started in the 1960s when American psychiatrist Aaron Beck developed cognitive behavior therapy (CBT). His daughter, Judith Beck, expanded on his work by proposing that negative core beliefs fall into two categories: *unlovability* and *helplessness*. Later on, a third category, *worthlessness*, was added. Many people with social anxiety hold negative core beliefs in more than one category.

Unlovability

In the unlovability bucket are the fears that you are not lovable, likable, or capable of intimacy. Some thoughts in this category include:

>> I'm undesirable.

>> I'm unattractive.

>> I'm different.

>> I'm boring.

If you have social anxiety, it's common to have negative core beliefs in the unlovability bucket. In fact, the negative beliefs in this category may be your most common. Developing positive core beliefs in this category may be difficult, but you can do it. Here's a sampling of some new beliefs to work on:

>> I'm reasonably likable, attractive, and desirable.

>> I'm interesting enough, and other people can see my positive attributes.

>> I can connect with others and will not end up alone.

Helplessness

The beliefs you hold with social anxiety may fall into the help-lessness category, including beliefs about inferiority, incompetence, and vulnerability. For example, thoughts in this category include:

>> I'm inferior.

>> I'm a failure.

>> I'm not good enough.

>> I'm vulnerable.

>> I'm incompetent.

If you have negative core beliefs in this category, you can work on changing your self-talk, as described in Chapter 10. You can also engage in exposures, discussed in Chapter 11, to help you discover that your negative core beliefs aren't generally true. Or, if there is some element of truth, you can learn how to cope with the social anxiety resulting from your beliefs. Some positive beliefs that could help you deal with your social anxiety include:

>> I'm as capable as other people.

>> I can handle feeling anxious.

>> I have strengths and weaknesses, and that's okay.

Worthlessness

Core beliefs of worthlessness are related to feeling as though you are insignificant or a burden to others. Negative beliefs in this category may be more common with severe social anxiety. Thoughts in this category include:

>> I'm bad.

>> I'm unworthy.

>> I'm defective.

>> I'm toxic.

WARNING

Negative core beliefs in the worthlessness category are extremely resistant to change. If you find your core beliefs of worthlessness too strong, turn to Chapter 15 to see if working with a therapist could benefit you. Some new beliefs to develop in this category include:

>> I'm worthy.

>> I have value.

>> I'm good enough.

Identifying Your Negative Core Beliefs

In Chapter 6, you assessed and rated the common negative thoughts and beliefs you have when you experience social anxiety. Those ratings can help you with the sections of this chapter where you'll delve more deeply into your core beliefs. You may already know what your core beliefs are from Chapter 6. If you need more help identifying them, try using the *downward arrow technique* to uncover them.

The downward arrow technique is an exercise that can help you identify and explore your underlying assumptions (what you think something means if something else happens) and your belief systems, such as your perceptions of threats that contribute to the misinterpretation of unwanted intrusive thoughts. You implement it by asking yourself questions to drill down to your beliefs and underlying assumptions at a deeper level. Examples of such questions include:

>> What will it mean if others think you are (fill in the blank)?

>> What does that say about you?

>> What if that were true?

>> What are you worried that might mean?

>> Why does that bother you?

>> What is the worst thing this thought might say?

>> Why is this situation, thought, or feeling so bad?

Figure 8-1 illustrates an example of how the downward arrow technique may be used to get to the core belief of someone with a fear of blushing in public. For each person, the starting thought could lead downward to a different core belief. In between the automatic thought and discovering your core belief, you'll discover some underlying assumptions. Sometimes, just working on the underlying assumptions can be enough to help you manage your social anxiety more effectively.

TIP

When you implement the downward arrow technique, you will know you have uncovered your core belief when you keep asking questions but always come back to the same answer (as if you are going in circles). At that point, your core belief has been revealed.

Now, fill in Table 8-2 using the downward arrow technique to discover one of your core beliefs.

Downward Arrow: Blushing in Public

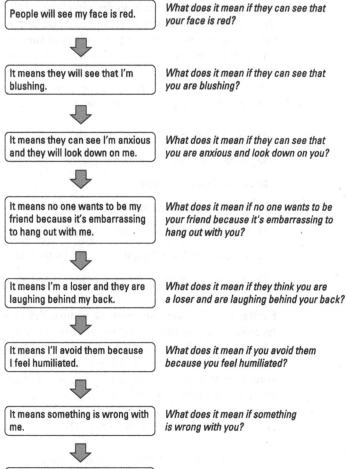

People will see my face is red.	*What does it mean if they can see that your face is red?*
It means they will see that I'm blushing.	*What does it mean if they can see that you are blushing?*
It means they can see I'm anxious and they will look down on me.	*What does it mean if they can see that you are anxious and look down on you?*
It means no one wants to be my friend because it's embarrassing to hang out with me.	*What does it mean if no one wants to be your friend because it's embarrassing to hang out with you?*
It means I'm a loser and they are laughing behind my back.	*What does it mean if they think you are a loser and are laughing behind your back?*
It means I'll avoid them because I feel humiliated.	*What does it mean if you avoid them because you feel humiliated?*
It means something is wrong with me.	*What does it mean if something is wrong with you?*
CORE BELIEF **I'm defective.**	

FIGURE 8-1:
The downward arrow technique.

Core beliefs about yourself

You probably have both positive and negative core beliefs about yourself with regard to social anxiety. When social anxiety kicks in, you may think others are judging you and that something is wrong with you. You may describe yourself in a negative way with words such as boring, ugly, dumb, loser, not good enough, incompetent, unworthy, undeserving, flawed, or unlovable. Or you may think you can't handle your feelings related to social anxiety.

TABLE 8-2   **Identifying a Core Belief**

Identify a situation that brings up social anxiety.	
Write down your negative thought(s) about this situation.	
What do these negative thoughts mean?	
• What will it mean if others think you are (fill in the blank)?	
• What does that say about you?	
• What if that were true?	
• What are you worried that might mean?	
• Why does that bother you?	
• What is the worst thing this thought might say?	
• Why is this situation, thought, or feeling so bad?	
What do you think your ultimate core belief is?	

What negative core beliefs do you have about yourself? What new positive core beliefs do you want to develop? List three negative and positive beliefs you hold about social anxiety in general.

Negative	Positive
I am_____.	I am_____.
I am_____.	I am_____.
I am_____.	I am_____.

Core beliefs about other people

What negative core beliefs do you hold about other people? You may believe people are judgmental, critical, untrustworthy, or manipulative. What are a few of your negative core beliefs about other people? What new positive core beliefs do you want to develop? List three negative and positive beliefs you hold about social anxiety in general.

Negative	Positive
People are_____.	People are_____.
People are_____.	People are_____.
People are_____.	People are_____.

Core beliefs about the world

What negative core beliefs do you hold about the world? You may think the world is a dangerous place, and you may be humiliated at any time. What are a few of your negative core beliefs about the world? What new positive core beliefs do you want to develop? List three negative and positive beliefs you hold about social anxiety in general.

Negative	Positive
The world is_____.	The world is_____.
The world is_____.	The world is_____.
The world is_____.	The world is_____.

Core beliefs about social performance standards

You may hold yourself to high standards of social performance. You may think you should always know what to say or be outgoing. What negative core beliefs do you hold about how you (and others) must perform socially? What new positive core beliefs do you want to develop? List three negative and positive beliefs you hold about social anxiety in general.

Negative	Positive
I must or should be_____.	It's okay to be_____.
I must or should be_____.	It's okay to be_____.
I must or should be_____.	It's okay to be_____.

Core beliefs about social anxiety itself

What negative core beliefs do you hold about anxiety and social anxiety? You may think social anxiety is bad and embarrassing. You may feel flawed or inadequate for having social anxiety. What are a few of your negative core beliefs about social anxiety? What new positive core beliefs do you want to develop? List three negative and positive beliefs you hold about social anxiety in general.

DEVELOPING NEW CORE BELIEFS

One way to develop new positive core beliefs is to look for evidence that the positive beliefs are true. Many times, the brain will let information in that supports its existing belief system. If you think you are unlovable, any proof of this will reinforce this negative belief. If you want to develop a new contradictory belief, you will need to actively look for evidence that the new belief is true. Exposures can help you test your beliefs and develop new ones as you learn through actual experience.

Negative	Positive
Social anxiety is_____.	Social anxiety is_____.
Social anxiety is_____.	Social anxiety is_____.
Social anxiety is_____.	Social anxiety is_____.

REMEMBER

It's not always necessary to try to directly change your core beliefs. You can work on developing more helpful self-talk (see Chapter 10) or engaging in exposures (see Chapter 11), which may result in more positive core beliefs about yourself, about others, and about the world.

How Core Beliefs and Schemas Differ

Though this book takes a standard approach to tackling social anxiety with cognitive and behavioral skills, it's worth mentioning that core beliefs and schemas are similar in that they are both deeply held beliefs that influence how you think, feel, and behave. Both start in childhood and are difficult to change, and the terms are often used interchangeably. However, schemas differ from core beliefs in that schemas are categories of life themes rather than the actual content of the beliefs. When schemas are activated, negative core beliefs can rise to the surface, making a situation feel very painful.

Here are some definitions:

>> **Schemas:** Patterns of thinking and interacting in the world as well as your felt beliefs about yourself and others.

>> **Core beliefs:** The cognitive portion of the schema.

In Chapter 3, I provide a list of schemas and discuss how schemas interact with thinking and behavioral reactions. Here's an example of how schemas, core beliefs, thoughts, and behaviors interact:

>> **Schema:** Social isolation. (The belief that you are isolated from the rest of the world, different from other people, and/or alienated from a community.)

>> **Core belief:** I'm different. I don't belong. I'm an outcast.

>> **Thoughts:** I'll never have friends. I'd rather be alone. I don't care if people like me anyway.

>> **Behaviors:** Avoid social opportunities.

TIP

Working on schemas is beyond the scope of this book. I mention them because it helps to understand that your schemas influence the core beliefs, thinking patterns, and behavioral reactions you have now. To learn more about schema therapy, visit the International Society of Schema Therapy website at https:// schematherapysociety.org.

3
Overcoming Social Anxiety

Discover how setting specific and realistic goals using the SMART goal technique can help you overcome your social anxiety and why your success depends on staying in a growth mindset.

Explore ways to face your social anxiety fears by doing exposures, including creating a fear ladder and addressing your fears at your own pace.

Look at common character strengths and figure out which ones apply to you.

Discover how to use positive psychology to help you use your strengths to live a meaningful life and advance your life's purpose.

Explore acceptance skills, ways to practice mindfulness, and how to cultivate compassion toward yourself.

Discover the different types of therapists and different types of therapy, and how to find the right therapist for you.

Chapter 9

Getting Ready to Change

Y ou may not think that getting ready to change is important to actually changing. However, being prepared is critical to making any improvements in life. The first step in overcoming social anxiety is to set specific, rather than general, goals. Then, you can work on overcoming any obstacles to reaching your goals. Also important is staying in a *growth mindset*, which means being open to learning and growing. With a growth mindset, you see mistakes as an opportunity to learn. (This may be the exact opposite of what you think right now, so keep an open mind.)

In this chapter, you look at how setting specific and realistic goals using the SMART goal technique can help you overcome your social anxiety. You also discover why your success depends on staying in a growth mindset. At the end of the chapter, you explore techniques for overcoming any obstacles to change you may discover along your path.

REMEMBER

Change can be hard. If it were easy, you would not be reading this book. You've come this far in trying to understand your social anxiety, so now it's time to set goals and get ready to overcome obstacles.

Defining SMART Goals

SMART stands for Specific, Measurable, Achievable, Relevant, and Timely. SMART goals can help you define changes you want to make and come up with a plan that will help you achieve them. They can be a helpful way to overcome the struggle of setting and following through on your goals. In this section, I describe each characteristic of a SMART goal and how you can set SMART goals for overcoming social anxiety.

Specific

A specific goal clearly identifies what you want to change. It answers the question, "What will I do?" A vague goal may be to "reduce social anxiety." A specific goal that answers the *what* question may be to "go to parties when I am invited" or "make eye contact." You probably have several goals you want to work on, and you can be specific about what you want to change.

TIP

Approach goals are stated in a positive, action-oriented way, such as "I will raise my hand and offer my opinions in meetings." *Avoidance goals* are far less motivating and specific, such as telling yourself, "I will stop being quiet in meetings." Approach goals tend to be more effective than avoidance goals. Try to set a goal for a specific action you want to take. When you tell yourself to do something in a positive way, it is more motivating and actionable.

Measurable

Goals should be measurable so that there is evidence of how far along you've come with achieving your goal. It should answer the question, "What will I track?" When you engage in a specific activity that usually triggers your social anxiety, your initial inclination may be to measure your success by whether your anxiety went down or not. Instead, a better way to measure your success is to note how many times you did something. For example, to make a goal measurable, you could keep track of the number of times you accepted invitations or how many times you spoke up in meetings.

It is important to find concrete ways to measure your success, track your progress, and know when you've met your goal. For example, you could keep a log of your accomplishments or use an app tracker.

Achievable

Goals should be something you can reasonably do. They should stretch you slightly so that you feel challenged but defined well enough to achieve them. An achievable goal answers the question, "Can I do it?"

TIP

Make sure your goals are reasonable for the level you are at right now. A good way to set achievable and reasonable goals is to develop a *fear ladder*, which is a list of situations that scare you, ranked from the easiest for you to do to the hardest for you to do. Be specific on what you will do to accomplish each goal. For example, an easy goal could be smiling at strangers while walking your dog in the park. A medium-level goal could be raising your hand and answering a question in class. A hard goal could be inviting a person out on a date. If you can achieve the easy goals first and then the medium goals, ultimately the hard goals will feel more achievable too. (See Chapter 11 for more details on how to create a fear ladder.)

Relevant

A relevant goal connects your goals to a larger purpose so that it feels meaningful and motivating. It answers the question, "Why will I do it?"

TIP

Sometimes, creating a pros and cons list of why you want to decrease social anxiety can be helpful in ensuring your goals are relevant. For example, maybe you are motivated to do the hard work of dating because you want to have a life partner and a family. Or perhaps reducing performance anxiety could enable you to make a difference in the world with meaningful work.

Timely

Timely goals answer the question, "When will I start and finish?" Timely goals can increase your sense of urgency, causing you to achieve your results more quickly. For example, a timely goal related to reducing your social anxiety may be that you will reach two specific goals by the end of this book. Or you can be more granular and make timely subgoals such as, "I want to ask someone on a date within two weeks," or "I want to attend a social event for at least an hour."

Setting SMART Goals

It's important to set SMART goals because, without a clear direction of where you are going, you may not achieve your goals except with luck, perhaps. A template for making your own SMART goals is shown in Table 9-1. Fill out the table to develop a SMART goal for yourself.

TABLE 9-1   SMART Goals Template

Specific (What will I do?)	
Measurable (What will I track?)	
Achievable (Can I do it?)	
Relevant (Why will I do it?)	
Timely (When will I start and finish?)	

REMEMBER

Don't let this process overwhelm you. Even if you can't fill out the template right now or if you can only add a couple of things, that's okay.

Staying In a Growth Mindset

With a *growth mindset,* you believe your ability can be developed through hard work and perseverance. Intelligence and talent are important but not the main ingredients. As a result, you develop a love of learning, resilience, and a tolerance for mistakes essential for high achievement. Your motto is: "Mistakes are an opportunity to learn."

TECHNICAL STUFF

The concept of the growth and fixed mindset was popularized in Carol S. Dweck's book, *Mindset: The New Psychology of Success* (Random House).

Those with a growth mindset:

- ❯❯ View mistakes as an opportunity to improve and do not give up easily.

- ❯❯ Embrace challenges and recognize setbacks as part of the learning process.

- ❯❯ Improve skills with time, effort, and practice and try new strategies.

- ❯❯ Realize that the only actual failure is not trying.

- ❯❯ Are encouraged and inspired by other people's successes.

- ❯❯ Appreciate feedback and aren't discouraged by criticism.

- ❯❯ Believe there is no such thing as failure because failure is necessary to learn and grow.

In contrast, with a *fixed mindset,* you believe intelligence and talent are innate and unchangeable. If you're not good at something, you think you will never be good at it, you lose interest, and you give up easily. When you stay primarily in a fixed mindset, you may achieve less than your full potential. Your motto is: "Why try?"

REMEMBER

It's important to stay in a growth mindset so you stay open to learning and growing. With social anxiety, you see mistakes as an opportunity to learn, and you fear judgment less.

Table 9-2 outlines the growth versus fixed mindset as it pertains to people with social anxiety.

TABLE 9-2   Growth versus Fixed Mindset in Social Anxiety

Growth Mindset	Fixed Mindset
Learning-oriented	Performance-oriented
Persists in the face of setbacks	Gives up easily
Learns from criticism	Avoids negative feedback
Inspired by the success of others and finds role models	Compares and feels threatened by others' success
Embraces challenges to confront social anxiety	Avoids exposures to social anxiety
Motto: "Mistakes are an opportunity to learn."	Motto: "Why try?"

Examining the Pros and Cons of Overcoming Social Anxiety

Identifying the pros and cons of overcoming your social anxiety can be a helpful way to become motivated to change. You may be surprised to discover that there are reasons that keep your social anxiety from changing. Bringing these reasons into awareness can be a helpful first step.

Tables 9-3 and 9-4 list examples of the pros and cons of overcoming your social anxiety versus staying the same. After reviewing each list, think about your own pros and cons of overcoming social anxiety. Circle the statements that apply to you and add any others you can think of.

Looking back at your pros and cons list, what are your top three reasons for changing? Write them down here:

1. _____

2. _____

3. _____

TABLE 9-3   Pros and Cons of Overcoming Social Anxiety

Pros	Cons
I'll feel more confident.	It will take work.
I'll make more friends.	I'll be nervous.
I might get a promotion at work.	People will see I am awkward.
Any other pros?	*Any other cons?*

TABLE 9-4   Pros and Cons of Staying the Same

Pros	Cons
I'll feel safe.	I will continue to feel lonely.
No one will notice me.	I'll get stuck in a dead-end job.
I won't have to take risks.	I will never know if I am likable.
Any other pros?	*Any other cons?*

Identifying the Obstacles to Change

To reach your goals, it's good to be aware of potential obstacles to change and have some strategies prepared to overcome them. In this section, I review some common obstacles to change and provide some ideas for handling them.

Managing anticipatory anxiety

Anticipatory anxiety is the anxious feelings you get when you think about doing something or right before you do it. These feelings are common and can cause you to avoid situations or cancel events. When anticipatory anxiety comes up for you, here are some ideas on how to handle it:

>> Find healthy distractions like walking, exercising, listening to music, or reading a book to take your mind off the situation.

>> Remind yourself that you can think of this social situation as an experiment and learn from it. There is no such thing as failure.

>> Think about how much you will enjoy the event after you go.

Getting over self-consciousness and inhibition

You may feel self-conscious when you try out new behaviors and participate in social situations. These feelings of self-consciousness may cause you to inhibit yourself socially by being quiet, having stiff body language, or avoiding eye contact. Here are some ideas to handle self-consciousness when it comes up:

>> Try to be present and in the moment.

>> Keep your focus outward on what is happening around you instead of inward toward yourself.

TIP

Grounding techniques help you stay present and focus your attention outward by using your five senses. For example, you can use your sight to notice the eyes of the person you're talking to, use your hearing to notice the inflection of their voice, use your sense of touch to feel your feet on the ground, use taste to try to figure out the ingredients in a dish you are sharing; or see if you can use your sense of smell to notice whether the other person is wearing any fragrance scents.

Handling negative thinking traps

As discussed in Chapter 7, thinking traps are unhelpful patterns of thought that people with social anxiety fall into. When your mind gets stuck in a negative way of thinking that's illogical or unhelpful, you could be in a thinking trap. Your mind starts to interpret things in a biased fashion. While the worst could happen, social anxiety causes you to focus on negative outcomes exclusively. Here are some ways to handle thinking traps when you get stuck in one:

>> Notice the thought pattern and identify the thinking trap.

>> Talk back to the thought pattern of the thinking trap and not only the content. For example, if you are catastrophizing, you can tell yourself, "Here I go again, thinking that the worst can happen."

>> Accept that the probability of your worst-case scenario is probably small while being aware of it. Do not over-focus on other scenarios that could happen.

Responding to negative automatic thoughts

Automatic thoughts are the words and images that pop up without you even realizing them. Automatic thoughts are the actual words you are hearing or images you are seeing in your brain. It often feels as if a devilish figure is sitting on your shoulder and whispering bad things in your ear. Here are some ideas for how to respond to negative automatic thoughts when they pop up:

>> Talk to yourself like you would to a good friend.

>> Reframe the negative thoughts in a more positive or helpful way.

>> Consider the accuracy of your anxiety-provoking images.

>> Embrace the possibility of anxiety-provoking thoughts or images ("Maybe I do look sweaty, but I'm learning to be ok with that.").

Eliminating safety behaviors

Safety behaviors are the coping mechanisms you do to make yourself feel better in social situations, but all they really do is perpetuate your social anxiety. Some examples of safety behaviors include staying quiet in groups, avoiding going places, and paying too much attention to yourself. Here are some ways to reduce safety behaviors:

>> Come up with a plan to gradually reduce safety behaviors over time.

>> Challenge yourself to do something small without engaging in a safety behavior and see what happens.

Tolerating anxiety

No one wants to feel anxious, especially when social anxiety can involve feelings of shame and humiliation. Being told to tolerate anxiety can feel heartless. You probably think that you just can't. But if you practice, you'll develop skills over time. In the meantime, here are some initial ideas about how to tolerate social anxiety:

>> Keep reminding yourself that, ironically, the only way to reduce social anxiety is to experience situations that make you feel anxious.

>> Practice getting in touch with your bodily sensations so that when you do feel them escalate, you are less scared of them and/or you know how to relax your body. You discover some body-focused skills in Chapter 14.

Reducing rumination after an event

Whether you have a successful social event or not, you are likely to overthink it afterward. The socially anxious mind is always looking for what went wrong. Sometimes, this overthinking is done for reassurance that the event went well, but this mental process tends to backfire. You will find any little thing you could have done better, or you will mind read what you think people thought of you with little to no evidence. Here are some ways to reduce rumination:

>> Notice when you start to ruminate and focus on something else. This is called *turning the mind*. Remember, you will have to turn your mind again and again.

>> Stay in the growth mindset. Sometimes, arguing with the ruminating mind does not work. It believes it made mistakes. Instead, remind yourself that even if you did make a mistake, it's an opportunity to learn.

Avoiding avoidance

Avoidance is the granddaddy of social anxiety. It is your most natural inclination when feelings of social anxiety set in. This is the most common and significant obstacle that will come up when you get anxious. You need to fight the urge to retreat if you want to tackle your social anxiety. Here are a few ways to handle avoidance urges:

>> Come up with a plan for less anxiety-provoking exposures first so you can slowly learn to handle your anxious feelings.

>> Focus on your reasons for changing and use motivating self-talk to help you work on confronting your fears.

IN THIS CHAPTER

» Turning your fearful thinking into resilient thinking

» Identifying and responding to your inner critic

» Understanding what doesn't work when trying to change self-talk

» Uncovering specific strategies to change self-talk

Chapter **10**

Changing Your Self-Talk

*C*ALM *thinking* refers to self-talk that's compassionate, accepting, logical, and motivating. Turning your fearful thinking into CALM thinking may seem impossible, but it can be done. The key is to notice your negative thoughts, identify your thinking traps, and then use reframing skills to create CALM self-talk. It's also helpful to identify which types of your inner critic drive your fears so that you can confront your inner critic firmly and forcefully. Certain strategies, such as repeating empty mantras, don't work. In this chapter, you discover specific cognitive strategies to help you quash negative self-talk and develop CALM thinking instead.

Self-talk is the voice in your head that reflects your thinking style.

REMEMBER

Reframing Fearful Thinking Into CALM Thinking

Fearful thinking refers to your negative thought pattern that produces social anxiety. *Reframing* means being able to change fearful thinking into *CALM thinking* — thoughts that are compassionate, accepting, logical, and motivating. Changing your self-talk isn't easy, and it takes continual practice. Reframing is like building a muscle; it takes time to see results. And like exercising, reframing is not something you do once and then stop and say that it doesn't work. Changing your fearful thinking into CALM thinking takes dedication; you need to commit to changing your mindset and finding messages that are believable to you.

Turning fearful thinking into CALM thinking involves three steps:

1. **Identify your negative self-talk.**

   What are you saying to yourself that's untrue or not helpful?

2. **Identify your thinking traps.**

   What are your common patterns of negative thinking that you need to correct?

3. **Correct your self-talk.**

   How can you create CALM thinking that's compassionate, accepting, logical, and motivating?

The definitions for each part of CALM thinking are as follows:

» **Compassionate:** Speaking to yourself in a gentler and kinder way.

» **Accepting:** Acknowledging the truth about yourself or the situation in a nonjudgmental way.

» **Logical:** Looking at your thinking traps and reframing your self-talk in a more realistic or helpful way.

>> **Motivating:** Reminding yourself of things that inspire you to meet your goals.

Looking at an example of fearful thinking

Following is an example of how to reframe fearful thinking into CALM thinking.

**CASE
EXAMPLE**

Linda is 22 years old and lives at home. She was attending community college but dropped out due to her social anxiety. Her family is active at their church, and Linda attends Sunday services every week. After church, she tries to stay and socialize with young adults in her youth group.

Step 1: What is Linda's fearful thinking?

I speak too slowly. Everyone can see I am nervous. They think I'm awkward. I am frustrated with myself because I'm an introvert. I can't get my thoughts out quickly like other people. I am a misfit.

Step 2: Identify her thinking traps.

Based on this self-talk, which thinking traps is Linda falling into? Table 10-1 lists the thinking traps and what each one means. (Refer to Chapter 7 for more about thinking traps.)

You may notice that Linda's fearful thinking falls into many different thinking traps. Here are a few:

>> **Emotional reasoning:** She feels frustrated, so she thinks there must be something wrong with her.

>> **Labeling:** She calls herself a misfit.

>> **Mind reading:** Linda thinks others are thinking she is awkward.

>> **Shining the spotlight:** Linda thinks everyone can see that she is nervous.

TABLE 10-1   Types of Thinking Traps

Thinking Trap	What It Is
All-or-nothing thinking	Thinking in opposites or absolutes
Catastrophizing	Thinking of the worst case with a downward spiral
Emotional reasoning	Using your feelings as evidence of the truth
Fortune-telling	Predicting that things will turn out badly
Jumping to conclusions	Making assumptions and ignoring the facts
Labeling	Using a negative word to describe yourself or another person
Mind reading	Assuming you know what others are thinking
Negative mental filter	Focusing on the negative and ignoring the positives
Overestimating probabilities	Thinking the risks are higher than in reality
Personalizing	Blaming yourself for things that are out of your control or not your fault
Shining the spotlight	Assuming others are paying more attention to you than they really are
Using "should" statements	Have rigid expectations about how situations and people should be, including yourself

Step 3: Correct Linda's self-talk.

How can Linda reframe her fearful thinking into CALM thinking with self-talk that's compassionate, accepting, logical, and motivating? Here's a new way Linda can start talking to herself:

>> **Compassionate:** What can you say to yourself that's gentler and kinder?

Many people are introverts, and it's a common trait. Introverts can be good listeners, and it makes me a more sensitive person. I may have difficult thoughts and feelings, but they don't have to rule the day.

>> **Accepting:** What part is true about yourself or the situation, and can you accept it in a nonjudgmental way?

While it's true that it takes me time to get my words out, I like meeting new people even if I have challenges.

>> **Logical:** What thinking traps do you notice? What can you say to yourself that's more realistic or helpful?

It doesn't make sense that I am making negative assumptions that other people think I am awkward and that I'm calling myself a misfit. I am in a thinking trap, and it's not helpful to be critical of myself.

>> **Motivating:** What can you remind yourself of that can inspire you to meet your goals?

I can focus on my values of kindness and being helpful to others. I have strengths in these areas. When I feel anxious, I can remind myself that people like me, and it can help me start up conversations.

Practicing changing your fearful thinking

You may be thinking, "This sounds easy on paper, but I can't do this myself." Thinking you can't do it could be the *negative mental filter* thinking trap talking. It is hard work to change fearful thinking into CALM thinking, but it can be done with time and practice. Complete the exercise that follows to practice changing some of your own fearful thinking into resilient thinking.

Step 1: Identify your negative self-talk.

What is your fearful thinking?

_____

_____

_____

Step 2: Identify your thinking traps.

Put a check mark next to the thinking traps your thinking falls into, and write a sentence about why your thinking falls into that trap.

___ All-or-nothing thinking: _____

___ Catastrophizing: _____

___ Emotional reasoning: _____

___ Fortune-telling: _____

___ Jumping to conclusions: _____

___ Labeling: _____

___ Mind reading: _____

___ Negative mental filter: _____

___ Overestimating probabilities: _____

___ Personalizing: _____

___ Shining the spotlight: _____

___ Using "should" statements: _____

Step 3: Correct your self-talk.

Reframe your fearful thinking by filling in Table 10-2 with new thoughts that are compassionate, accepting, logical, and motivating.

TABLE 10-2   Reframing Your Fearful Thinking

Compassionate: What can you say to yourself that's gentler and kinder?	
Accepting: What part is true about yourself or the situation, and can you accept in a nonjudgmental way?	
Logical: What thinking traps do you notice? What can you say to yourself that's more realistic or helpful?	
Motivating: What can you remind yourself of that can inspire you to meet your goals?	

Identifying Your Inner Critic

You are likely familiar with the concept of the inner critic — the part of you that judges, criticizes, blames, or punishes yourself or others. It can be so insidious that you may not even notice it. The inner critic is a bully and can make you feel constantly anxious. The inner critic thinks its job is to help you. It's hypervigilant about spotting danger so you can be prepared if something bad happens or avoid what your critic perceives as dangerous.

Your inner critic is responsible for your thinking traps. It may tell you to catastrophize, exaggerate, mind read, or magnify the bad and minimize the good. For example, your inner critic may tell you that if you catastrophize, you will be prepared if you fail. Or if you mind read, you can avoid bad people.

REMEMBER

The inner critic generally forms in childhood. It can develop from receiving critical messages from parental figures, teachers, or anyone who bullies or abuses you. It can arise when your core emotional needs are not met, and then schemas, or negative life themes, develop.

Social anxiety brings with it several types of inner critic modes, which I describe in the following sections. As you read through the descriptions, ask yourself the following:

>> Which critic modes apply to you?

>> What do these critic modes usually say to you?

Demanding critic: Work harder and harder

The demanding critic pushes you always to be the best. It tells you to overwork and overachieve. It makes you feel stressed and exhausted all the time because work is prioritized over leisure. It constantly compares your achievements to others. Your self-worth becomes your accomplishments. You may also push others as you push yourself.

Perfectionistic critic: Avoid mistakes

This critic tries to get you to do things perfectly so that you won't be judged or criticized by others or yourself. It says mistakes and flaws are unacceptable. It fixates on imperfections and has trouble seeing the big picture. It is extremely judgmental and hard on you when an actual or perceived failure does happen. You may also look down on others if they are not perfect.

Punishing critic: Suffer the consequences

The punishing critic tells you that you must suffer the consequences if you do something wrong. It has extremely high moral and ethical standards. It punishes you for small infractions or perceived failures. You may also have a punitive attitude toward others.

WARNING

The punishing critic can lead you or others to self-harm. If you are engaging in self-harm, such as cutting, look ahead to Chapter 15 for information on working with a therapist.

Shaming critic: You are unworthy

The shaming critic attacks your self-worth and causes you to feel humiliated. When this critic shows up, you feel inherently flawed, bad, or worthless. Toxic shame makes you believe there is something deeply wrong with you. You feel depressed and insecure when this critic shows up. If you shame others, too, then it becomes toxic to the people around you.

Guilt-inducing critic: Takes care of others

The guilt-inducing critic tells you that your needs are not as important as the needs of others. Expressing your needs is not allowed and is viewed as selfish. It says you must take care of others at your own expense.

Controlling critic: Don't be a fool

The controlling critic tries to control what you say and do so you don't embarrass yourself or make a fool of yourself. It results in you being overly rigid and emotionally constricted. It says to keep your thoughts and feelings to yourself so others can't judge you.

Talking back to your inner critic

REMEMBER

The inner critic is a bully so you must talk back to it a little more forcefully than when you are only reframing your fearful thinking. You can use similar strategies to talk back to your inner critic as you did when you confronted fearful thinking. The main difference with talking back to your inner critic is that you have to be firm and forceful because the inner critic can be relentless.

Talking back to your inner critic involves three steps:

1. Identify which inner critic mode has shown up.

2. Identify what the inner critic is telling you.

3. Talk back to the inner critic by being firm and forceful to the inner critic while being compassionate, accepting, logical, and motivating to yourself.

Looking at an example of the inner critic

Following is an example of how the inner critic may show up and how to talk back to it.

CASE
EXAMPLE

Jim is 32-year-old up-and-coming finance director. Deep down, he is very shy, and he constantly worries about what others think of him. He works overtime a lot because he double- and triple-checks his work due to the fear of making mistakes that others could notice and judge him. His wife complains that he gets home too late on weekdays and that he's checked out on weekends. He compares himself to others and thinks he is not good enough. Most of the time, he thinks he is an imposter, and if people knew how incompetent and anxious he was, they'd look down on him.

Step 1: Identify which inner critic has shown up.

Which inner critic has shown up for Jim?

Jim has a very demanding and perfectionistic critic. His demanding critic does not let him relax, compares him to others, and keeps pushing him to do more and more. His perfectionistic critic fears making mistakes.

Step 2: Identify what the inner critic is telling you.

What is Jim's inner critic telling him?

>> You are not good enough.

>> If you make a mistake, you'll be exposed and fired.

>> You are weak because you are anxious. If people knew how anxious you were, they'd look down on you.

Step 3: Talk back to the inner critic.

Let's look at how Jim can talk back to his inner critic:

>> Be firm and assertive to the inner critic.

  You can't talk to me like that anymore. It's not helpful. In fact, it's demotivating me. You need to stop pushing me all the time because I'm getting exhausted and it's not sustainable.

>> Be compassionate, accepting, logical, and motivating.

  While I do worry a lot, it does not need to consume my every thought and action. It makes no sense to keep comparing me to others because I am me with my own strengths and weaknesses. I need to remember that mistakes are an opportunity to learn and to be less fearful.

Practicing talking back to your inner critic

The next time your inner critic shows up, see if you can identify and talk back to it. This can be hard to do in the moment until you've had practice, but you can always work on talking back to your critic after the fact. Consider using a pen and paper because writing things down can reinforce a new skill.

Recognizing Unhelpful Types of Self-Talk

You may think the following types of self-talk are helpful for reframing fearful thinking, but they actually do not work. Read on to see why.

Arguing with your inner critic

Sometimes developing new self-talk does not work because you find yourself arguing with yourself. You may feel as though your compassionate self is sitting on one shoulder and the inner critic is on the other and you are trapped in the middle. You get so confused that you do not even know what's true. Instead of arguing, validate what's true while acknowledging what isn't and end the argument there.

Telling yourself to stop feeling anxious

Using self-talk to directly reduce your feelings of social anxiety can backfire. Instead of telling yourself you "shouldn't" feel anxious, try reminding yourself of your strengths and be compassionate and accepting of yourself.

Turning a negative into a positive

If you think, "I am a bad person," you may think it makes sense to then say, "I am a good person." However, your mind may not take in the positive thought without evidence. Instead, provide specific examples that support that claim and enable new beliefs to enter your mind. For example, "I am a good person because I helped a friend today" is more convincing and believable.

Repeating mantras

Mantras are words or phrases you repeat to yourself again and again. I am calm. I am present. I am happy. While these mantras sound great, unless there is some powerful self-talk supporting them, you may not believe them. So try to develop CALM thinking and come up with a short summary statement with examples that support it.

Strategies to Reframe Your Thinking

Reframing is the fundamental self-talk skill that helps you move from fearful thinking to resilient thinking. It involves three steps: identifying your negative self-talk, identifying your thinking traps, and correcting your self-talk by being compassionate, accepting, logical, and motivating. But sometimes you can't reframe your thoughts so directly. In this section, I describe some additional strategies you can use to help you reframe your thinking.

Noticing your thoughts

The first step in reframing your thinking may also be the most obvious: Notice your thoughts. Observe them without changing them. Noticing thoughts without judgment or criticism is the first step in gaining perspective.

Thinking flexibly

Flexible thinking means being able to change your approach or perspective when you're facing new or challenging situations. It means being able to think outside the box and consider multiple options or solutions to a problem. Flexible thinking is your ability to revise plans when faced with obstacles or mistakes.

Signs that you may need to work on thinking more flexibly include:

>> Feeling overly anxious in more familiar social situations

>> Getting overwhelmed when plans change or something unexpected happens

>> Being unable to see different perspectives

>> Getting stuck in thinking traps

>> Using avoidance to handle anxiety instead of facing fears

TIP

Ways to foster flexible thinking include:

>> Be aware of what you are thinking. Get unstuck from unhelpful beliefs. Use compassionate, accepting, logical, and motivating self-talk.

>> Do something you know how to do but do it differently. Be spontaneous. Change up your routine.

>> Pursue new challenges. Learn a new language. Cook a new dish.

>> Approach scary situations gradually.

>> Change your environment. Take a vacation. Walk around the block.

Decatastrophizing by rating possible outcomes

When you catastrophize, you may exaggerate the importance of a problem or assume that the worst possible outcome is true or likely to happen.

TIP

Here are a few questions that can help you pinpoint your catastrophic thinking and gain perspective:

>> What is your catastrophic worry?

>> What are some possible outcomes in addition to the one you are predicting?

>> If you had 100 points, how would you divide the 100 points, and how many points would you assign to each possible outcome?

>> How likely do you think it is now that your original catastrophe will happen?

You can practice these steps with your own catastrophic thinking. Write down a catastrophic worry in the space provided and then fill in Table 10-3 with the possible outcomes. The table has space for four possible outcomes, but you may have more or less.

Your catastrophic worry: _____

TABLE 10-3 **Rating Possible Outcomes**

Possible Outcomes	Points Assigned (out of 100)

What is the likelihood of your prediction of your catastrophic outcome now? What is your new belief?

_____

_____

Decatastrophizing by imagining coping

Sometimes rating all possible outcomes as described in the previous section will reduce your overfocus on the worst-case scenario because the exercise helped you realize that the worst is possible but unlikely to happen. However, if you are still worried, the following is a strategy to help you come up with a realistic coping plan and then set aside your worry.

TIP

Think about a catastrophic worry and answer the questions that follow:

1. What is your worry?

_____

_____

2. How likely do you think it will happen? What evidence supports and doesn't support your thinking?

Evidence for: _____

Evidence against: _____

3. If your worry comes true, what is the worst that can happen?

_____

_____

4. If it happens, how can you cope with it?

_____

_____

Now set aside your worry because you have a plan to cope!

Perspective-taking

Perspective-taking is the ability to look at a situation from another point of view. For example, you could ask yourself what a friend would think or what you would think if you weren't worried.

TIP

To use perspective-taking to help reframe your thinking, think of a worry and answer the questions that follow:

1. What is the situation you are worrying about?

_____

_____

2. How can you take a new perspective on this worry? Here are some questions to help you take a new perspective:

What would I tell a friend if they had this worry?

_____

_____

How might I feel about this situation when I'm 95?

_____

_____

What would I tell myself if I weren't so worried?

_____

_____

Creating distance from your thoughts

Another way of gaining perspective is to write down your negative thoughts. This technique helps create a sense of distance from the thought, which can provide perspective. Here's an example:

> **Thought:** I am a loser.
>
> **I am having the thought that** I am a loser.
>
> **I have noticed that** I keep thinking I'm a loser.
>
> **I am aware that the thought of** being a loser keeps popping up.

Now try it yourself:

> **Thought:** _____
>
> **I am having the thought that** _____
>
> **I have noticed that** _____
>
> **I am aware that that the thought of** _____

Noticing your strengths

Learning to notice your own strengths may be an entirely new skill for you if your inner critic is exceptionally strong. To help build this skill, keep a daily list of your successes and write down one or two positive actions you did or thoughts you had each day. It can be something you did, imagined yourself doing, or thought. For example, your list may be as simple as this:

Monday	I texted a friend and remembered that I am kind.
Tuesday	I made eye contact with the Starbucks clerk.
Wednesday	I ordered at a restaurant. I gave myself credit for it.
Thursday	I imagined myself asking someone out on a date. I am grateful I am healthy.

Reinforcing Your Positive Self-Talk

Once you have turned some of your fearful thinking into resilient thinking, the following tools can help you remind yourself of your positive self-talk.

Keeping a diary

In the moment, it may be hard to reframe your negative thoughts, and you may find yourself stuck in a thinking trap. Sometimes, when you feel calmer, it helps to take some time later to write down the thoughts that got you stuck and reframe them. A thought record could be as simple as two columns with your original negative thought on the left and your new thought that is compassionate, accepting, logical, and motivating on the right.

Negative thought:	New thought:

Using written coping cards

Another way to remind yourself of your new CALM thinking is to write your thoughts down so you can review them during the day. You can write your thoughts on an index card or a piece of paper and post them somewhere where you will see them. You can also keep a notes app on your phone to look at it or send yourself a daily reminder of your new self-talk.

Using audio coping cards

It often helps to listen to yourself talking to yourself. You can record your new CALM thinking on your phone and play it back to yourself daily or as needed. If you don't like the sound of your voice, you can ask a trusted friend or family member to record it for you as if they were talking to you in a supportive way.

IN THIS CHAPTER

» Identifying and ranking your fears

» Setting up exposures and predictions to face your fears

» Reviewing what you discovered after the exposures

» Finding other ways to face your social anxiety fears

Chapter **11**

Facing Your Fears

The number one goal of this book is to help you gain confidence and a sense of mastery of your emotions so that social anxiety does not control you. One way to change how you think and feel is by deliberately seeking out the situations you have been avoiding. This is called *exposure*. You have to be willing to accept a certain level of anxiety and uncertainty as you face your fears. Exposing yourself to your social anxiety fears helps you learn that you can survive with social anxiety. Doing exposures also helps you learn whether your fears actually come true. Confronting your fears in real life is the only way to start getting over them.

In this chapter, you explore ways to face your social anxiety fears by doing exposures. You discover how to conduct exposures by creating a fear ladder and addressing your fears at your own pace. You also find out about other ways you can work on your social anxiety. I hope that with these tools under your belt, you will be able to reduce your fear of social situations and increase your confidence that you can cope with your anxiety.

Exploring the Benefits of Exposures

Doing exposures to face your fears may sound scary. Just hearing the word "exposure" may immediately cause you to feel fearful. Exposures may sound terrifying because you may imagine having to stay in a situation that causes you anxiety for a long time while you wait for your anxiety to go down — and it may not go down at all. After all, you've probably already been told to get over your fear and *just do it.*

REMEMBER

Some of the misperceptions underlying social anxiety are the beliefs that other people are judgmental, negative evaluation is intolerable, and you can't handle feeling anxious. You may find the feelings of anxiety themselves to be intolerable and, therefore, try to avoid social situations altogether to avoid feeling nervous or anxious. With exposure therapy, you need to suspend these beliefs and jump in and see what happens.

One of the fundamental principles of doing exposures is being able to get used to having anxiety without escaping it. The idea is if you can stay in a situation long enough and keep repeating exposures, your anxiety will naturally go down over time. Some options are to simply jump in and expose yourself to the situation that causes you anxiety or to expose yourself to it gradually.

The second important principle of exposure is being able to learn from it. As you challenge your automatic reactions to social anxiety, your brain forms new associations that signal safety and control rather than danger. You may learn you can tolerate and cope with anxiety better than you expected, or you may learn that your fear did not come true.

TIP

Even if the outcome of an exposure was not great, you can still examine what you learned instead of assuming everything went poorly. You may or may not get rid of your fear responses, but by looking at what you learned after an exposure, you gain new information that balances your fears so that you can better participate in life.

As you expose yourself to your fears, the overwhelming feelings of anxiety will start to lose their power. When you face your fears in real life and learn from the experiences, you may notice a newfound sense of empowerment taking root. Following are the benefits of doing social anxiety exposures:

>> You are able to process what you learn at an emotional level — you may know something is true but do not feel it at an emotional level. For example, you may know you are likable but that belief may not feel true. Through exposures, you can learn that what you think and what you feel are consistent.

>> Exposing yourself to your fears can be more powerful than simply trying to change your thinking through positive self-talk. For example, exposures may create new self-talk about your ability to cope with your social anxiety without you purposefully trying to change your self-talk.

You may find that the self-talk strategies outlined in Chapter 10 are effective, and that's all you need to help you overcome a fear. You can go into scary situations prepared with ways to talk to yourself differently, and this helps you tolerate anxiety just fine.

On the other hand, you may feel that you just can't get yourself to think differently. This is when setting up exposures can help you see whether your beliefs about your fears change over time.

REMEMBER

When you start to confront your fears, being in a growth mindset is essential. As discussed in Chapter 9, a *growth mindset* is the belief that you can improve with effort and that talent can be developed. A *fixed mindset* is a belief that you are born with inherent traits that you can't change. Though genetics and childhood experiences influence the development of social anxiety, you are not stuck with social anxiety. By using the skills in this book to change your mindset and confront your fears, you can change your relationship with social anxiety.

Doing Exposures to Face Your Fears

Following is an overview of the steps involved in doing exposures to face your fears. If these steps feel complicated or overwhelming, remember that you can do them at your own pace.

1. Create a target list of the fears you want to work on.

2. Identify safety behaviors to stop.

3. Build a fear ladder.

4. Engage in an exposure.

5. Debrief after the exposures.

6. Repeat the exposure or do a new one.

Creating a target list

The first step in doing exposures is to develop a target list of the situations you want to work on. They could be situations you entirely avoid or that you endure with a lot of anxiety. If you identified situations that make you feel anxious in Chapter 6, you can use this list as a starting point. If you are not sure of exactly what causes your social anxiety, you could also do some real-life monitoring for a few days to see what comes up using the Social Anxiety Log in Chapter 6.

Looking at an example target list

CASE EXAMPLE

The following example looks at a hypothetical person named Jennifer. Jennifer is an engineer at a large technology company. Jennifer developed severe social anxiety as a teenager when her family moved and she had to make new friends at a new school. In her job, Jennifer gets excellent performance reviews for her technical skills, but she gets marked down for her interpersonal skills. Her boss told her that she needs to interact with her coworkers more, attend company events, and network with people in other departments.

Table 11-1 lists some of Jennifer's feared situations. She rated them based on the following:

>> How scary they are from 1 to 10, with 10 being the scariest

>> How much she avoids them from 1 to 10, with 10 being the most avoidance

>> How important they are for her to overcome from very important (VI) to important (I) to not important (NI)

TABLE 11-1 **Jennifer's Feared Situations**

Situation	Fear Level	Avoidance	Importance
Talking to coworkers	7	7	VI
Sharing opinions in meetings	10	9	I
Networking	8	10	VI
Attending company events	8	10	VI
Talking to her boss	4	2	NI
Looking nervous in front of others	8	5	VI
Public speaking	10	10	NI
Working with unfamiliar people	8	4	I

Based on this list, Jennifer would be most motivated to do exposures to help her talk to coworkers, network, attend company events, and look less nervous in front of others because she rated these items as very important. However, these are all pretty scary things to do because she rated them a 7 or 8 on the fear scale. When Jennifer creates her fear ladder in the next step, she'll break these down so that there are some easier steps she can take first. While public speaking makes her very scared and she completely avoids it, she does not find it to be important right now because it's not required as a part of her current job.

Creating your own target list

Now, create your own list of fears you want to work on. If you created a list of the situations that make you feel anxious in

Chapter 6, you can use that list as a guide to help you fill out Table 11-2. Remember to indicate how important each situation is for you to overcome, from very important (VI) to important (I) to not important (NI).

TABLE 11-2 **Your Feared Situations**

Situation	Fear Level	Avoidance	Importance

REMEMBER

When you create a target list of the situations you want to work on, it's important to also identify the safety behaviors you need to drop. Remember that safety behaviors interfere with learning and can prevent you from feeling confident that you can handle social anxiety. For more about safety behaviors, see Chapter 5.

Identifying safety behaviors to stop

CASE EXAMPLE

Here are a few safety behaviors Jennifer wants to drop:

>> Avoidance (not going to lunch with coworkers, not speaking up in meetings, not going to company events)

>> Talking softly

>> Looking down

>> Wearing too much makeup (to hide blushing)

>> Being overly nice

Now, create a list of the safety behaviors you may have. What are some of the safety behaviors you need to drop? If you identified safety behaviors in Chapter 6, look back at that list for guidance.

Your avoidance and other safety behaviors:

_____

_____

_____

Building a fear ladder

It's now time to create your fear ladder. A *fear ladder* is a list of things from easiest to hardest that you want or need to do to overcome your social anxiety. In this step, you set a goal — a fear you want to tackle — and come up with baby steps to work on your goal. You'll rate each baby step on a scale from 0 to 10 based on how much anxiety each step makes you feel if you did not avoid it or did it without safety behaviors, with 0 being no anxiety and 10 being very high anxiety. You'll then put the items to create a ladder from least to most scary.

REMEMBER

You don't have to face your fears in the order of your fear ladder. You can pick and choose what to do. In this regard, think of your fear ladder as a fear menu. Also, you don't need to stay in an exposure until your anxiety completely goes away. The goal of exposure is to have a learning experience. You may learn that your feared prediction does not come true. Or if it does come true, you discover that you can handle it.

Looking at an example fear ladder

CASE EXAMPLE

Table 11-3 illustrates a fear ladder for Jennifer. The fears Jennifer wants to overcome include talking to coworkers (fear rating = 7), networking (8), attending company events (8), and looking nervous in front of others (8). She decides to focus on getting more comfortable interacting with coworkers and came up with steps from least to most scary to help her reach this goal. As part of working on getting comfortable with her coworkers, she will be exposing herself to her own anxiety as well as looking nervous in front of others.

Jennifer's goal: Get comfortable interacting with coworkers.

TABLE 11-3   Jennifer's Fear Ladder

Level of Difficulty	Anxiety Rating	Situation
Hardest	10	Attend a happy hour with coworkers after work.
	8–9	Go out to lunch with a group of coworkers.
Moderate	6–7	Join a group of coworkers in a casual conversation in the office.
		Ask a coworker to go to lunch.
	4–5	Start a conversation with a coworker about what they did over the weekend.
		Sit in the break room while coworkers are chatting over coffee.
Easiest	2–3	Ask a coworker a work-related question.
		Say hello to coworkers.

Creating your own fear ladder

Now, set up your own fear ladder in Table 11-4. Pick a goal you want to work on, and then see if you can break this goal into baby steps. Place your feared situations on the fear ladder from least to most scary. These should be examples of exposures you may want to try to handle anxiety better. Don't worry if you don't have an item for each rung on the ladder.

Your goal: _____

TABLE 11-4   Your Fear Ladder

Level of Difficulty	Anxiety Rating	Situation
Hardest	10	
	8–9	
Moderate	6–7	
	4–5	
Easiest	2–3	

Engaging in exposures

The next step is to start facing your fears. In this step, you'll pick one item from your fear ladder and create a specific exposure for it. You don't have to go in the order of your fear ladder. You can jump around if you want.

Refer to the earlier example of Jennifer wanting to become more comfortable interacting with her coworkers. She decided first to do a few of her easy exposures, which included saying hello to coworkers and asking a work-related question. She is feeling more comfortable now and is ready to try something harder. She decides to work on starting a conversation with a coworker about what they did over the weekend.

Before the exposure

Before the exposure, it is important to come up with a specific pre-exposure plan. You first decide on the exposure you want to practice, and then you make a prediction of what you think could happen. This is called your *feared outcome*. Next, you identify what safety behaviors you'll need to give up to make sure you are fully exposing yourself to your fear. If it is too hard to completely give up your safety behaviors on the first try, you can phase them out as you keep repeating the exposure.

CASE EXAMPLE

Here's an example of Jennifer's pre-exposure plan:

What exposure do you want to experiment with?

I will talk to my coworker Sally on Monday morning at break time.

What safety behaviors will you have to give up?

I need to overcome my urge to avoid. I need to make direct eye contact and speak a little louder.

What feared outcome(s) are you most worried about and how likely do you think it is they'll happen?

I think I will be extremely nervous (100%).

I worry my mind will go blank (70%).

Sally will not be interested in talking to me (70%) and will think I am boring (90%).

Fill in the following information for the specific exposure you want to try:

What exposure do you want to experiment with?

_____

_____

What safety behaviors will you have to give up?

_____

_____

What feared outcome(s) are you most worried about and how likely do you think it is they'll happen?

_____

_____

During the exposure

During the exposure, your goal is to stay focused on the task and the person you are interacting with. You need to be outward-looking and not focused internally on your anxiety or mind reading about what they may be thinking about you. It's okay to name your emotions, but don't try to fight or resist your anxiety. Instead, let your feelings and bodily sensations be there with you. Be okay with not knowing what will happen, and treat this exposure as an experiment. There is no failure. Your goal is to tolerate your feelings and push through them.

Sometimes, it can be helpful to rate your anxiety level before, during, and after the exposure. This is not to push the anxiety away or to measure success on how anxious you feel. Instead, it can be part of the learning process to be curious about how your anxiety waxes and wanes during exposures and as you do new exposures.

Debriefing after the exposure

After the exposure, you want to explore what you actually did and what you learned. First, think about how the outcome differed from what you expected and if there were any surprises. Then, evaluate how well you did with letting go of your safety behaviors. Finally, review what you learned.

REMEMBER

The positive information you learned with the exposure is something you want to keep reinforcing because this is how your brain gains control over social anxiety and learns that anxiety is not dangerous.

CASE EXAMPLE

Here's how Jennifer debriefed after the exposure:

How was the outcome different than what you expected? What surprised you?

I spoke to Sally, and while I was nervous, it wasn't as hard as I thought. My mind did not go blank, and I was able to hold a conversation. Sally appeared interested, smiled at me, and kept the conversation going. I was surprised because the conversation went well, and it did not seem like Sally thought I was boring.

Did you engage in safety behaviors?

I had some trouble with eye contact, but I was aware that eye contact may be hard, so I reminded myself to focus externally on Sally instead of on myself.

What did you learn from this exposure?

I learned that the more I practice, the more confident I'll get. I'm starting to believe that while I am not the most talkative or confident person right now, people still like me and want to talk to me. I learned it's okay to be nervous, and I was surprised that the longer I spoke with Sally, the less anxious I felt.

Answer the following questions with your results:

How was the outcome different than what you expected? What surprised you?

_____

_____

Did you engage in safety behaviors?

_____

_____

What did you learn from this exposure?

_____

_____

Repeating the same exposure or doing a new one

Now that you've done an exposure or two, it's important to keep repeating exposures and doing new ones. The more you repeat old exposures and do new ones and vary the conditions of how and where you do your exposures, the more you will improve.

EXPERIMENT

Table 11-5 outlines an exposure worksheet you can use to repeat exposures and design new ones. Make as many copies of this form as you need. Keep making your exposures harder over time. Remember that you are winning when you are feeling anxiety and not trying to escape it.

TABLE 11-5   Exposure Worksheet

Before the Exposure	
What exposure will you do?	
What safety behaviors will you have to give up?	
What feared outcome(s) are you most worried about and how likely do you think it is they'll happen?	
After the Exposure	
How was the outcome different than what you expected? What surprised you?	
Did you engage in safety behaviors?	
What did you learn from this exposure?	

Maximizing the Effectiveness of Your Exposures

The overall goal of exposures is to surprise yourself and learn something new about the situations that make you nervous and your ability to cope with them. The more an experience stands out in your memory as positive, the better you'll be at handling your fears in the future. There are several ways you can make your exposures more effective.

Expect to feel anxious

When you are pushing yourself with exposures to social anxiety, you can expect to feel some anxiety. That's a sign you are doing the exposure correctly. Your job is to stay in the situation even if you feel anxious so you can learn that anxiety is not dangerous and that you can handle it.

Focus on learning

Staying in an exposure for a long enough time can be helpful because you will learn you can handle anxiety. However, you do not need to be in the exposure for a specific amount of time because your anxiety may or may not decline during the exposure. But that does not mean exposure is not working. Exposure works when you learn from the experiences. Instead, focus on staying in each exposure long enough to learn something new about handling anxiety and see if your worry prediction comes true.

Drop safety behaviors

For exposures to work, you need to drop your safety behaviors, reassurance-seeking, distraction, and anything that prevents you from feeling anxious. Be aware of your common safety behaviors and have a plan for dropping them. If you are not able to drop them all at once, be sure to have a gradual plan for reducing safety behaviors over time.

Vary your exposures

Varying exposures helps you learn that you can handle anxiety in different circumstances and will help you gain confidence. You can vary your exposures in many ways, such as by changing how long you do the exposure, where you do it, when you do it, or who's around. Try to see whether you can make your exposures harder because that will help to increase your confidence.

Don't try to fight your anxiety

Exposure is more effective when you name your emotions rather than try to change them. Focus on noticing your anxiety while staying focused on what you are doing. Instead of resisting your anxiety, notice and name your feelings and bodily sensations. For example, if you are feeling guilty that maybe you said the wrong thing and insulted the other person, you can notice and name it as guilt. Just naming your feeling as guilt can help you be less reactive and regulate your emotions better.

Stop ruminating

Ruminating is when you keep going over a specific thought again and again. It can feel hard to let go of overthinking things after an exposure. After an exposure, you may over-focus on what you think you did wrong. This is where the debriefing step is helpful. It's important to turn your mind to what went well during your exposure and keep a growth mindset.

Use encouraging self-talk after exposures

Remember to be compassionate, accepting, logical, and motivating after your exposures to reinforce what you learned. Don't use too much positive self-talk before or during your exposures because it can become a safety behavior and prevent you from learning that you can handle anxiety. However, after your exposures, positive self-talk can help encode the learnings in your memory.

GENERALIZING: APPLYING WHAT YOU LEARNED TO OTHER SITUATIONS

Generalizing means using a skill you learned in one situation in another one, such as with different people, in different settings, and at different times. If you become comfortable speaking to one coworker, you can use what you learned during that exposure to speak to other coworkers or to people in different settings, such as at the grocery store or on the telephone. Or if you get comfortable giving a speech to a small audience, you may feel comfortable speaking in front of other small groups and eventually feel confident giving a speech to a larger audience. The goal of exposures is to be able to generalize what you learn so that you can tackle your social anxiety over the long term.

Keep a diary

It can be helpful to keep a diary of your exposures so that you can track your progress. Jot down some notes about what you learned after every exposure. This can help you build confidence, especially when you look back at your first exposures and see how far you've come.

Getting Comfortable with Your Anxious Feelings

A big worry for many people with social anxiety is a fear of their physical symptoms — especially if they think someone else can see that they are anxious. Many people just do not want to feel anxious, whether anyone can see their anxiety or not. It's uncomfortable to feel anxious. However, to help you overcome your anxiety, you need to expose yourself to your anxious feelings and get comfortable with and accepting of having the feelings and the bodily sensations associated with your social anxiety. The technical term for exposure to bodily sensation is called *interoceptive exposure*.

The benefit of exposure to your bodily sensations is that you learn what they mean, which can help you move forward even when you feel uncomfortable sensations in your body. For example, you may feel a racing heart and tightness in your chest and interpret it as a heart attack. By doing exposures to your bodily sensations, you learn that these feelings indicate anxiety.

EXPERIMENT

You can recreate your physical sensations to learn how to manage the physical symptoms of anxiety and fear. Some examples of such physical exposures include:

>> Running in place to increase your heart rate and have your face turn red

>> Going out in the hot sun until you perspire and you can feel your clothes getting wet

>> Rubbing your hands together to create sweaty palms

>> Spinning around in a chair until you feel light-headed

>> Hyperventilating for 1 to 2 minutes because it'll usually create several panic-like at once such as shortness of breath, a fast heart rate, feelings of faintness, and light-headedness

>> Staring at yourself closely in the mirror to create a sense of unreality

Letting People See You Are Anxious

To become comfortable with anxiety and judgment, you could go out to where there are people and see if you can cope with your bodily sensations in public. You can see whether other people even notice your bodily sensations and, if they do, determine whether their noticing is catastrophic. Eventually, you could do this exposure with friends, coworkers, acquaintances, or strangers.

Using Your Imagination as an Exposure

The most obvious type of exposure is to design one that you can do in real life. However, sometimes you either can't do something in real life or you rated everything on your list as being so scary that doing an exposure is too overwhelming to try. In these cases, it is helpful to design an exposure you can do in your imagination.

Imaginal exposure involves imagining a situation you want to confront as if you were in a movie. As you create a scene in your head, you want to make the situation feel as real as possible. This involves using all of your senses to imagine what you see, hear, smell, touch, and taste. You can also imagine how you feel emotionally and physically and what you are thinking. You confront your fears in your imagination or with a script that you can read, or you can create an audio you can listen to. Just like with real-life exposure, you want to see what you learn about how you handle anxiety.

CASE EXAMPLE

Sally is a college student. She is working on speaking up in class. She has pretty severe social anxiety. Her anxiety is a 9 out of 10 when she is in class, and she is terrified to even make eye contact when the professor asks a question. So Sally does some imaginal exposures starting with how she is feeling in class using all of her senses. Then she works her way on her fear ladder in her imagination from making eye contact to raising her hand to answering a question. Then, she can slowly practice in real life.

If you are finding some of the exposures on your fear ladder are too hard, see if you can use imaginal exposure to help you get started with facing your fears. Just like with real-life exposures, it involves the same steps. You can pick an item from your fear ladder that feels too scary to do now and expose yourself to it in your imagination before venturing into the real world.

Finding Other Ways to Work on Social Anxiety

The most effective way to work on overcoming social anxiety is to directly confront it with exposures. However, you may struggle in other areas, such as being overly self-conscious, feeling shame, avoiding, or thinking that you can't use your skills when you get overwhelmed. In this section, I discuss a few strategies you can try to minimize or overcome these challenges.

Role-playing

A useful activity is to practice facing your fears on your own or with a friend before doing an exposure. You can practice your social skills by taking two roles: one is yourself, and another is someone you want to interact with in real life. You or your friend can play the other person and practice what you will say to them and how they will respond. You can also role-play by being more assertive. You can start with easy situations in your role-playing and advance to interacting with more challenging people.

Attention training

When you are having social anxiety, you tend to be self-conscious. You may start to monitor yourself and your attention turns inward. You may be judging yourself negatively and how you are coming across in the moment. This can cause a self-fulfilling prophecy as you miss parts of the conversation and you have trouble focusing on things around you. When you work on training your attention, you are trying to teach yourself to pay attention to the things around you instead of what's going on in your head and body.

EXPERIMENT

Practice attention training by going into a public place and noticing the sounds around you — people talking, traffic sounds, music, a ticking clock, and any number of things. As you gain control of your attention, you may become more effective at looking outward and being present in social interactions.

Shame busting

Shame-busting exercises (also known as *social mishap exercises*) may be the scariest of any strategy to try, but it is well worth it. In this strategy, you design extremely silly or ridiculous exposures to help yourself overcome feeling shame or embarrassment in doing them.

EXPERIMENT

You could design an outing to a shopping mall and put some things on your list to do there, such as:

>> Go to the cashier with an item you want to buy and tell the cashier you forgot your wallet.

>> Go to a frozen yogurt stall and ask if they sell hamburgers.

>> Go to a lingerie shop and ask for help purchasing something for your partner (or imaginary partner).

The ideas for shame-busting exercises are endless. They can be fun to do with a trusted friend because you will laugh so much that how could it not reduce your feelings of shame?

Social-skills training

If you feel that part of your social anxiety stems from not having certain social skills, then learning and practicing social skills could be part of your plan. In reality, you may not lack social skills. It may be that you get so overwhelmed with your social anxiety that you have trouble using your skills. Some things you can practice include making eye contact, what to say in conversations, how to be assertive, having more open and friendly body language, and any number of skills that you feel overwhelmed by when you get social anxiety.

Chapter **12**

Using Positive Psychology to Create New Beliefs

I f you have social anxiety, you likely look at yourself through a deficit lens, which means you tend to focus on your weaknesses rather than on your strengths. Instead of focusing on what you think is wrong, you can use positive psychology to help you overcome your social anxiety by developing and using your strengths. In this chapter, you explore common character strengths and figure out which ones apply to you. You then discover how to use positive psychology to help you use your strengths to live a meaningful life and advance your life's purpose. You also look at tools that can help reinforce your positive beliefs and increase your confidence and resilience.

Defining Positive Psychology and the Three Types of Happiness

Positive psychology is the scientific study of how people can lead meaningful lives by cultivating their strengths and enhancing their life experiences. As a science, positive psychology emerged in the 1970s and gained steam in 1998 when Dr. Martin Seligman, Ph.D., formally publicized it during his presidency of the American Psychological Association. In his book, *Authentic Happiness* (Atria Books), Dr. Seligman proposed that there are three types of happiness: having a pleasant life, an engaged life, and a meaningful life. All types contribute to having a fulfilling and happy life.

A pleasant life

In a pleasant life, you are doing things that bring you pleasure. The pleasant life involves doing things frequently and consistently that make you feel good at the moment. It requires a lot of repetition because it's short-term. A pleasant life involves healthy activities like watching a movie, eating a favorite food, listening to music, and going for a walk. Activities that bring you pleasure are important to engage in — rather than avoid — when you have social anxiety. When you are not fully engaged in everyday enjoyable activities, social anxiety may get worse.

WARNING

Though it's important to do things that make you feel good to manage social anxiety, a pleasant life becomes unhealthy when you get hooked on the immediate gratification from harmful activities like abusing drugs or alcohol, overeating, gambling, or excessively engaging in sex, social media, and other addictive or impulsive behaviors. Unhelpful activities like these can serve as a form of emotional avoidance if you are engaging in them to escape from feeling anxiety.

An engaged life

When you lead an engaged life, you feel a sense of flow, or being "in the zone," which is when you become completely absorbed by what you are doing. You can live an engaged life by finding your interests and passions. When you are in the zone, you feel less self-conscious because you are in the moment and looking outward instead of inward, and you may even lose track of time. Engaging in interests and passions can help you overcome social anxiety when you are with like-minded people. It can motivate you to stop avoiding social situations when you look forward to participating in activities that create flow.

A meaningful life

A meaningful life involves using your strengths and virtues for a higher purpose. As with an engaged life, when you are living a meaningful life, you feel more confident and are more likely to be able to motivate yourself to overcome your social anxiety because you are serving a purpose greater than yourself. Your purpose may be serving your family to the best of your ability. Other people may identify a cause outside of themselves, such as animal rights, the environment, politics, social justice, creating a company that provides jobs, or any number of big-picture causes they care about.

Understanding Universal Character Strengths

Discovering your greatest strengths can help you overcome social anxiety, and knowing your strengths can help you face your fears, work toward your goals, and lead a meaningful life with or without social anxiety.

In the early 2000s, the VIA Institute on Character — a nonprofit organization dedicated to bringing the science of character strengths to the world — supported a three-year, 55-scientist study that identified 24 character strengths that have been scientifically tested and validated as being universal for all human beings (see Figure 12-1). As a result of that study, the Institute developed a free, quick, and scientific survey of character strengths that is available online at https://via character.org.

The 24 positive character strengths are organized into six virtue classes:

>> **Wisdom:** Creativity, curiosity, open-mindedness, love of learning, perspective

>> **Courage:** Honesty, bravery, persistence, zest

>> **Humanity:** Kindness, love, social intelligence

>> **Justice:** Fairness, leadership, teamwork

>> **Temperance:** Forgiveness, modesty, prudence, self-regulation

>> **Transcendence:** Appreciation of beauty, gratitude, hope, humor, spirituality

The following sections outline ways you can use your character strengths to overcome social anxiety.

FIGURE 12-1: Twenty-four character strengths.

Wisdom

The virtue of wisdom includes many strengths that can influence your thinking and help you form new beliefs and actions to overcome social anxiety. Table 12-1 outlines the main wisdom character strengths.

TABLE 12-1 Wisdom Character Strengths

Character Strength	What It Is	Using It for Social Anxiety
Creativity	Using your imagination and having original ideas	Coming up with innovative ways to reframe your negative thoughts and change your avoidance patterns
Curiosity	Having a strong desire to know or explore new things	Shifting from fear to exploration of your social anxiety
Open-mindedness	Considering something without being biased	Examining your social fears from all sides and not jumping to conclusions
Love of learning	Having joy and excitement when acquiring knowledge	Mastering new skills to overcome social anxiety
Perspective	Being able to see the big picture	Recognizing that social mishaps are not the end of the world

Courage

Strengths encompassed by the courage virtue help you overcome resistance in achieving your goals (see Table 12-2). They help you push through, rather than avoid, your social anxiety fears.

Humanity

Strengths encompassed by the humanity virtue enable you to form and build interpersonal relationships essential for social connection (see Table 12-3).

Justice

Table 12-4 outlines the strengths of the justice virtue. These strengths involve balancing one's own needs with those of others.

TABLE 12-2 **Courage Character Strengths**

Character Strength	What It Is	Using It for Social Anxiety
Bravery	Showing mental strength to face danger, fear, or difficulty	Facing challenges and painful emotions when you have social anxiety
Honesty	Telling the truth and acting with integrity	Using realistic self-talk when having social anxiety
Persistence	Continuing to do or try something even though it is difficult	Persevering through setbacks with social anxiety exposures
Zest	Being enthusiastic and full of energy	Having passion and enjoyment in life in spite of social anxiety

TABLE 12-3 **Humanity Character Strengths**

Character Strength	What It Is	Using It for Social Anxiety
Kindness	Being generous, helpful, and considerate of others	Doing things for others, even if it makes you anxious
Love	Having feelings of affection	Building close relationships with family and friends
Social intelligence	Understanding your own and other's actions	Letting go of mind reading

TABLE 12-4 **Justice Character Strengths**

Character Strength	What It Is	Using It for Social Anxiety
Fairness	Treating others in a just and impartial way	Seeking balanced and equitable social environments
Leadership	Inspiring others to do their best	Finding small ways to encourage others
Teamwork	Being part of a group to achieve goals	Fostering a sense of belonging to reduce social isolation

Temperance

Strengths within the virtue of temperance outlined in Table 12-5 help you to be balanced in your thinking and in control of your behavior.

TABLE 12-5 Temperance Character Strengths

Character Strength	What It Is	Using It for Social Anxiety
Forgiveness	Accepting mistakes and letting go of resentment and anger	Ending rumination and beating yourself up after social situations
Modesty	Being humble about your abilities and accomplishments	Not overly minimizing your successes
Prudence	Being careful and not taking poor risks	Taking small steps to reduce your assessment of danger with social anxiety
Self-regulation	Managing your behavior and emotions about things happening around you	Regulating your social anxiety so you do not over-react to situations

Transcendence

Strengths within the transcendence virtue enable you to rise above suffering and pain and find meaning in the universe (see Table 12-6).

TABLE 12-6 Transcendence Character Strengths

Character Strength	What It Is	Using It for Social Anxiety
Appreciation of beauty	Noticing beauty and excellence	Allowing yourself to be imperfect
Gratitude	Being thankful	Appreciating the small things you do that help you cope with social anxiety
Hope	Believing good things are possible	Imagining being able to handle social anxiety

(continued)

TABLE 12-6 *(continued)*

Character Strength	What It Is	Using It for Social Anxiety
Humor	Being comical, funny, or amusing	Getting the courage to be light-hearted
Spirituality	Believing in a higher power or purpose	Creating meaning that provides comfort in times of social distress

Identifying Your Character Strengths

Identifying your character strengths can help you live a more meaningful life and motivate you to achieve it. Refer back to the list of character strengths outlined in the previous section and see if you can identify three to five of the top character strengths you feel you have or strengths you want to develop. Then, fill in Table 12-7 to guide you in using those strengths to overcome social anxiety.

TABLE 12-7 **Your Personal Character Strengths**

Strength I Have or Want to Develop	How I Do or Can Embody This Strength	How This Strength Can Help Me Overcome Social Anxiety
1.		
2.		
3.		
4.		
5.		

TIP

If you have trouble identifying your character strengths from the descriptions provided earlier, the VIA Institute on Character survey of character strengths may be helpful. You can find it at www.viacharacter.org. Over 30 million people have taken the survey.

It's important to not overuse or underuse your character strengths. You want to use your character strengths optimally and in the appropriate amount for the circumstances. In 2016, a study in the journal *Personality and Individual Differences* found that the overuse of humility, the underuse of zest, humor, self-regulation, and both the under- and overuse of social intelligence were associated with social anxiety.

People with social anxiety tend to be too humble, mind read what others are thinking, and not engage fully in life. As such, identifying your strengths and using them in a balanced way can help you overcome social anxiety and create a meaningful life. In layman's terms, you need to inject some fun into life — not too much, just the optimal amount.

Finding Meaningful Pursuits

Finding a meaningful and fulfilling life can feel daunting, but it is essential to helping you overcome your social anxiety. Knowing your strengths and purpose can catapult you to overcome avoidance and engage in your passions.

Owen looked at the character strengths in this chapter. He identified creativity and love of leaning as two of his strongest character strengths. He worked as an accountant, and while he liked his job and his team, the work itself was not fulfilling on a deeper level. He loved art, and as a child, he was pretty good at drawing, but as he got older, he was never sure what to do with this talent. He decided to use his character strengths to motivate himself to attend a social event at an art museum. Eventually, he met a few people who shared his love of art, and he became more comfortable going to the events. He even started taking a drawing class and hoped to eventually participate in a local gallery exhibition.

Following are a few steps and questions to ask yourself to help you find activities that are meaningful to you:

1. **Identify your strengths and virtues.**

   What are the best things about you? What are you good at? What are your natural talents? What are the virtues you deliberately cultivated in yourself? Refer to Table 12-7 that you filled in or take the online survey at https://www.viacharacter.org.

_____

_____

2. **Identify some meaningful interests and activities.**

What are some causes bigger than yourself that you feel are truly worth serving? What are some of your interests and passions? How would you spend your time if you could do anything?

_____

_____

3. **Match your strengths with meaningful pursuits.**

How can you use your strengths to pursue a meaningful cause? Can you pick something actionable that matches your strengths with something meaningful that you want to do?

_____

_____

4. **Work to overcome your social anxiety.**

How can you engage in your meaningful cause? How will your character strengths propel you forward to overcome any social anxiety preventing you from achieving this goal?

_____

_____

Creating New Positive Beliefs

You can overcome social anxiety by using your character strengths to create new positive beliefs. Character is the sum of all we are, including our thoughts, feelings, and actions. Knowing your character strengths, you can change how you handle social situations and create new positive beliefs. The following exercises show you how to use your character strengths to create new positive beliefs that can help you overcome your social anxiety.

Reframe evidence in a positive way

The first way to create positive beliefs that can help you overcome social anxiety is to reframe an old belief in a positive way.

CASE EXAMPLE

Jennie has social anxiety over her fear that people would know when she is nervous because her face turns red. Jennie decided to try to use her character strengths to overcome her fear of judgment by others. Table 12-8 shows how Jennie reframed her old beliefs into new beliefs.

TABLE 12-8   How Jennie Reframed Her Beliefs

Character Strength	Old Belief	New Belief
Appreciation of beauty	I am embarrassed when my face turns red.	I still have a pretty face even when I am blushing.
Enthusiasm	I look scared when I blush.	The extra color makes me look energetic.
Love	I should avoid others when I am anxious.	I need to connect with people instead of avoiding.
Humility	Others can see I am nervous, and they look down on me.	The spotlight is not on me. Other people are busy with their own thoughts.

Now, see if you can use some of your character strengths to reframe an old belief to create a new belief. Use Table 12-9 as a template.

TABLE 12-9   Your Reframed Beliefs

Character Strength	Old Belief	New Belief

Examine past evidence

Another way to build a character strength that can help you overcome social anxiety is to review all the past evidence that supports your strengths. You can make a bulleted list using your memory. If you can't think of anything, ask a trusted friend or family member to help you.

CASE EXAMPLE

Richard was a college student and had never asked a girl on a date. There was an attractive girl in his English class. He worked up the courage to sit on her side of the auditorium, but he could not get himself to talk to her. He thought he was not handsome or interesting enough and that she would reject him if he tried. Other people told Richard he was kind, but he discounted that quality and believed the old saying that "nice guys finish last."

Here's the list of evidence that Richard came up with that shows he is kind and that others value kindness:

›› In high school, I was part of the production team and helped out every day. My friends said I did a good job, and they appreciated my help.

›› Over the summer, I tutored an elementary school student, and his mother said he improved his test scores.

›› Last week, my roommate asked me if I could be his wingman at a party. Even though I am shy, I decided to go to support him. My roommate was grateful the next day and said he could not have gone without me.

Though he was still not convinced a girl would want to date him because he was kind, looking at past evidence and getting input from others helped him see he was more interesting than he thought.

Focus on what you are doing well

When you can see what you are doing well, it can help you to think differently as well as work up the courage to face your fears. You can pick a character strength that you already have and keep a brief daily log of your accomplishments related to it.

CASE EXAMPLE

Daniel was shy and did not speak up for himself in work meetings. He realized that he needed to develop the character strength of bravery to help him overcome his fear of judgment. He decided to keep a journal of the evidence that supported his bravery. He included things he did both inside and outside of work, as well as personal accomplishments that made him feel brave. He made sure to write brief notes every day in his journal. Here is what he came up with:

Monday	Went for a strenuous run that increased my heart rate. Discussed an idea one-on-one with my boss.
Tuesday	Had lunch with my coworker and shared an opinion.
Wednesday	Wrote notes about my new project so I could be prepared for Friday's staff meeting.
Thursday	Took my dog on a walk and smiled at the people who walked by.
Friday	Answered a question about my project at the staff meeting when I was called on.

By the end of the week, he realized that he was already using his character strength of bravery, and it gave him more courage to continue to try hard things. Within a month, he was able to share an opinion in a meeting, something he had never done before.

Reinforcing Positive Beliefs

In addition to the skills already introduced, you can use several additional tools to create and reinforce new positive beliefs.

Keeping a journal

Journaling does not have to be cumbersome and long. You can use journals or logs to write brief bullet points about something you want to remember and reinforce. For example, you can create a daily log to recall times when you used a character strength. At the end of each week, you can review what you wrote and think about what this evidence is saying.

Using your strengths

Once you identify a few character strengths you have or want to build, it's important to find opportunities to use them. For example, you may want to invite someone to go out for coffee. You can use your character strength of kindness to motivate you to ask.

Visualizing yourself at your best

Top athletes are trained to use visualization techniques. They picture themselves succeeding by focusing on what they want to happen instead of what they don't want to happen. Athletes visualize themselves winning the game, scoring the winning point, or making a basket or a touchdown. Visualizing success becomes a self-fulfilling prophecy and creates a positive snow-ball effect.

You can use visualization, too. With this skill, you imagine yourself doing something successfully in the future or recalling how you handled a difficult situation before. In your mind, you practice in advance for a situation so that you feel prepared, which results in building self-confidence.

Here are the steps for practicing visualization successfully:

1. Picture the scene in your mind.

2. Decide what you want to do or see happen. For example, do you want to make a presentation or do you want to make a phone call?

3. Use all of your senses as you imagine yourself doing it. Imagine yourself engaging in each step as if you were watching yourself in a movie.

4. After your visualization, write a summary of yourself succeeding in the situation. Reviewing your notes before the event can be incredibly helpful in reinforcing your success in your mind.

5. Practice visualization exercises before stressful events.

Setting positive intentions before social interactions

Setting an intention is different than making a goal. An intention is a way you want to live in the moment. Goals are specific things you want to achieve in the future. You can remind yourself every morning of what your intention is for that day. For example, you may be invited to a party, and you set the intention to be mindful and focus on the other person when you are engaged in conversation.

TIP

It's helpful to set an intention for the day. In the morning, you can bring to mind a brief but clear statement of what you want to have in your life. Then, you envision yourself living your intention. For example, you may set an intention for a way of being such as to be nonjudgmental that day, to look at things through a positive mental filter, or to be grateful for your strengths. You can also set an intention to do something that day, such as be more friendly and open with someone or create positive vibes with your smile.

Savoring positive experiences

When you savor, you intentionally and mindfully engage in thoughts that increase your positive feelings about the moment or past events. Effective savoring involves your five senses — the feelings, sights, sounds, tastes, and smells. You engage fully and appreciate the details of the experience.

When you savor, you pause and intentionally focus on the positive aspects of an experience. For example, if you connect with someone at an event, you can savor the experience of talking to them. You can use your five senses by imagining how they looked at you, the sounds of their voice, or the features of their face. You can recall the positive feelings you had in the exchange.

Savoring past events also involves reminiscing, which means remembering past events with pleasure. For example, you can look at photos, read texts or emails related to the situation, or talk to people who were involved. This will remind you of the moments you want to remember and savor what brought you enjoyment.

REMEMBER

Unlike reminiscing, rumination involves repetitive negative thoughts that dwell on past mistakes. Rumination is common with social anxiety. Instead, you want to be able to switch your mind toward reminiscing on what went well and your enjoyment of past situations.

Practicing self-compassion

Self-compassion means expressing kindness and caring toward yourself. You practice taming the inner critic when you fail at something, make a mistake, or feel judged, awkward, or inadequate. Self-compassion helps you cope with adversity and talk to yourself in a gentle and kind way. Instead of letting your inner critic beat you up, self-compassion helps you cope in challenging social situations and build resilience to keep trying to overcome your social anxiety.

One of the leading experts on self-compassion is Dr. Kristin Neff, Ph.D. She defined three parts to self-compassion:

» **Mindfulness:** Being aware when you're struggling without being judgmental or overreacting.

» **Self-kindness:** Being understanding and supportive toward yourself instead of harshly self-critical.

» **Connectedness:** Remembering you are not alone. Everyone makes mistakes and has challenges.

You can learn more about cultivating self-compassion at Dr. Neff's website at https://self-compassion.org.

Chapter **13**

Embracing Your Social Anxiety

E mbracing your social anxiety is a powerful step toward overcoming your social anxiety. One important way to embrace your anxiety is to live your life by your *values* — those principles and qualities in yourself you hold in high regard. Your values can serve as a motivating force for you to overcome social anxiety. Embracing your social anxiety also means moving toward acceptance instead of avoidance. In this chapter, you discover how to identify your values so that you can use them as motivators. You also explore acceptance skills, ways to practice mindfulness, and how to cultivate compassion toward yourself. Taken together, these skills comprise some ways to embrace your social anxiety.

Identifying Your Values

Your values help define who you are and who you want to be. When you are aware of your values — those principles and qualities that are important to you — you can use them to guide you in life decisions. If a value important to you is to be confident and cheerful to others, you can use that value to help you overcome social anxiety. Your values can become motivators to be or act a certain way.

REMEMBER

When your behavior aligns with your values, you're living authentically, which can give you confidence and pride. When you feel confident, you are often willing to take more risks. You are willing to accept the uncomfortable feelings that come with social anxiety in order to live your values.

To identify the values important to you, follow these steps:

1. **Identify your feelings and experiences.**

    Happiness: Identify times when you were happiest. What were you doing? Who were you with? What was going on? What other feelings came with being happy?

    _____

    _____

    _____

    Pride: Identify times when you were proud. Why were you proud? What was happening? What did you accomplish? Do you have personality traits that make you proud?

    _____

    _____

    _____

    Meaning: What were some of the most meaningful times of my life? When did I feel most fulfilled and satisfied? What was happening? Why did this experience feel fulfilling and meaningful?

    _____

    _____

    _____

Inspiration: Who inspires you? Who are your role models? What do you admire and respect about that person? In what positive ways would you like to emulate them?

_____

_____

_____

Anger: What people or things bring out strong negative emotions in you? What is it about these people or situations that made you angry?

_____

_____

_____

2. **Identify and prioritize your values.**

Values: Look at each of the values listed in Table 13-1 and circle the top ten that are most consistent with your core beliefs and character strengths. Remember, less is more, so focus on the values that seem most important to you.

Prioritize: Rank the values you circled in order of importance, with the most important values at the top. You can do this by pairing two values at a time and seeing which one ranks higher. Then keep doing this until you have them rank-ordered.

1.

2.

3.

4.

5.

6.

7.

8.

9.

10.

Reaffirm: Double-check that your top values are a fit. Do they fit your vision for yourself and your life? Do they make you feel good about yourself? Would you be proud to share your values with others?

3. **Use your values to overcome social anxiety.**

   Ask yourself how you can use your values to help you overcome social anxiety. Think about the top three values that could help you overcome social anxiety.

   - Why does this value matter to you, and how does it motivate you?

   - How can this value help you approach social anxiety instead of avoiding it?

   - To live authentically, how can you use this value to do difficult things?

   Write a short statement answering these questions for each of your top values. You can even be specific about what you need to do to overcome social anxiety using this value.

   Value 1:

   _____

   _____

   _____

   Value 2:

   _____

   _____

   _____

   Value 3:

   _____

   _____

   _____

TABLE 13-1 Values List

Accountability	Excellence	Intelligence	Performance	Risk-taking
Achievement	Fairness	Intuition	Perseverance	Safety
Ambition	Family	Joy	Personal development	Security
Belonging	Friendships	Justice	Philanthropy	Self-control
Caring	Flexibility	Kindness	Popularity	Service
Charity	Freedom	Knowledge	Power	Spirituality
Collaboration	Fun	Leadership	Professionalism	Stability
Courage	Generosity	Learning	Punctuality	Success
Creativity	Growth	Love	Quality	Teamwork
Curiosity	Happiness	Loyalty	Recognition	Thankfulness
Dependability	Health	Making a difference	Relationships	Traditionalism
Diversity	Honesty	Motivation	Reliability	Wealth
Empathy	Humor	Optimism	Religion	Well-being
Encouragement	Individuality	Open-mindedness	Resilience	Wisdom
Enthusiasm	Innovation	Passion	Respect	
Ethics	Integrity	Perfection	Responsibility	

Accepting You Have Social Anxiety

When you are experiencing social anxiety, your first instinct may be to try to push it away. Your self-talk may be: "Why is this happening to me?" "I don't want to feel this way." "How can I get it to stop?" The more you refuse to accept social anxiety, the larger it will grow. Accepting that you have social anxiety does not mean you are giving up.

Defining acceptance

Acceptance of your social anxiety means you acknowledge the facts and see what is happening despite wishing you did not feel socially anxious. Once you accept that you are experiencing social anxiety, you are able to decide on the most effective response. Some aspects of acceptance include:

>> You understand that your social anxiety is real and deserves to be acknowledged.

>> You recognize that life can be meaningful even with social anxiety.

>> You are able to be nonjudgmental of your present-moment experiences of social anxiety.

>> You can accept your thoughts and feelings, whether positive or negative, while participating in the present moment without evaluating it.

>> You live in the present moment and let go of fear-based thinking patterns.

Understanding acceptance is not giving up

You may balk at the acceptance concept. You may think, "If I accept I have social anxiety, doesn't that mean I am just giving up?" You may think that if you accept your social anxiety, you will never change. So, instead of accepting it, you continue to fight against your thoughts and feelings.

REMEMBER

Acceptance is not about giving up on your goals and dreams and tolerating a life that is not in tune with your values — you can still try to improve. By accepting that you have social anxiety, you can move forward rather than getting paralyzed by the anxious feelings leading to giving up.

When you give up, you stop making an effort. You resign yourself to failure. You tell yourself your feelings of social anxiety are intolerable and you can't move forward. You can't feel this way anymore so you stop trying. Giving up feels negative and final.

When you accept your social anxiety, You are no longer resisting your feelings of social anxiety. You recognize that social anxiety is a part of you, but only one part, and you don't need to hide it. You are moving toward your goals in a non-judgmental manner. Acceptance feels open and full of possibilities. You know you are enough just as you are. You are not attached to an outcome.

Using acceptance strategies

The aim of acceptance is to create a rich and meaningful life while accepting the pain that comes with it. The goal is to reduce your struggle to control or eliminate your social anxiety while participating in meaningful life activities consistent with your values. You can use self-talk, relaxation, mindfulness, loving-kindness meditation, self-compassion, and all the other skills described in this book to develop acceptance of yourself and your social anxiety.

TECHNICAL STUFF

Certain types of therapy focus on acceptance. Dialectical Behavior Therapy (DBT), for example, focuses on radical acceptance — fully accepting your reality — as a way to reduce your emotional suffering. Acceptance and Commitment Therapy (ACT) focuses on acceptance as a way to embrace the full range of your thoughts and emotions rather than trying to avoid or deny them.

Practicing Mindfulness

Mindfulness is a practice that involves noticing what's happening in the present moment without judgment. It's a helpful tool for managing social anxiety. It allows you to be present with your thoughts and feelings of social anxiety without judging or interpreting them.

Following are several examples of practicing mindfulness with social anxiety:

>> Having a moment-by-moment awareness of your socially anxious thoughts, feelings, bodily sensations, and the social environment you are participating in.

>> Paying attention to your thoughts and feelings about social anxiety without judging them or believing there's a right or wrong way to think or feel.

>> Being present with what *is* rather than rehashing the past about social performance or imagining future social interactions.

Knowing the difference between mindfulness and meditation

Too often, people think that to be mindful, they have to commit to a dedicated meditation practice. So, they reject mindfulness because they envision having to sit and do nothing for a certain amount of time. They say, "Mindfulness doesn't work for me."

While meditation can bring about mindfulness, meditation is not what mindfulness actually is. *Meditation* is a formal practice that you can do to focus your mind on the present and bring your mind back to the present when your mind strays. It typically entails a dedicated daily or weekly practice of anywhere from 10 to 30 minutes each time you practice. On the other hand, *mindfulness* is a quality you can embody by learning to be aware of what's around you and how your body feels. There are many ways to learn to become mindful without doing a formal sitting meditation.

Cultivating informal mindfulness in daily life

You can practice mindfulness in many different ways. It only takes minutes to go from being unmindful to mindful in your daily life. When you are mindfully doing the dishes, can you feel the temperature of the water? Can you smell the soap? When taking a mindful walk, what do you smell? What do you hear? When petting your cat, can you feel the softness of its fur and the sound of its purring? You can turn any activity into a mindful one by focusing on your five senses. Notice what you are seeing, hearing, smelling, tasting, or touching while engaging in the activity.

Mindfulness can be a helpful tool for overcoming social anxiety. For example, when you are in a conversation with someone, can you focus on them instead of your uncomfortable feelings? Can you see the color of their eyes? Can you hear the sound of their voice? When your mind wanders back to your inner feelings in the moment, can you bring your attention back to the other person?

Practicing formal mindfulness

As discussed in the previous section, mindfulness can be cultivated informally by simply being in the moment and aware of what's around you. However, you can also practice mindfulness on a formal basis as well. A formal mindfulness meditation practice involves intentionally setting aside time to focus on only one thing, such as your breath, a sound, or a sensation. The benefits of mindfulness meditation can include things like stress reduction, relaxation, better ability to cope with pain, lowered blood pressure, better sleep, and less rumination. It may be something you practice for 5 minutes in the morning to set the tone for your day. Or you can practice mindfulness at bedtime to relax your mind. With even a few minutes of mindfulness meditation in a day, you could see some benefits.

To practice formal mindfulness, follow these steps:

1. **Get comfortable.**

   Set aside at least 5 minutes and find a quiet space.

2. **Observe the present moment and choose a focus of attention, such as your breath, a sound in your room, or the environment.**

   Aim to pay attention to the present moment without judgment.

3. **Return to the present moment and refocus your attention on your breath or the sound.**

   Practice returning your attention again and again to the present moment until the time you set aside has passed.

TIP

Be kind to yourself. Make a mental note of judgments and let them pass. Don't criticize yourself when your mind has wandered off. Expect it to happen. The practice of mindfulness is about refocusing your attention.

REMEMBER

A mindfulness practice is not the same as formal meditation. Mindfulness can be cultivated in your everyday life in simple ways. The key is to be present and aware. This can help you with your social anxiety because then you will be inside yourself less, which shifts your focus outward, and this can help with self-consciousness, rumination, and other unhelpful patterns.

Showing Compassion for Yourself

With social anxiety, compassion toward yourself is important because fear of judgment is one of the core issues. When you are feeling socially anxious and down on yourself, you may have self-critical thoughts. Instead of dwelling on the negative, you can use the CALM thinking skills discussed in Chapter 10, focusing on the "C" for compassion. The other skill that can be useful for developing compassion is loving-kindness, which is a form of meditation that includes directing positive thoughts and feelings toward yourself. How to practice loving-kindness is described later in this chapter.

Self-compassion means having kindness and understanding for yourself even when you feel inadequate, defective, or like a failure in some way. Instead of criticizing yourself, showing compassion for yourself means you speak of yourself in a supportive, helpful way. The following example uses the "C" in the CALM thinking technique to develop more helpful and compassionate self-talk:

What can you say to yourself that's gentler and kinder?

Keeping this question in mind, write a self-compassionate statement about yourself. Think about something you'd like to remind yourself of on a daily basis. An example could be, "I am working on my social anxiety and doing a lot to work on self-talk and face my fears. Change takes time, and I need to be patient."

_____

_____

_____

Performing Loving-Kindness Meditation

Loving-kindness meditation is a practice that involves connecting with positive feelings by wishing yourself and others well. It's first practiced toward yourself because you can have difficulty loving others when you do not love yourself first. After that, you can practice extending loving-kindness to others.

To get started, sit in a comfortable and relaxed manner. Take two or three deep breaths and let them out slowly. Try to let go of any thoughts and worries. Imagine your breath moving through your heart and the center of your chest. You can envision an image of yourself as you start this meditation and keep it in your mind in order to strengthen your practice.

Now, slowly repeat the following phrases (or other phrases that fit for you) in your mind or out loud:

>> May I be happy.

>> May I be peaceful.

>> May I be healthy.

>> May I be free from suffering.

Feelings of warmth, friendliness, or love may come up within your body and mind. Try to savor and connect to these feelings. Repeat this process a few times. Try to let the positive thoughts and feelings grow as you repeat the phrases.

TIP

If using "I" seems too difficult, envision yourself sitting in front of you. Then you can use phrases from the "you" perspective to give loving-kindness to yourself. For example, you can say, "May you be happy," "May you be peaceful," and so on.

If you'd like, you can stop here and just let yourself experience the positive feelings you have toward yourself. Otherwise, you could also practice extending loving-kindness to others. To do this, bring to mind a friend or someone in your life who you care for or who has deeply cared for you. Then slowly repeat phrases of loving-kindness toward them:

>> May you be happy.

>> May you be peaceful.

>> May you be healthy.

>> May you be free from suffering.

You can repeat this process with other friends, family members, neighbors, coworkers, animals, or others. If you are ready for a challenge, try directing loving-kindness to a difficult person. This is not forgiveness; it's a way of letting negativity leave your life.

TIP

You can personalize loving-kindness to your needs. For example, try using different phrases to create your own intentions for yourself or others. Some examples include: May I be well, May I find joy, May I be strong, May I be confident, May I be free of anxiety, May I be free of pain, May I be free from sadness, and May I be free from harm. The possibilities are endless, but I recommend sticking to just a few in a single meditation in order to focus your intentions for this period of practice.

Chapter **14**

Taking Care of Yourself

When you have social anxiety, you may experience physical symptoms of anxiety in your body that can feel uncomfortable. Sometimes, your bodily sensations can even feel dangerous if you misinterpret them as something else. You may avoid social situations in order to not feel these symptoms. While taking care of your body is not the "cure" for social anxiety, having good self-care can reduce your baseline level of anxiety so you can cope better when you get triggered by your social anxiety. In this chapter, you discover how social anxiety affects your body, find out ways to get in touch with your bodily sensations, and explore ideas for calming your body and engaging in life.

Identifying the Physical Sensations of Social Anxiety

Social anxiety can cause you to experience actual physical sensations that may cause your fear to increase. You may also mistake these sensations for a physical problem, such as having a heart attack or being sick. Once you feel physical symptoms of anxiety start to arise, this awareness can become self-perpetuating, causing more anxiety to surface.

Anxiety can affect your body in many ways, such as a racing heart, feeling like you are not present, difficulty breathing, fatigue, upset stomach, high blood pressure, and many more. When you learn to identify and connect with — and not avoid — your uncomfortable bodily sensations, you begin to change your relationship to discomfort and fear. You may be able to stay more present even if you do not like what you are feeling. Two exercises that can help you identify the physical sensations of social anxiety you may be feeling are the body scan exercise and progressive muscle relaxation.

Body scan exercise

The body scan exercise is a mindfulness exercise that can help you discover where the tension is in your body and release the tension brought on by stress or an intense emotional state. It involves mentally scanning your body from your toes up through your head as you focus your attention on each part, noticing different sensations. You learn to explore pleasant and unpleasant sensations and notice what happens when you are not trying to fix or change anything.

To practice the body scan exercise, follow these steps:

1. **Get ready.**

   Find a quiet place without too many distractions. Choose a comfortable position for your body scan. Sit or lie down.

2. Breathe.

Take a few deep breaths. Inhale slowly and deeply for a few breaths, then exhale slowly by about double the length of your inhale.

3. Notice.

Be aware of how you feel physically as you are seated or lying down. Notice the surface and how it feels against your body.

4. Scan.

Start at your toes and work your way up. Scan your toes, calves, knees, thighs, hips, abdomen, arms, chest, shoulders, neck, and head.

5. Acknowledge.

As you scan each part of your body and notice sensations, acknowledge any emotions or tension associated with it. Pause on each body part and take a few deep breaths. Imagine yourself letting go of the pain or breathing it away.

TIP

If you prefer a guided exercise, search for "body scan meditation" in your favorite search engine to find several 5- to 10-minute guided exercises.

Progressive muscle relaxation

Unlike the body scan exercise, where you are not trying to change anything about your bodily sensations, with progressive muscle relaxation (PMR), you are teaching yourself how to relax specific muscle groups. PMR can help you to lower your overall tension and stress levels. Eventually, you can use PMR to help you relax in the moment when you are feeling anxious in real life.

REMEMBER

PMR involves a two-step process. The most important part of PMR is to focus on and notice the difference between tensing and relaxing your muscles.

Here are the two steps for practicing PMR:

1. **Tense.**

   Choose a specific part of your body where you are feeling tension. Take a slow, deep breath in and squeeze the muscles as hard as you can for about 5 seconds.

2. **Relax.**

   Quickly exhale and release the tension from the previously tensed muscles. You should feel the muscle becoming loose as the tension flows out.

Taking Care of Your Body

Taking care of your body is an essential part of self-care. It involves the basics like getting enough sleep, exercising, eating well, relaxing, and more.

Getting enough sleep

Getting enough sleep is essential for managing social anxiety. You may have trouble falling asleep or staying asleep because your mind is reliving all your social interactions from the day. You may be ruminating on how you think you embarrassed yourself or imagining how you said something stupid or mind reading what you think others are thinking about you. Most of your worries will be unrealistic or exaggerated. You may also be worrying about your social engagements for tomorrow and falling into numerous thinking traps. (For help in identifying your thinking traps, see Chapter 7.)

When you do not get enough sleep, the next day you are susceptible to feeling more anxious. Before you know it, you're in a cycle of sleepless nights and anxiety that's damaging to your mental health and well-being. It may even develop into a fear of not getting enough sleep and then you develop sleep anxiety in addition to social anxiety. These two types of anxiety feed off of each other.

TIP

Working on your social anxiety can calm your mind, leading to better sleep. It is also important to establish a regular bedtime routine. Here are some common recommendations for improving your sleep routine:

>> Go to bed and wake up at the same time every day, even on weekends.

>> Stop doing work and using electronics a few hours before bedtime.

>> Don't have caffeine after mid-day.

>> Limit alcohol and heavy food before bedtime.

>> Don't do mentally stimulating activities in bed, such as using your phone or computer.

>> Establish a relaxing routine to get your body ready to sleep, such as taking a warm shower, meditating, or reading a book.

Exercising

Exercise is beneficial to reducing social anxiety by helping improve your mental and physical well-being. Some benefits of exercise include:

>> Distracts you from the thoughts that are causing your social anxiety.

>> Decreases muscle tension, lowering the body's baseline state of anxiety.

>> Gets your heart rate up and changes your brain chemistry by increasing positive brain chemicals like serotonin and others.

>> Helps control the amygdala — the over-reactive part of the brain responsible for leading you into thinking traps.

TIP

Some ways to engage in exercise include:

>> Choose something you enjoy so you will do it.

>> Start small and build up to something that gets your heart rate going.

>> Exercise outdoors in nature when possible because you'll get double the anxiety-reducing benefits.

Doing yoga

Practicing yoga is great way to feel relief from stress, generalized anxiety, and social anxiety. Yoga helps to calm your sympathetic nervous system also known as fight, flight, or freeze. This part of your body has a heightened reaction to perceived threats, leading to anxiety, agitation, stress, worry, heart palpitations, and other unhelpful mental and physical symptoms. Yoga helps to stimulate the parasympathetic nervous system, which causes you to feel safe and calm.

TIP

You can find many free videos online to help guide you through basic yoga moves. You can also find several popular paid apps in the app store on your smartphone or other devices. Just 5 to 10 minutes of yoga a day can benefit you and help rest the mind and body.

Eating well

You are what you eat! It's important to learn how your body reacts to different nutrients. Some people feel calmed by eating carbohydrates, while for others, eating carbohydrates leads to binge eating. Here are a few basic ideas about healthy eating:

>> **Eat healthy, balanced meals.** It goes without saying that this, along with exercise, is the most critical thing you can do for your overall physical and mental health.

>> **Don't overeat.** Monitor your hunger and fullness level like it's a gas tank. Don't get too empty, but also don't keep refilling the tank too soon.

>> **Eat earlier in the day.** Breakfast is often considered the most important meal of the day. You are more likely to avoid excessive night-time and binge eating if you space out your meals throughout the day.

>> **Eat protein.** It can help you feel satisfied longer and keep your blood sugar steady so that you avoid highs and lows in your mood.

>> **Eat complex carbohydrates.** They can increase the amount of serotonin in your brain, which has a calming effect.

>> **Avoid too much sugar.** Foods that contain simple carbohydrates, such as sugary foods and drinks, have been linked to increased anxiety.

>> **Drink plenty of water.** Even mild dehydration can affect your anxiety level.

>> **Limit or avoid alcohol.** It may feel as though alcohol is calming but as it is processed by your body, you may become irritable and have trouble staying asleep.

>> **Limit or avoid caffeine.** It can make you feel jittery and nervous. If you must have caffeine to get going, have it early in the day to avoid it interfering with falling asleep.

>> **Pay attention to food sensitivities.** You can keep a simple good journal to understand what foods work for you and which ones don't.

Relaxing

It's important to make time for activities that are purely for fun and for nurturing yourself. You may be "on" all the time and put relaxation on the back burner. Relaxation is productive. It leads to mental clarity, moments of peace, less fatigue, and reduced stress and anxiety. When you don't take time to rejuvenate, your energy levels diminish.

TIP

Relaxation can come from any of your interests. You can have a formal practice of relaxation such as meditating, doing a body scan, practicing yoga, and others. Or you can just do things you enjoy like reading a book or watching a movie. Getting out in nature and being mindful about what you see, feel, hear, and smell can be extremely nurturing.

Deep breathing

You always hear about breathing as being essential to well-being. It seems cliché to mention it. However, breathing in the right way can help reduce the physical and mental symptoms of social anxiety. By being mindful of your breath, you can reduce stress and anxiety and feel calmer inside and out.

TIP

Many of the uncomfortable physical sensations of anxiety, such as chest pain, heaviness, sweating, muscle tension, and so on, are the result of hyperventilation. Hyperventilation can be so subtle that we don't even notice that we are doing it, but it nonetheless triggers our fight/flight response. By regulating your breathing, you can relieve many of the physical symptoms of anxiety.

Shallow breathing can make you feel anxious and stressed. It's important to practice deep breathing. The advantage of using your breath as a technique for taking care of your body is that it is always with you, and you can manipulate it to have a soothing effect. Here's how to practice deep breathing:

1. Place one hand on your stomach and the other hand on your chest. Imagine there's a balloon in your stomach that you're filling and deflating.

2. Breathe in through your nose for a slow count of four. Feel your stomach rise as you inhale.

3. Breathe out more slowly with a slow count of six using pursed lips. You should feel the balloon in your stomach deflating while the hand on your chest will stay mostly still.

Participating in Leisure Activities and Hobbies

Hobbies and leisure activities can be great for building self-esteem. For you, someone with social anxiety, participating in hobbies and leisure activities is a great way to meet people and build a sense of community where you feel supported and safe.

TIP

You can group activities and hobbies into several categories, such as:

>> People (family, friends, church)

>> Entertainment (movies, reading, music, theater, dancing)

- Creating (drawing, writing, painting, knitting, cooking, baking)

- Sports (football, volleyball, basketball)

- Games (board games, cards, chess, video games)

- Exercise (running, weight lifting, aerobics classes)

- Outdoors (fishing, hiking, skiing, gardening)

- Travel (long weekends, international trips)

Within these categories, there's probably something that may interest you, or maybe there is something else that is not listed here. If you already have leisure activities and hobbies, good for you! You can do activities on your own or participate with others. This will help you to work on your social anxiety in a way that makes you feel more confident.

Finding Purpose and Meaning

Purpose is an overarching intention that is personally meaningful to you and important to the world beyond you. You can try to find ways to blend your passion, talents, and care for the world in a way that fills your life with meaning. When you are engaging in meaningful activities, you may feel less socially anxious in your body and mind because you are doing things you enjoy and love. See Chapter 12 for more on using positive psychology to help you live a meaningful life and advance your life's purpose.

WARNING

Fear is one of the biggest obstacles to finding your purpose. The fear of failure, rejection, and not being enough can stop you in your tracks. To find your purpose, you have to move past these fears. Limiting beliefs are another form of fear that can either hold you back or propel you forward toward meaning.

Many years ago, I read *Man's Search for Meaning* by Viktor Frankl. Originally published in 1946, it chronicles the author's experience in a Nazi concentration camp during World War II. In it, Frankl says people can survive the worst of circumstances by finding purpose and meaning in their existence. Frankel said many of those who survived the camps were able to imagine a purpose for themselves in the future. Many were able to imagine conversations with their loved ones.

REMEMBER

Through Frankl's experience in surviving the concentration camp, he concluded that there are three ways to find meaning in life, including:

>> Work, especially when it's both creative and aligned with a purpose greater than yourself.

>> Love, which can be caretaking for family and friends and other ways in the service of others.

>> Suffering, and the attitude we take toward suffering.

Getting Social Support from Family and Friends

Social support involves having a network of family and friends that you can turn to in times of need including one-on-one relationships and through social and religious organizations. Social support has been shown in research to be a protective factor against anxiety and depression. Don't forget that social support is a two-way street. It's important to give social support to others so when you need it, others are willing to help you, too.

TIP

There are different types of social support. Here are a few types of social support most people need:

>> Emotional support, such as listening and validating when you're feeling anxious or down.

>> Physical help when you are ill and otherwise unable to do things for yourself.

>> Guidance, advice, information, and mentoring when you're making decisions or big changes in your life.

IN THIS CHAPTER

» Exploring different types of therapy

» Finding a therapist with expertise in social anxiety

» Knowing the difference between therapists and psychiatrists

Chapter **15**

Working with a Therapist

I f you think you need professional help for your social anxiety, you may be wondering where to begin. There are many types of therapists and different types of therapy. For example, you may wonder what the difference is between a therapist, a psychologist, and a psychiatrist. What do CBT, DBT, ACT, or any number of other acronyms mean? What type of therapy is most effective for social anxiety? In this chapter, you explore answers to these questions.

Understanding Evidence-Based Treatment of Social Anxiety

Cognitive behavior therapy (CBT) is the gold standard for helping people with social anxiety. CBT represents a family of cognitive and behavioral therapies. You can think of CBT as an umbrella with various types of therapy falling underneath it.

CBT is a practical, goal-oriented form of therapy that is focused on the present and future to help you solve current problems as well as resolve long-standing issues that are affecting you today. CBT helps you let go of unhelpful ways of thinking and problematic behaviors. The two main ingredients of CBT to cope with and reduce social anxiety are cognitive reframing to change your self-talk and exposures to face your fears.

TIP

When looking for a CBT therapist, make sure the therapist is practicing CBT using the gold standard features of CBT for social anxiety. The therapy should

>> Be goal-oriented with an action plan and progress-tracking

>> Incorporate cognitive reframing and exposure therapy

>> Be focused, with an agenda for every session

>> Be personalized to your needs and not manualized

>> Include between-session assignments to practice skills

>> Be efficient and time-oriented (although the exact number of sessions depends on your needs)

>> Be active and collaborative, and your therapist should provide you with feedback

>> Be compassionate and patient-oriented

TIP

Ask the therapist where they received their training in CBT to see if they are incorporating the features of CBT for anxiety, especially exposure therapy.

Identifying Different Types of Therapy

When deciding what type of therapy you want, make sure the therapy includes a focus on both helping you change your thoughts and core beliefs as well as facing your fears with exposures. Most therapists have a certain way they try to help people, which is called their *clinical orientation*. If someone does not offer the essential components of CBT, you may not want to choose them. In the following sections, I provide some background on different types of cognitive and behavioral therapies to help you find the right type of therapy and therapist for you.

Cognitive therapy

Many people think that cognitive therapy is all about trying to think positively or that the therapist is trying to convince you to think a different way. In fact, cognitive therapy is about changing the way you feel by changing the way you think. Cognitive therapists use various techniques to help you think in more realistic and helpful ways and encourage you to try new behaviors to promote greater confidence.

In reality, skilled cognitive therapists use guided discovery to help you uncover your thinking and behavioral patterns that are getting you stuck with social anxiety. Then, your therapist helps you get unstuck by teaching you how to reframe your negative or unhelpful thoughts.

Exposure therapy

Exposure therapy is the behavioral element of CBT that involves confronting your fears in real life. In exposure therapy, you can create a fear ladder that lists your fears from the easiest to do to the hardest. You can choose what you want to do, and you do not need to complete the steps in order. All forms of CBT combine cognitive therapy with some exposure and behavioral experiments to confront your fears in real life. (For more about exposure therapy, see Chapter 11.)

Acceptance and commitment therapy

Acceptance and commitment therapy (ACT) uses acceptance, mindfulness, commitment, and behavior-change strategies to help you think more flexibly and live more in tune with your values. Most forms of cognitive behavior therapies include having a flexible mindset and using your values for motivation, but ACT provides a unique framework for doing this.

Dialectical behavior therapy

Dialectical behavior therapy (DBT) is a form of CBT that focuses on helping people manage intense emotions. It is a structured program lasting six months to a year that combines skills-based group training with individual therapy. The skills taught include mindfulness, distress tolerance, emotion regulation, and inter-personal effectiveness.

Radically open dialectical behavior therapy

Radically open dialectical behavior therapy (RO DBT) is a varia-tion of standard DBT that focuses on helping individuals with an over-controlled personality style with emotional expression and flexibility. Many people with social anxiety probably lean toward being over-controlled because some of the traits overlap with social anxiety. These include being reserved or socially distant; expressing emotions that don't match how you're feeling, such as smiling when you are anxious; inhibiting your emotional expression, such as having a flat face when being complimented; or comparing yourself to others.

Schema therapy

Schema therapy is an evolution of CBT that is designed to help people identify and change long-term firmly held beliefs and behavioral patterns. Schema therapy was originally designed to work with personality disorders, but it has evolved into a ther-apy that can help with other problems like chronic depression and anxiety. Research on applying schema therapy to problems like social anxiety is recent but promising. Schema therapy may be a good fit if you have severe social anxiety and/or avoidant personality disorder.

Mindfulness-based cognitive therapy

Mindfulness-based cognitive therapy (MBCT) combines CBT strategies with mindfulness and meditative practices. MBCT is done over eight weeks in a group setting, and much of the practice is done outside the group on your own with guided meditations and finding ways to cultivate mindfulness in your daily life. This style of therapy may help you learn to be more present and in the moment.

Group therapy

Cognitive behavior therapy in a group setting is considered a gold standard for social anxiety. You are learning to confront your fears with other people. This can trigger social anxiety in and of itself because group therapy is an exposure. On the other hand, when the group supports you in a warm and caring way, such support can help you overcome your negative thoughts and develop a resilient mindset.

Social skills training

Social skills training (SST) focuses on helping you develop interpersonal, communication, and assertiveness skills. It enables you to express feelings and understand verbal and nonverbal cues. The skills are taught through teaching, role-playing, feedback, and practice in both an individual and group setting.

VIDEO THERAPY VERSUS IN-PERSON THERAPY

Traditionally, therapy has been provided only in person. The advantage of in-person therapy for social anxiety is that it can help you overcome in-person avoidance. Some CBT therapists may do exposures with you before you do them on your own, such as walking with you to a coffee shop.

However, the use of telemedicine has been growing, and it exploded during the COVID-19 pandemic. Research shows that video therapy

(continued)

(continued)

can be just as effective as in-person therapy. Some advantages of video therapy include:

- You don't have to spend time on the road driving to and from a therapist's office.

- You can access experts anywhere in their state or the world (provided the therapist is appropriately licensed).

- Seeing your face as well as your therapist's face on video can be anxiety-provoking and serve as an exposure.

- Skilled therapists can do exposures with you on video in your home environment, which is not possible with traditional in-person therapy.

- Skilled therapists can do outside exposures with you because you can take your smartphone anywhere.

Identifying Different Types of Therapists

Finding the right therapist takes some research and patience. There are manysza different types of therapists. Some therapists are generalists, while others are highly trained and certified in a specific type of therapy. Some therapists have a master's degree, while others have a doctorate (yet they are not medical doctors). All of the mental health professionals listed in Table 15-1 can diagnose mental health conditions and can work with any person as long as they have experience with that specific population or disorder.

TIP

When deciding on the right therapist for you, make sure exposure is a central component of the therapy because that is one of the most important parts of therapy for social anxiety.

REMEMBER

To legally provide therapy, mental health professionals need to be licensed. This is to protect you, just like a medical doctor needs a license to practice medicine. Every country has its own laws and regulations. In the United States, a therapist must be licensed in the state in which you are located or have some type of reciprocal agreement with your state. An unlicensed therapist in training can see patients, but they must be working under the supervision of a therapist with a license.

TABLE 15-1 **Types of Therapists**

Therapist	Description
Clinical Social Worker	A mental health professional who has a master's degree in social work with training in social and economic factors, and can see individuals, couples, families, and children
Marriage and Family Therapist	A mental health professional who holds a master's degree and has expertise in marriage, families, and children but can work with individuals, too
Professional Clinical Counselor	A mental health professional who has a master's degree and focuses on individuals and couples but can also work with families and children with additional training
Psychiatrist	A medical doctor who prescribes medicine and sometimes offers therapy, although most psychiatrists do not
Psychologist	A mental health professional who holds a doctorate degree and whose education focuses on aspects of mental health beyond just therapy, such as research and testing

REMEMBER

When you are looking for a therapist for social anxiety, it is more important to determine whether they have significant experience with social anxiety and certification in CBT than what their degree is. In practice, there's not much difference between a psychologist, a marriage and family therapist, a professional clinical counselor, or a clinical social worker other than their degree.

Knowing What Makes a Good Therapist

When working with a therapist, the most important criterion that determines whether you found the right therapist is the relationship you and your therapist form, so it is important to do your research to find the best fit for you. There are many qualities to look for depending on your personality and style. Some things you may not be able to judge after the first session, but at the very least, you should feel comfortable when you talk to your therapist over the phone and meet for the first time. Research shows that the number one way to determine whether you found the right therapist is how well you connect with and trust this person.

In general, good therapists have the following characteristics:

>> Is a good listener and curious about your feelings and experiences

>> Is observant and provides feedback that shows empathy and understanding

>> Uses gentle inquiry and guided discovery to help you understand your thinking and behavioral patterns

>> Is confident in their approach and that they can help you

>> Has expertise in the treatment of social anxiety

>> Is prepared for sessions and remembers what you discussed in previous sessions

>> Holds you accountable, provides assignments to do in between sessions, and reviews those assignments at the next session

>> Is trustworthy, reliable, and consistent

>> Has strong ethical boundaries

Resources for Finding a Therapist

There are many ways to find a therapist. You can get referrals from people you know, or you can use online resources to find therapists with expertise in social anxiety.

TIP

Be sure to ask the therapists you are considering what their approach to helping you overcome social anxiety will be.

Referrals

Traditionally, the most common way to find a therapist is through a referral from a friend, family member, or doctor. This is a great place to start. If you can't find a therapist this way or you prefer greater confidentiality, you can consider searching for a therapist online yourself.

Search engines

Today, more and more people go online to look for therapists themselves. Many people use online search engines such as Google or Bing and see who comes up with their search terms. You can search for "social anxiety therapy" plus your location to find therapists licensed in your area. A big advantage of this approach is you can find an expert in what you need help with, but you will need to be careful in screening the therapists you find.

National Social Anxiety Center

If you are looking for a therapist for social anxiety, a helpful resource is the National Social Anxiety Center (https://national socialanxietycenter.com), which lists member clinics from many parts of the United States on its website. All of the therapy clinics listed have been screened to be sure they understand the best practices for helping people with social anxiety. Each clinic has at least one therapist who is certified in CBT by the Academy of Cognitive Therapy.

Academy of Cognitive and Behavioral Therapies

All therapists listed on the Academy of Cognitive Therapy's website at www.academyofcbt.org are certified in CBT. One advantage of searching this list is that you can find CBT therapists from all over the world. However, a downside to this resource is that many of the CBT therapists listed practice different forms of CBT. Some have a balanced approach and focus on cognitive and behavioral strategies more evenly. Others may focus more on acceptance and mindfulness strategies, and some may focus more on more behavioral strategies.

TIP

If you are screening therapists from the Academy's website, be sure to ask about their approach to working with social anxiety. While all of the therapists listed practice CBT, there are many types of CBT, so be sure you understand what you will be doing with your therapist.

International Society of Schema Therapy

If you have severe social anxiety or avoidant personality, you may want to consider working with a schema therapist. The International Society of Schema Therapy at https://schema therapysociety.org offers a helpful search feature to find a schema therapist. Two things to keep in mind with this resource are that the therapists may not be well versed in social anxiety specifically, and many of the therapists listed are not actually certified in schema therapy.

TIP

You will need to ask a lot more questions to make sure the therapists you are considering are experts in schema therapy with experience with social anxiety and avoidant personality. Ideally, you should find an Advanced Certified Schema Therapist with expertise in social anxiety disorder.

Psychology Today

If you search for a therapist, the Psychology Today (PT) therapist directory will almost always pop up pretty high in the rankings because PT (www.psychologytoday.com) pays to rank high on the search engines. PT is a great resource for finding therapists in specific locations because most therapists have a directory listing. However, be aware that PT doesn't do any kind of screening or background checks. As with any other resource, you will need to carefully screen therapists listed on PT using the criteria in this chapter.

Other associations

Other places you can find therapists include the therapist directories provided by the Association for Behavioral and Cognitive Therapies (www.abct.org) and the Anxiety and Depression Association of America (https://adaa.org).

WARNING

Many therapists say they practice CBT when what they actually mean is that they throw in some cognitive or behavioral techniques or some other random CBT strategies to traditional talk therapy. They may not have an agenda at every session or have you practice things on your own outside of therapy. They may not incorporate exposure therapy, which is critical to overcoming social anxiety. Keep in mind what an evidence-based approach to CBT looks like, and be sure to find out exactly what a therapist will do when they claim to practice CBT.

Finding a Psychiatrist

It is not uncommon for people to be confused about the difference between therapists and psychiatrists. Psychiatrists are medical doctors with special training in psychiatry. Their main role is to prescribe medication. Some may offer therapy along with medication, but the majority partner with a therapist for the therapy side.

WARNING

Doctorate-level therapists may have the letters "Dr" in front of their names, but they are not medical doctors and can't prescribe medication.

When finding a psychiatrist, most people get a referral from their insurance company or their primary care doctor. These days, it is hard to find psychiatrists with openings, so you may want to talk to your primary care physician (PCP) first to get evaluated for a psychiatric issue. Your PCP can prescribe psychiatric medication if needed. If your PCP thinks you need a more extensive psychiatric evaluation, then they will refer you to a psychiatrist.

4

Tackling Specific Types of Social Anxiety

Find out how to change your self-talk around public speaking and how to face your fears by conducting exposures in public speaking situations.

Explore basic principles of conquering your dating anxiety, including changing your self-talk and facing your fears in real life.

Discover the common types of social anxiety at work and worries that professionals often have.

Find out how social anxiety impacts children and how to help your child if they struggle with it.

Chapter **16**

Fear of Public Speaking

The fear of public speaking — also known as *glossophobia* — is one of the most common forms of social anxiety. Some 15 to 30 percent of the general population has public speaking anxiety, according to the *Diagnostic and Statistical Manual of Mental Disorders, Fifth Edition* (DSM-5). Many experts say that around 75 percent of people have some level of anxiety about public speaking. The underlying issue behind this fear is the fear of judgment and negative evaluation, which is the same as in other types of social anxiety.

In this chapter, you find out how to change your self-talk around public speaking and how to face your fears by conducting exposures in public speaking situations. You learn specific steps for conducting public speaking exposures, how to debrief to maximize what you learn from the exposures, and the importance of repeating exposures.

Getting Control of Your Public Speaking Anxiety

To get control of your fear of public speaking, you need to work on your mindset and what you think and do when you get nervous. The following strategies are helpful whether you have mild, moderate, or severe public speaking anxiety:

>> **Change your self-talk:** Notice when you are in an unhelpful thinking pattern and use the CALM thinking skills to create more compassionate, accepting, logical, and motivating self-talk.

>> **Face your fears:** Identify your fears and come up with exposures that can help you learn from the experiences.

These topics are covered in Chapters 10 and 11. In this chapter, you apply these principles to your fear of public speaking.

Identifying Speaking Situations that Make You Nervous

Some common public speaking situations that tend to make people nervous include making small talk, talking to strangers, having longer conversations, participating in meetings, speaking up in class, speaking to authority figures, giving presentations to small groups, or giving formal presentations to large groups. You may also worry about showing physical signs of anxiety, such as blushing, having shaky hands, or sweating in public.

TIP

Chapter 4 discusses the common situations that may make you feel anxious, and many of these situations involve public speaking. Review Chapter 4 to determine if any of these situations apply to you.

Changing Your Mindset About Public Speaking

In this section, you discover how to identify your thinking traps and change your self-talk around your public speaking anxiety. You'll read about a hypothetical person who has a fear of public speaking. You'll follow this person as she works on changing her mindset using the CALM thinking skills and faces her fears by doing exposures. In doing so, you explore how to face your own public speaking fears.

CASE EXAMPLE

Meet Molly. Molly is a 24-year-old recent college graduate. She's a sales representative in the pharmaceutical industry. She's been in her job for about a year, and her first job review was excellent. In terms of development, Molly's manager said she needs to be more aggressive with doctors and work on looking less nervous when she participates in meetings or gives presentations internally within her direct group.

Molly is representing a new medication that has become a blockbuster in her industry, and she's one of the few salespeople who knows a lot about it. She has been asked to give a presentation to the senior executives in her company.

Identifying thinking traps

Thinking traps are patterns of thinking that are unhelpful and often not true. When you can identify your thinking traps and the negative thoughts that result from them, you can begin to change your self-talk and your mindset. Table 16-1 lists the common thinking traps. (Refer to Chapter 7 for definitions of each one.)

TABLE 16-1   **Common Thinking Traps**

All-or-nothing thinking	Jumping to conclusions	Overestimating probabilities
Catastrophizing	Labeling	Personalizing
Emotional reasoning	Mind reading	Shining the spotlight
Fortune-telling	Negative mental filter	Using "should" statements

CASE EXAMPLE

Molly had the following fearful thoughts and thinking traps about giving a presentation:

> **Situation:** Giving a presentation.
>
> **Feelings:** Nervous, anxiety, trepidation, worry, fear.
>
> **Fearful thoughts:** She will lose her train of thought and her voice will tremble. Then people will look down on her and think she's terrible.
>
> **Thinking traps:** Fortune-telling, labeling, mind reading.

Changing self-talk

CASE EXAMPLE

Molly realized that she has a perfectionistic inner critic who tells her that she has to do a perfect presentation or people will look down on her. Molly used the reframing skills outlined in Chapter 10 to change her fearful thinking into self-talk that is more compassionate, accepting, logical, and motivating. Table 16-2 illustrates how Molly used the CALM thinking skills to reframe her fearful thinking.

TABLE 16-2 Molly's CALM Thinking

Compassionate: What can you say to yourself that's gentler and kinder?	I am doing my best and facing my fear. I need to give myself credit for my effort and for taking risks.
Accepting: What part is true about yourself or the situation, and can you accept in a nonjudgmental way?	I do get nervous during presentations, and that's okay.
Logical: What thinking traps do you notice? What can you say to yourself that's more realistic or helpful?	Most people won't notice or care if I am nervous. But if they do notice, it's an opportunity to practice facing my fear of judgment.
Motivating: What can you remind yourself of that can inspire you to meet your goals?	I am getting really good performance reviews, and I can keep practicing public speaking. The more I practice, the easier it will be.

Think of a situation where you experienced social anxiety around public speaking. Write down some of your feelings, fearful thoughts, and thinking traps related to the situation.

Situation: _____

Feelings: _____

Fearful thoughts: _____

Thinking traps: _____

Now, use the reframing skill to fill in Table 16-3 with thoughts that are compassionate, accepting, logical, and motivating.

TABLE 16-3 Reframing Your Fearful Thinking

Compassionate: What can you say to yourself that's gentler and kinder?	
Accepting: What part is true about yourself or the situation, and can you accept in a nonjudgmental way?	
Logical: What thinking traps do you notice? What can you say to yourself that's more realistic or helpful?	
Motivating: What can you remind yourself of that can inspire you to meet your goals?	

Facing Your Fears with Public Speaking Exposures

Facing your fears with exposures is critical to overcoming public speaking anxiety, or at least to help you become less fearful and more functional when speaking in a public setting. With exposures, you can learn that either your fears are not true and/or that you can cope with your anxious feelings when they come up. Exposures are helpful when you can't talk yourself out of the fear of public speaking. Exposures will show you that you can learn new beliefs by facing your fears. By staying in learning mode after each exposure, you will keep improving.

As you do exposures for public speaking anxiety, you follow the same steps for facing your fears described in Chapter 11:

1. Create a target list of the fears you want to work on.
2. Identify safety behaviors to stop.
3. Build a fear ladder.
4. Engage in an exposure.
5. Debrief after the exposures.
6. Repeat the exposure or do a new one.

Creating a target list

CASE
EXAMPLE

Molly decided it was time to work on her fear of public speaking by conducting exposures, so she created a target list of the fears she wants to work on. She realized that by doing exposures and staying in a learning mode, she could create a new mindset around her fear of public speaking.

Table 16-4 lists Molly's feared situations around public speaking. She rated them based on the following:

>> How scary they were from 1 to 10, with 10 being the scariest

>> How much she avoids them from 1 to 10, with 10 being the most avoidance

>> How important they are for her to overcome from very important (VI) to important (I) to not important (NI)

TABLE 16-4 **Molly's Public Speaking Fears**

Situation	Fear Level	Avoidance	Importance
Giving presentations	10	10	VI
Talking in team meetings	6	8	VI
Making small talk	3	2	I
Meeting with customers	5	2	VI
Talking to authority figures	8	8	I
Showing anxiety at work	9	8	VI

Molly has to give a formal presentation to senior executives soon, so she decided to target her exposures to accomplish this goal. Even though her fear level around giving presentations is rated a 10, she knew she couldn't avoid giving this presentation because she'd already agreed to do it. She also realized that she needed to work on being more comfortable speaking with people in authority positions and working on her fear of showing anxiety. Because her end goal is terrifying to Molly, she'll break her exposures down into easier steps she can tackle first when she creates her fear ladder.

Now, create your own list of public speaking fears you want to work on. If you created a list of situations that make you feel anxious in Chapter 6, you can use that list as a guide to help you fill out Table 16-5. Remember to indicate how important each situation is for you to overcome from very important (VI) to important (I) to not important (NI).

TABLE 16-5 **Your Public Speaking Fears**

Situation	Fear Level	Avoidance	Importance

TIP

For more information about creating a target list of situations you want to work on, see Chapter 11.

Identifying safety behaviors to stop

It's important to identify the safety behaviors you need to drop. Safety behaviors interfere with learning and can prevent you from feeling confident that you can handle public speaking anxiety. Review Chapter 5 for some helpful hints on safety behaviors.

CASE
EXAMPLE

Some of the safety behaviors Molly decided she needed to stop included avoidance, such as purposely not speaking to anyone who made her nervous or she found intimidating. She also wore a lot of makeup to camouflage any signs of blushing. Many times she stayed quiet in meetings to avoid feeling the anxiety of speaking up and feeling judged. Whenever she did have to do an informal presentation, she brought note cards that she read.

As a next step, come up with the safety behaviors you do that are related to your fear of public speaking. If you identified safety behaviors in Chapter 6, look back at that list for guidance. Include the situations you clearly avoid. Then add other behaviors you do to make yourself feel safe but that might be maintaining your public speaking anxiety.

Your avoidance and other safety behaviors:

_____

_____

_____

Building a fear ladder

CASE
EXAMPLE

Based on Molly's goal, she came up with a few possible exposures she could work on both in and outside of work. She created the fear ladder shown in Table 16-6.

Molly's goal: Get comfortable with speaking and presentations.

TABLE 16-6 Molly's Fear Ladder

Level of Difficulty	Anxiety Rating	Situation
Hardest	10	Giving a formal presentation to a large group of executives and others
	8–9	Giving an informal presentation in front of her peers
		Practicing a presentation in front of a few trusted friends
Moderate	6–7	Sharing an opinion at a small meeting
	4–5	Asking a question at a meeting
Easiest	2–3	Giving a toast at her parents' small upcoming anniversary party
		Talking to a new person at a happy hour with friends

Now, create your own fear ladder in Table 16-7 for your fears of public speaking. Try to come up with some activities that are easy, moderate, and hard to do to help you prepare for the goal you set for public speaking.

Your goal: _____

TABLE 16-7 Your Fear Ladder

Level of Difficulty	Anxiety Rating	Situation
Hardest	10	
	8–9	
Moderate	6–7	
	4–5	
Easiest	2–3	

Engaging in public speaking exposures

As Molly worked on her fear ladder, she was getting more comfortable with speaking in public. She decided he wanted to work on giving an informal presentation in front of her peers. In the following sections, use Molly's example as a guide to conduct your own public speaking exposures.

Before the exposure

Before the exposure, be specific about the exposure you want to practice. Then, add in the feared outcome, which is your prediction of what you think could happen. Include the safety behavior you must give up to ensure you fully expose yourself. If it is too hard to give up all your safety behaviors, you can phase them out in future exposures as you repeat them.

CASE EXAMPLE

Here's Molly's pre-exposure plan:

What exposure do you want to experiment with?

I will give an informal presentation to my peers.

What safety behaviors will you have to give up?

I'll need to give up wearing so much makeup and not read my notecards verbatim.

What feared outcome(s) are you most worried about and how likely do you think it is they'll happen?

I'll be nervous and blush (90%).

I will lose my train of thought (80%).

People will look down on me when they notice I'm anxious (80%).

EXPERIMENT

Now, fill in the following information for the specific exposure you are ready to try.

What exposure do you want to experiment with?

_____

_____

What safety behaviors will you have to give up?

_____

_____

What feared outcome(s) are you most worried about and how likely do you think it is they'll happen?

_____

_____

During the exposure

During exposures for public speaking anxiety, you need to focus outward instead of inward on your feelings and bodily sensations. You need to stop scanning your body for bodily sensations and let them be there with you without judging them. Stay focused on who you are talking to or on sharing information during presentations. Your goal is to tolerate your feelings and push through them.

Ultimately, you want to stop mind reading, especially as you are speaking. If you are speaking to someone one-on-one or in a small group, try to make eye contact and smile. If you are giving a formal presentation to a large group, when you look out at the audience, assume the positive instead of assuming everyone thinks you are nervous and are judging you negatively.

TIP

Sometimes, it is helpful to rate your anxiety before, during, and after your public speaking exposures. It can be part of the learning process to notice how your anxiety increases or decreases during public speaking exposures and as you repeat exposures.

Debriefing after the exposure

After the exposure, think about what you did and what you learned. Ask yourself how the outcome was different than what you expected and whether there were any surprises. Evaluate how well you did with letting go of safety behaviors. The most important part is to summarize what you learned. You want your exposures to keep reinforcing what went well. This is how your mind learns about public speaking and that the feelings you have before and during public speaking exposures are not dangerous.

**CASE
EXAMPLE**

Here's how Molly debriefed after the exposure:

How was the outcome different than what you expected? What surprised you?

I was nervous but I did not lose my train of thought. No one seemed to care if I was nervous and blushed because they came up to me afterward and said that I did a good job.

Did you engage in safety behaviors?

I wore less makeup. I took notecards with me, but I only referred to them and did not read them.

What did you learn from this exposure?

I learned that I could feel anxious but that my bodily sensations were not deal-breaking. I realized that my habit of mind reading and other thinking traps were changing as I focused outward and kept practicing exposures.

Answer the following questions with your results:

How was the outcome different than what you expected? What surprised you?

_____

_____

Did you engage in safety behaviors?

_____

_____

What did you learn from this exposure?

_____

_____

Repeating the same exposure or doing a new one

It's important to keep repeating exposures and doing new ones. You need to vary how you do exposures to get maximum feedback and build confidence with public speaking. For example, you can vary who you give presentations to, the content of your presentations, and how you do them (such as with or without notes or using PowerPoint slides). You can practice making impromptu comments in different types of meetings and with different people present or changing where you give presentations or opinions. If you don't have enough places to practice public speaking, consider going to a Toastmasters meeting where you can practice both impromptu and formal presentations. For more about Toastmasters, visit www.toastmasters.org.

TIP

Make copies of the Exposure Worksheet in Chapter 11 to keep repeating your public speaking exposures.

Ending Negative Patterns with Public Speaking

Unhelpful thinking and behavioral patterns often come up when you are experiencing public speaking anxiety. They can include thinking traps as well as avoidance behaviors. If you catch these patterns early, you can change your thoughts and actions. The following sections highlight some common negative patterns that come up with the fear of public speaking. You may experience others that aren't mentioned.

Avoiding opportunities for public speaking

When you have opportunities for public speaking, whether it's a formal or informal exposure, it's important to jump in and practice. For example, if you are in college and the professor asks the class a question, raise your hand and give your best try at answering. If you are in a work meeting, make a comment without planning it. See what happens. You can use the Exposure Worksheet in Chapter 11 to assess unplanned exposures, too.

Being overly self-critical

Your inner critic will try to make you feel judged and make you think negative thoughts about how you did. It will criticize your performance and cause your thinking traps to become activated. Your inner critic will say that having feelings and bodily sensations when you are speaking in public are dangerous. Be sure to spot your inner critic when it shows up and don't argue with or listen to it.

Dwelling afterward

You may dwell afterward on how you think your comments or presentations went. Dwelling afterward is also known as rumination. Filling out the Exposure Worksheet in Chapter 11 can help you stop dwelling and move into learning mode.

Catastrophizing

If you think others are judging you, perhaps you think of worst-case scenarios. As a high school student, you may think that if others think what you said was stupid, then they won't want to be your friend. If you are a mom, you may worry about sharing your opinions with other moms because they may talk behind your back. To end negative thinking patterns, you can work on recognizing these thoughts as thinking traps and spotting them before they start to exaggerate the risk of speaking in public.

Chapter **17**

Social Anxiety with Dating

L et's face it. Finding a lifetime partner is a universal desire of almost all human beings. You have a lot of love to give if only you weren't so nervous about taking steps to meet the right person. Unfortunately, your dating anxiety can thwart this goal. You may be scared to contact potential matches on a dating app. Or perhaps you get to the point of going on a date and have trouble making eye contact or maintaining the conversation. To build your confidence in dating, you need to work on your mindset and what you think and do when you get nervous.

In this chapter, you discover how to increase your confidence to help you achieve your goal of meeting the right person. You explore basic principles of conquering your dating anxiety, including changing your self-talk and facing your fears in real life. By the end of this chapter, you'll understand how to turn every exposure into an experiment where there is no failure.

Getting Control of Your Dating Anxiety

The basic principles for overcoming dating anxiety involve several of the same principles outlined in Chapters 10 and 11: changing your self-talk, facing your fears, and continuing to learn.

>> **Change your self-talk:** Spot your thinking traps and develop more compassionate, accepting, logical, and motivating self-talk.

Seeing your dating fears from a new perspective can help you develop a more positive mindset. For example, you may fall into a mind reading thinking trap and imagine that your date is judging you. With helpful self-talk, you can show yourself compassion and say something like, "Of course, I am nervous because dating is new to me. I know I am imagining what my date is thinking about me. I'll never know for sure unless they directly tell me. Even if I imagine that they think I am weird or unattractive, it does not make it true." A new thought like this can help you feel calmer before, during, and after a date.

>> **Face your fears:** Face your fears by exposing yourself to your dating fears in real life to see if your predictions come true.

Sometimes, you can't change your self-talk by talking yourself out of it. This is where real-life exposures using a learning approach can help. You can label each date as an "experiment" because with an experiment, there is no such thing as failure, and each exposure can give you more confidence to try again. By thinking of dates as experiments, they can be less scary. You set up a test and see what happens.

>> **Keep learning:** Debrief after every experience and see what you have learned.

Maybe you learned you can tolerate anxiety when you are meeting someone new and it's not as scary as you expected. Or maybe you were pleasantly surprised to learn that your date had fun and would like to see you again. Keep engaging in more dating experiences to continue learning and improving. Remember that even a bad date or a rejection can help you learn an important lesson. Learning to tolerate rejection can be a powerful tool for the future.

Identifying Dating Situations that Make You Nervous

Some common dating situations that tend to make people nervous include looking at dating apps and contacting a match, asking someone on a date, meeting someone in person, asking for a second date, showing signs of anxiety on the date, continuing communication with that person, asking the other person to be in a committed relationship, and comparing themselves to their date's previous partner.

TIP

Chapter 4 discusses common situations that may make you feel anxious, and many of these situations can happen with dating. Review Chapter 4 to determine if any of these situations apply to you.

Changing Your Mindset About Dating

In this section, you discover how to identify your thinking traps and change your self-talk about dating. You'll read about a hypothetical person with dating anxiety and follow this person as he works on changing his self-talk and facing his fears around dating. By applying the principles illustrated in this example, you can practice facing your fears about dating, too.

CASE EXAMPLE

Meet Jason. Jason is a 32-year-old man who has only had one girlfriend. That girlfriend broke up with him because he was distant and did not communicate well. Shortly after the breakup, she started dating one of Jason's acquaintances. Jason often compared himself to that guy, which made him feel inferior because Jason was shorter than him and stuttered when he was anxious. Jason thinks he is short for a man because he's about 5 feet 4 inches. He thinks women will not like him because he is short. He often compares himself to people he sees day-to-day at work and on TV.

Jason has a good job as a software engineer at a major company, but he's worried about getting laid off. He hesitates to take action toward dating because he thinks he has nothing to offer anyone, especially if he gets laid off from his job. No matter what he's tried, Jason can't get over his self-consciousness about his height. Jason also stutters sometimes when he is anxious, so he is worried that his date will notice and think he's weird. He worries he will represent himself online as someone with a good job and who is taller than he is, and then when he goes on a date, the woman will think he's a fraud. Not only that, he fears he will have trouble talking to her if he starts to stutter. Jason is terrified of asking someone on a date, or even looking at dating apps online, so he goes back and forth between approaching and avoiding dating situations.

Identifying thinking traps

Thinking traps are patterns of thinking that are unhelpful and often not true. When you can identify your thinking traps and the negative thoughts that result from them, you can begin to change your self-talk and your mindset. Table 17-1 lists the common thinking traps. Chapter 7 discusses thinking traps in more detail.

TABLE 17-1 Common Thinking Traps

All-or-nothing thinking	Jumping to conclusions	Overestimating probabilities
Catastrophizing	Labeling	Personalizing
Emotional reasoning	Mind reading	Shining the spotlight
Fortune-telling	Negative mental filter	Using "should" statements

CASE EXAMPLE

Jason's fearful thoughts and thinking traps about dating are listed in Table 17-2. Jason's negative thoughts contain more than one thinking trap, but because there is a lot of overlap, only one is identified for each thought for clarity. This helps illustrate the themes in Jason's negative thinking about himself and others.

TABLE 17-2 ## Jason's Thinking Traps

Fearful Thoughts	Thinking Trap(s)
Women don't like short men and will find me to be unattractive. I'll never find a partner.	Catastrophizing
I'm going to stutter. They'll see that I am nervous and they'll think I am weird.	Labeling
They'll think I am a loser if I don't have a job.	Mind reading
I won't be able to hold a conversation because I'm socially inept.	Fortune-telling

What are some of your own worries about dating? Think about your self-talk and the messages you give yourself before, during, and after dating situations. Look back at Table 17-1 and the definitions in Chapter 7 to identify your thinking traps and write them down in Table 17-3.

TABLE 17-3 ## Your Thinking Traps

Fearful Thoughts	Thinking Trap(s)

Changing self-talk

CASE EXAMPLE

Jason realized that he has a demanding inner critic who tells him that his dates will judge him. His inner critic tells him that he's inferior, a loser, and a fraud. The inner critic goes on and on in his head, making it hard for Jason to move forward with any actions toward dating. Jason has the following fearful thoughts about interacting with a potential date on a dating website:

Situation: Clicking the "like" button to show interest in a person on a dating app.

Feelings: Nervous, worried, dejected, depressed.

Fearful thoughts: No one wants to date a short man. They'll think I'm unattractive. If I stutter, they'll think I'm a loser. I'm going to end up alone, so why try?

Thinking traps: Catastrophizing, labeling, mind reading, fortune-telling.

Jason used the reframing skills outlined in Chapter 10 to change his fearful thinking into self-talk that is compassionate, accepting, logical, and motivating. Table 17-4 illustrates how Jason used the CALM thinking skills to reframe his fearful thinking.

TABLE 17-4 **Jason's CALM Thinking**

Compassionate: What can you say to yourself that's gentler and kinder?	Dating is hard. I am feeling vulnerable and scared. No one wants to put themselves out there. I am doing a good job by trying.
Accepting: What part is true about yourself or the situation, and can you accept in a nonjudgmental way?	It's true that I am short for a man, and I do stutter when I am nervous. These are parts of myself that I need to work on accepting and embracing as part of myself.
Logical: What thinking traps do you notice? What can you say to yourself that's more realistic or helpful?	I am catastrophizing because it's unlikely that I'll end up alone because I am short or stutter sometimes. It takes time to find a partner. When I am thinking realistically, I know that I have a lot to offer someone.
Motivating: What can you remind yourself of that can inspire you to meet your goals?	I can continue to take steps to make progress with my dating anxiety. As I get more experience with dating, I will gain confidence.

Think of a dating situation where you experienced social anxiety. Write down some of your feelings, fearful thoughts, and thinking traps related to the situation.

Situation: _____

Feelings: _____

Fearful thoughts: _____

Thinking traps: _____

Now, use the reframing skill to fill in Table 17-5 with thoughts that are compassionate, accepting, logical, and motivating.

TABLE 17-5 ## Reframing Your Fearful Thinking

Compassionate: What can you say to yourself that's gentler and kinder?	
Accepting: What part is true about yourself or the situation, and can you accept in a nonjudgmental way?	
Logical: What thinking traps do you notice? What can you say to yourself that's more realistic or helpful?	
Motivating: What can you remind yourself of that can inspire you to meet your goals?	

Facing Your Dating Fears with Exposures

Exposures are helpful when you can't talk yourself out of the fear of dating. Exposing yourself to your dating fears lets you feel your fear without escaping it. Just by allowing yourself to be in a scary situation, you may learn that you can handle anxiety and that your anxiety goes down with time.

Sometimes, however, you need to do more than just expose yourself to the fears and hope that your dating anxiety goes away. Research shows that engaging in exposures with specific experiments to test your predictions can be more effective than exposure by itself. This combination can be more powerful in changing your beliefs about yourself and others.

As you do exposures for your dating anxiety, you follow the same steps for facing your fears described in Chapter 11:

1. Create a target list of the fears you want to work on.

2. Identify safety behaviors to stop.

3. Build a fear ladder.

4. Engage in an exposure.

5. Debrief after the exposures.

6. Repeat the exposure or do a new one.

Creating a target list

CASE
EXAMPLE

Jason decided it was time to face his fears with dating, so he created a target list of the fears he wants to work on. He realized that by exposing himself to his fears, he could create a new mindset around dating as long as he stayed in a learning mode.

Table 17-6 lists Jason's feared situations around dating. He rated them based on the following:

>> How scary they were from 1 to 10, with 10 being the scariest

>> How much he avoids them from 1 to 10, with 10 being the most avoidance

>> How important they are for him to overcome from very important (VI) to important (I) to not important (NI)

Now, create your own list of dating fears you want to work on. If you created a list of situations that make you feel anxious in Chapter 6, you can use that list as a guide to help you fill out Table 17-7. Remember to indicate how important each situation is for you to overcome from very important (VI) to important (I) to not important (NI).

TABLE 17-6 Jason's Dating Fears

Situation	Fear Level	Avoidance	Importance
Looking at profiles	3	6	VI
Interacting with someone through the dating app	7	7	VI
Telling someone his height	10	10	NI
Meeting someone in person	10	10	VI
Asking for a second date	10	10	I
Stuttering on a date	8	5	I
Sending the first message	8	9	VI
Writing his profile	5	5	VI
Talking or texting outside the dating app	10	10	VI
Liking people on the dating app	5	5	VI
Deciding what dating apps to use	3	4	VI

TABLE 17-7 Your Dating Fears

Situation	Fear Level	Avoidance	Importance

For more information about creating a target list of situations you want to work on, see Chapter 11.

TIP

Identifying safety behaviors to stop

Safety behaviors interfere with learning and can prevent you from feeling confident that you can handle your dating anxiety.

It's important to identify the safety behaviors you need to drop. Review Chapter 5 for more information about what safety behaviors are and how to let go of them.

**CASE
EXAMPLE**

Some of the safety behaviors Jason decided he needed to stop were wearing shoes that make him look taller, excusing himself if he feels he's going to stutter, being too quiet on a date, holding his coffee cup too tightly, taking medication before a date to help calm his anxiety, and not making eye contact. He also engaged in many avoidance behaviors, such as not taking the initiative to follow up with someone online so that he didn't have to go on a date.

Now, see if you can come up with the safety behaviors you do that are related to your dating anxiety. If you identified safety behaviors in Chapter 6, look back at that list for guidance. Start by adding behaviors you do to make yourself feel safe but that might be maintaining your dating anxiety. Don't forget to include the situations you clearly avoid.

Your avoidance and other safety behaviors:

_____

_____

_____

Building a fear ladder

**CASE
EXAMPLE**

Based on Jason's goal of asking someone on a date, he came up with a few possible situations he could work on. He created the fear ladder shown in Table 17-8 that outlines his plans to conduct dating exposures and eventually tackle his hardest fear. The most important tasks he wanted to do were ask someone on a date and go on a date in person, so he focused his fear ladder on things to do to reach this initial goal.

Jason's goal: Go on a date.

TABLE 17-8 Jason's Fear Ladder

Level of Difficulty	Anxiety Rating	Situation
Hardest	10	Meeting in person
	8–9	Asking someone on a date
		Talking or texting outside the dating app
Moderate	6–7	Sending the first message on a dating app
		"Liking" people on a dating app
	4–5	Writing his profile
		Looking at profiles
Easiest	2–3	Deciding what dating apps to use
		Thinking about using a dating app

Now, create your own fear ladder in Table 17-9 for your specific fears of dating. Try to come up with some things that are easy, moderate, and hard to do to help you prepare for the exposures you want to do to face your dating fears.

Your goal: _____

TABLE 17-9 Your Fear Ladder

Level of Difficulty	Anxiety Rating	Situation
Hardest	10	
	8–9	
Moderate	6–7	
	4–5	
Easiest	2–3	

Engaging in dating exposures

As Jason worked on the items on his fear ladder, he was getting more comfortable with dating situations in general like responding to matches on dating apps and talking with potential dates online, but he still hadn't asked anyone on a date. He decided he wanted to work on asking someone out for coffee. He is going to set up this exposure as an experiment so that he would be more confident trying and staying in a learning mode.

Before the exposure

Before the exposure, be specific about what you want to do. You can pick something off your target list or even think of something new that you want to try. Make a prediction of what will happen in this experiment. Remember to take an observer stance while staying focused on your date instead of looking inward and judging yourself during the date.

**CASE
EXAMPLE**

Here's Jason's pre-exposure plan:

What exposure do you want to experiment with?

I'll ask Debbie out for coffee on Friday. She's 5'2", so that gives me a little more confidence in meeting her since I'm taller than her.

What safety behaviors will you have to give up?

I don't think I can give up too many safety behaviors yet because this exposure will be extremely challenging. I am overcoming avoidance by asking and potentially meeting her in person. I am going to try not to take medication before the date, and I will try to keep the conversation going.

What feared outcome(s) are you most worried about and how likely do you think it is they'll happen?

I'm worried Debbie will say no (80%).

If she says yes, I am worried she'll think I am boring if I can't hold a conversation and unattractive because I am short (90%).

I will feel inadequate and awkward (100%).

Jason identified what he would do and what he was worried could happen. He included the safety behaviors he'll need to give up to make sure he is fully exposing himself. It was a bit hard for Jason to give up all of his safety behaviors on this first date, so he decided on what he felt he could give up now with a commitment to phase more of them out in future exposures as he repeats them.

EXPERIMENT

Now, fill in the following information for the specific exposure you are ready to try.

What exposure do you want to experiment with?

_____

_____

What safety behaviors will you have to give up?

_____

_____

What feared outcome(s) are you most worried about and how likely do you think it is they'll happen?

_____

_____

During the exposure

During exposures for dating anxiety, you need to focus outward instead of inward on your feelings and bodily sensations. For example, if Jason starts to stutter, he needs to continue to focus on talking with Debbie instead of assessing his stuttering and what she must think of him. Stop scanning your body for bodily sensations and let them be there with you without judging them. Your goal is to tolerate your feelings and push through them.

TIP

Sometimes, it is helpful to rate your anxiety before, during, and after your dating exposures. It can be part of the learning process to notice how your anxiety increases or decreases during dating exposures and as you repeat them. The goal is not to reduce your anxiety directly but to notice your feelings and how anxiety waxes and wanes.

Debriefing after the exposure

When debriefing after the exposures, think about what you did and what you learned. Ask yourself how the outcome was different than what you expected and whether there were any surprises. Evaluate how well you did with letting go of safety behaviors. The most important part is to summarize what you learned. You want to keep reinforcing what went well with your exposures. This is how your mind learns that the feelings you have before and during exposures are not dangerous.

Here's what Jason learned after the exposure:

How was the outcome different than what you expected? What surprised you?

Debbie was very engaged and talked a lot about herself and her family. Debbie said she'd like to see me again.

Did you engage in safety behaviors?

I did an overall good job of letting go of the safety behaviors I planned. I nodded and smiled as she talked. I tried to make some eye contact. I did wear the shoes that make me a couple of inches taller, but if I get to know Debbie better, I might be ready to let go of that safety behavior. I didn't take medication before the date.

What did you learn from this exposure?

I learned that I could do okay on a date and that I could keep a conversation going even though I was nervous. I was pleasantly surprised when Debbie asked to see me again. I was still anxious about contacting her, but I decided to follow up to meet again.

Answer the following questions with your results:

How was the outcome different than what you expected? What surprised you?

_____

_____

Did you engage in safety behaviors?

_____

_____

What did you learn from this exposure?

_____

_____

Repeating the same exposure or doing a new one

It's important to keep repeating dating exposures and doing new ones. You need to vary how you do exposures to get maximum feedback and build confidence with dating. For example, you can keep practicing going on dates, vary the types of type of people you contact, go on dates in different venues, use different dating apps, wear different kinds of clothes on dates, talk about different subjects, and much more.

TIP

Make copies of the Exposure Worksheet in Chapter 11 to keep repeating your dating exposures.

Ending Negative Patterns with Dating

Unhelpful thinking and behavioral patterns often come up when you experience dating anxiety. They can include thinking traps as well as avoidance behaviors. If you can catch these patterns early, then you can change what you think and do. Following are some examples of common negative patterns that come up with the fear of dating. There may be others that apply to you that aren't mentioned.

Avoiding opportunities for dating

When you have opportunities to confront your dating fears, whether it's a formal or informal exposure, it's important to jump in and practice. You can use the Exposure Worksheet in Chapter 11 to see what you have learned and stay in learning mode.

Being overly self-critical

Your inner critic will try to make you feel judged and make you have negative thoughts about how you did. It will criticize how you look and talk and cause your thinking traps to become activated. Be sure to spot your inner critic when it shows up and don't argue or listen to it.

Dwelling afterward

You may dwell afterward on how you think your date went. Dwelling afterward is also known as rumination. Filling out the Exposure Worksheet in Chapter 11 can help you stop dwelling and move into learning mode.

Catastrophizing

If you think others are judging you, perhaps you think of worst-case scenarios. For example, you may think you are too unattractive to ever have a partner or get married. To end this negative thinking pattern, you can work on recognizing these thoughts as thinking traps and spot them before they start to exaggerate the risk of dating.

Chapter **18**

Social Anxiety in the Workplace

Worrying about how you are coming across to other people at work is perfectly normal. After all, you likely have an annual performance review, and your company may even conduct multisource reviews (sometimes called a 360-degree review) during which your colleagues provide feedback on you in addition to your boss. It is common for both situations to cause some stress. The real problem arises when your social anxiety takes over and becomes the norm.

If you have excessive worry about what your colleagues think of you, compare yourself to others, feel like a failure or an imposter, fear people in authority, or worry a lot before, during, and after work meetings and interactions, you may have social anxiety at work. In this chapter, you discover some common types of social anxiety at work and worries that professionals often have. You then explore how you can change your thinking traps at work with CALM thinking and by doing exposures to face your fears.

Getting Control of Your Social Anxiety at Work

The basics of taking control of your social anxiety at work involve the same techniques for facing your fears you explore in Chapters 10 and 11: changing how you think, facing your fears through exposures, and, ultimately, accepting yourself.

>> **Change your self-talk:** The fundamental tool to change your fearful thinking into CALM thinking that is compassionate, accepting, logical, and motivating is to notice your negative thoughts, identify your thinking traps, and use reframing skills to create more compassionate, accepting, logical, and motivating self-talk. It's also helpful to identify which types of inner critics drive your fears so that you can confront them assertively.

>> **Face your fears:** Facing your social anxiety fears is the only way to start getting over them. By rating your fears on a fear ladder from the easiest to do to the hardest to confront based on your fear level, you can proceed at your own pace. It's critical to stay in a growth mindset. You also need to start believing that mistakes are an opportunity to learn so that you are willing to take some risks.

>> **Practice self-compassion:** Self-compassion means expressing kindness and caring toward yourself when you feel judged, awkward, or inadequate, fail at something, or make a mistake. Practicing self-compassion helps you develop resilience and has the potential to greatly improve your social anxiety.

Identifying the Types of Social Anxiety at Work

Social anxiety shows up in work situations in numerous ways. In this section, I describe a few ways you may already be familiar with and some you may not expect.

Fear of negative evaluation day to day

Worrying about what others think of you is the core feature of social anxiety, and it is a significant part of social anxiety at work. There are many examples of how the fear of negative evaluation can come up day to day. You may worry a lot that your coworkers or bosses will view your ideas negatively, so you do not speak up in meetings. You may worry that when you give presentations, others are thinking that you are incompetent and that you should not be in your job. Or maybe you do not connect socially with your coworkers because you don't feel like you fit in, and so you don't go out to lunch with them and avoid happy hours with the team.

Fear of being visibly nervous

A common but lesser-known fear is when people are worried that others at work will notice that they are anxious. If this applies to you, it can feel paralyzing. You imagine that others can see you sweating or blushing. Or you think they can hear your voice trembling or crackling when you speak. You view social anxiety as a weakness, so you try hard to hide your symptoms. The more you try to hide them, the worse they get. To compound this problem, it is true that people at work often look down on others with social anxiety. This makes your fear more realistic and scary.

Fear of speaking at work

The number of performance situations at work that could cause social anxiety is endless. The most common work situation that causes anxiety is any speaking situation, whether it's sharing an opinion in a meeting, giving a talk to a small group, training employees, or giving a formal presentation to a large group. It could even extend to less expected types of speaking situations like calling a customer or talking to coworkers at work. Fear of speaking in public can range from slight nervousness to paralyzing fear and panic. In Chapter 16, you find out more about this fear.

Worry about performance reviews

You may have a lot of worry at performance review time. In extreme cases, you may worry about what your boss will say during your performance review, and you have trouble sleeping the night before. You ruminate in advance, imagining what your boss will say and write about you, and who provided your boss with feedback and what they said. You catastrophize about being put on a performance improvement program or even fired. Even if you are a high performer and have had good performance reviews before, you still expect a bad review this time. Afterward, you may discount the positive and still fear future reviews.

Fear of being observed or watched

You may worry that other people are watching you at work. For example, if you sit in a cubicle, you may worry about calling someone because you think other people will listen to you. Whether you have to clock in or not, you may quickly enter and exit the building because you think your coworkers are watching what you do. While there may be times when your manager at work does need to pay attention to you, you may be exaggerating this fear that all eyes are on you.

Anxiety about social interactions and performance situations

You may spend a lot of time worrying about what will happen tomorrow at work. You may look at your calendar with trepidation, or you may avoid looking because it makes you so anxious. You ruminate every evening about the next day and have trouble sleeping. You wake up feeling uneasy and anxious and sometimes you aren't even sure why. This can feel like generalized anxiety, but in your case, because you have social anxiety, your excessive rumination is about what people will think of you and your excessive worry about negative evaluation, and not only about the stress of how much work you have to get done.

Fear of not knowing what to say

At work, you may worry about your mind going blank or being caught off guard when asked a question. This may happen in specific situations, such as public speaking, but it could happen across many situations, like going to lunch with coworkers, seeing people in the hallways, or being in a meeting. Your core fear is that you won't know what to say, which will be embarrassing and cause others to look down on you. While it could be true that sometimes you really can't think of something clever or interesting to say, it's rare that you say nothing at all.

Fear of authority figures

You may do pretty well with handling your social anxiety at work with subordinates and peers, but your anxiety intensifies when you have to deal with authority figures. It may feel as though you have a sudden lack of confidence when a superior suddenly appears or you are in a meeting with senior executives. You may struggle with talking to bosses or others in positions of authority. This can be very damaging to your career prospects. At its core, it's a fear of being judged and possibly even losing career prospects if superiors judge you as inferior. Fear of authority figures can sometimes be rooted in being raised in a strict family with rules and punishments, where you learned to fear authority figures.

Worry about your executive presence

You may worry about not having the elusive quality of executive presence at work. *Executive presence* refers to the ability to inspire confidence and show people have the leadership qualities to advance to higher levels in your organization. You want to show your subordinates, peers, and upper management that you are capable and knowledgeable in your field of expertise and a great communicator with the political skills to sway people in your company. Because executive presence can be hard to show in real life and can seem like a magical quality, you may feel anxiety about not having this quality and just not being cut out to advance.

Fear of writing

You may be nervous about sending emails at work. You may worry that if your email contains a typo or grammatical error, people will think you are not knowledgeable and don't know what you're talking about. You may also worry about what others will think of your reports and spend an inordinate amount of time making sure they are perfect.

REMEMBER

It is easy to hide behind technology. Using messaging systems and working from home can help you hide your social anxiety. However, these safety behaviors make it worse. You need in-person interactions to truly conquer social anxiety.

Changing Your Mindset About Social Anxiety at Work

In this section, you discover how to identify your thinking traps and change your self-talk at work. You'll look at an example of a typical professional with social anxiety and follow this person as he reframes his thinking and engages in exposures at work to face his fears. You review the skills you learned about CALM thinking in Chapter 10 and practice them yourself for your social anxiety at work.

CASE EXAMPLE

Meet Dave. Dave is a successful director at a large company who suffers from social anxiety at work. He's moved into a new division and was just promoted to this job. It's a big step up, but he's been with the company for over ten years. He's worked in three other divisions and was promoted in every job. Dave is well-liked and has worked with many of the same people at different points in his career.

Dave feels inadequate, not good enough, like an imposter, and he worries about how people perceive him. These feelings started as he began working with more high achievers over his academic and business career. Dave is from a small town and started his schooling at a community college. He remembers working as a bartender in college and then going on to a state university. He eventually got two master's degrees, one in business and one in software engineering, from an elite university.

Now, he's at one of the top corporations in the country, working with many people with high-powered pedigrees and this makes him feel insecure even though his resume and accomplishments are outstanding. When he's working with others, he is often triggered into thinking that his coworkers are better than him or that they are more aggressive than he is. When this happens, he goes right back to feeling as if he were still in college.

Identifying thinking traps

You may recall from Chapter 7 that thinking traps are patterns of thinking that are distorted. Your thoughts may include some elements of truth, but thinking traps make you believe your negative thoughts without questioning them. Recognizing your twisted thinking and being aware that it could be a thinking trap can help you reframe your fearful thinking into resilient thinking. Table 18-1 lists the common thinking traps.

TABLE 18-1   Common Thinking Traps

All-or-nothing thinking	Jumping to conclusions	Overestimating probabilities
Catastrophizing	Labeling	Personalizing
Emotional reasoning	Mind reading	Shining the spotlight
Fortune-telling	Negative mental filter	Using "should" statements

CASE EXAMPLE

Dave's automatic thoughts and core beliefs that lead to his social anxiety at work are outlined in Table 18-2. Notice how his worries correlate to the thinking traps discussed in Chapter 7.

TABLE 18-2 **Dave's Thinking Traps**

Fearful Thoughts	Thinking Trap(s)
I'm the wrong guy for this job. I can't live up to expectations for this role. Others will think I shouldn't be in this role.	Fortune-telling Mind reading
I'm a failure. I am not as smart, capable, or talented as others. I don't get things as much as others.	Labeling Negative mental filter
I am not as articulate. My vocabulary is not as eloquent. It's my fault because I did not pay attention in English classes when I was young.	Personalizing
I am an anxious person incapable of communicating in stressful situations. I get nervous and lose my train of thought. My point does not come across well. I forget what I want to say. I must be a bad communicator.	Emotional reasoning
People will see that I am nervous. If I look nervous, others will look down on me. My worst fears will then come true.	Shining the spotlight Catastrophizing
I have high standards for myself. I am not getting up to speed quickly enough. I should know more by now. I'm an imposter.	Using "should" statements

What are some of your own worries at work? Think about your self-talk and the messages you give yourself before, during, and after social situations at work. Look back at Table 18-1 and the definitions in Chapter 7 to identify your thinking traps and write them down in Table 18-3.

TABLE 18-3 **Your Thinking Traps**

Fearful Thoughts	Thinking Trap(s)

Changing self-talk

CASE EXAMPLE

Dave realized he had a demanding and perfectionistic inner critic and had the following fearful thoughts about sharing his opinion in meetings:

Situation: Sharing my opinion in a meeting

Feelings: Nervous, worried, anxious

Fearful thoughts: I am not as smart, capable, or talented as others. People will know that if I speak up in this meeting.

Thinking traps: Mind reading, negative mental filter, catastrophizing

Dave used the reframing skills discussed in Chapter 10 to change his fearful thinking into self-talk that is compassionate, accepting, logical, and motivating. Table 18-4 illustrates how Dave used the CALM thinking skills to reframe her fearful thinking.

TABLE 18-4 **Dave's CALM Thinking**

Compassionate: What can you say to yourself that's gentler and kinder?	I need to remind myself that I am very accomplished, but my value should not come from my accomplishments alone. I have many inherent characteristics like kindness and loyalty that are more important than external achievements.
Accepting: What part is true about yourself or the situation, and can you accept in a nonjudgmental way?	It's true that I had to support myself at an early age, and it was tough for me to get to where I am today. I probably still feel insecure because of this.
Logical: What thinking traps do you notice? What can you say to yourself that's more realistic or helpful?	It's not true that I am not as smart or talented as others. I have achieved a lot and I am just as capable. I've been promoted throughout my career and I get lots of positive feedback. This is all proof that I can't possibly be a failure.
Motivating: What can you remind yourself of that can inspire you to meet your goals?	I am still new at my job, and I am learning and getting up to speed. I will stay in learning mode and remember that mistakes are an opportunity to learn.

Think of a situation where you experienced social anxiety at work. Write down some of your feelings, fearful thoughts, and thinking traps related to the situation.

Situation: _____

Feelings: _____

Fearful thoughts: _____

Thinking traps: _____

Now, use the reframing skill to fill in Table 18-5 with thoughts that are compassionate, accepting, logical, and motivating.

TABLE 18-5 **Reframing Your Fearful Thinking**

Compassionate: What can you say to yourself that's gentler and kinder?	
Accepting: What part is true about yourself or the situation, and can you accept in a nonjudgmental way?	
Logical: What thinking traps do you notice? What can you say to yourself that's more realistic or helpful?	
Motivating: What can you remind yourself of that can inspire you to meet your goals?	

Facing Your Fears with Exposures at Work

Exposing yourself to your fears is at the heart of how to overcome social anxiety at work. Sometimes, you can't just talk yourself out of social anxiety. Exposures can show you that your fears are not true and/or that you can cope with your anxious feelings when they come up. You'll be in learning mode and improving with every exposure opportunity.

As you do exposures for your social anxiety at work, you follow the same steps for facing your fears described in Chapter 11:

1. Create a target list of the fears you want to work on.

2. Identify safety behaviors to stop.

3. Build a fear ladder.

4. Engage in an exposure.

5. Debrief after the exposures.

6. Repeat the exposure or do a new one.

REMEMBER

Doing exposures is the only way to overcome social anxiety.

Creating a target list

CASE EXAMPLE

Dave decided it was time to take action to overcome his social anxiety and deepen his new positive beliefs about himself. The first step he took was to create a target list of situations he wants to work on.

Table 18-6 lists Dave's feared situations at work. He rated them based on the following:

>> How scary they are from 1 to 10, with 10 being the scariest

>> How much he avoids them from 1 to 10, with 10 being the most avoidance

>> How important they are for him to overcome from very important (VI) to important (I) to not important (NI)

Based on this list, Dave would be the most motivated to do exposures to help him prepare for and speak in meetings because he rated these items, as well as being able to cope with his anxious feelings and speak in front of superiors, as very important. However, these are all pretty scary things to do for Dave because he rated them from 8 to 10 on the fear scale. When he creates his fear ladder in the next step, he'll break these down so that he can take some easier steps first.

TABLE 18-6   **Dave's Fears at Work**

Situation	Fear Level	Avoidance	Importance
Speaking to or in front of superiors	8	7	VI
Being around peers he views as more successful	8	7	I
Giving performance reviews to his staff	6	5	I
Voicing opinions in meetings	8	8	VI
Asking questions in meetings	8	8	VI
Giving presentations	7	6	I
Introducing himself at meetings	5	3	I
Experiencing panicky feelings during meetings	10	1	VI
Being unprepared	9	3	VI
Interacting with John, one of his employees	8	4	I

Now, create your own list of fears at work you want to work on. If you created a list of situations that make you feel anxious in Chapter 6, you can use that list as a guide to help you fill out Table 18-7. Remember to indicate how important each situation is for you to overcome from very important (VI) to important (I) to not important (NI).

TABLE 18-7   **Your Fears at Work**

Situation	Fear Level	Avoidance	Importance

For more information about creating a target list of situations you want to work on, see Chapter 11.

TIP

Identifying safety behaviors to stop

After you create a target list of the situations you want to work on, it's also important to identify the safety behaviors you need to drop. Remember that safety behaviors interfere with learning and can prevent you from feeling confident that you can handle social anxiety. For more about safety behaviors, see Chapter 5.

CASE EXAMPLE

Some of the safety behaviors Dave decided he needed to stop included avoidance of talking to his employees when he thought it would be a difficult conversation. He also had to stop being quiet in meetings and find opportunities to ask questions and make comments. He tried to stick to the facts when he did talk in meetings and needed to practice loosening up. He always had a bottle of water in case his throat clenched up. While bringing water to meetings was not necessarily a bad behavior, it became a safety behavior for Dave because it was as if he assumed he would have trouble speaking.

Now, create a list of the safety behaviors you may have. First, think about what you avoid. Then think about other things you do that make you feel safe but that may be keeping your social anxiety alive. If you identified safety behaviors in Chapter 6, look back at that list for guidance.

Your avoidance and other safety behaviors:

_____

_____

_____

Building a fear ladder

CASE EXAMPLE

Dave realized that the things he viewed as most important to work on first were many things that happened during meetings. He remembered times when his anxiety in meetings got so high that he felt the room was closing in on him, he'd lose his train of thought, and his voice got shaky. One time when this happened, some peers commented on him looking nervous, which only validated his fear. Therefore, Dave's fear ladder was focused on being ready for meetings and speaking in meetings. Table 18-8 outlines the fears Dave wants to work on by conducting exposures at work.

Dave's goal: Be more comfortable in meetings.

TABLE 18-8 **Dave's Fear Ladder**

Level of Difficulty	Anxiety Rating	Situation
Hardest	10	Experiencing panicky feelings during meetings
	8–9	Being unprepared for meetings
		Voicing strong opinions in large meetings
		Asking questions he thinks he should already know
Moderate	6–7	Making a comment in a meeting
		Asking a simple question in a small meeting
	4–5	Being prepared for meetings
		Introducing himself at meetings
Easiest	2–3	Attending meetings
		Talking to peers outside of meetings

Now, create your own fear ladder in Table 18-9 related to your social anxiety at work. You may not have something for every rung of the ladder, or you may have a few activities on the same rung.

Your goal: _____

TABLE 18-9

Your Fear Ladder

Level of Difficulty	Anxiety Rating	Situation
Hardest	10	
	8–9	
Moderate	6–7	
	4-5	
Easiest	2–3	

Engaging in exposures at work

Dave worked on some items on his fear ladder and was getting a bit more comfortable at work. Now, he decided he wanted to work on being more comfortable voicing opinions in meetings. In the following sections, use Dave's example as a guide to conduct your own exposures at work.

Before the exposure

Before the exposure, be specific about the exposure you want to practice. Then, add your prediction of what you think could happen. This is called your *feared outcome.* Next, identify what safety behaviors you'll need to give up to make sure you are fully exposing yourself. If it is too hard to completely give up your safety behaviors, you can phase them out as you keep repeating exposures.

**CASE
EXAMPLE**

Here's Dave's pre-exposure plan:

What exposure do you want to experiment with?

I will practice sharing my opinion at the next meeting. I have a meeting coming up with my peers on a new product launch they are working on.

What safety behaviors will you have to give up?

I need to overcome avoidance and motivate myself to participate.

What feared outcome(s) are you most worried about and how likely do you think it is they'll happen?

I'll get nervous and lose my train of thought (80%).

Others will see that I am nervous and look down on me (80%).

I'll forget what I was going to say (60%).

EXPERIMENT

Now, fill in the following information for the specific exposure you are ready to try.

What exposure do you want to experiment with?

_____

_____

What safety behaviors will you have to give up?

_____

_____

What feared outcome(s) are you most worried about and how likely do you think it is they'll happen?

_____

_____

During the exposure

During the exposure, your goal is to stay focused on the task and the person you are interacting with. You need to be outward-looking and not internally focused on your anxiety or mind reading about what they may be thinking about you. It's okay to name your emotions, but don't try to fight or resist your anxiety. Instead, let your feelings and bodily sensations be there with you. Be okay with not knowing what will happen, and treat this exposure as an experiment. There is no failure. Your goal is to tolerate your feelings and push through them.

TIP

Sometimes, it is helpful to rate your anxiety level before, during, and after the exposure. This is not to push the anxiety away or to measure success on how anxious you feel. Instead, being curious about how your anxiety waxes and wanes during exposures and as you do new exposures can be a part of the learning process.

Debriefing after the exposure

After the exposure, explore what you actually did and what you learned. First, think about how the outcome differed from what you expected and whether there were any surprises. Then, evaluate how well you did with letting go of safety behaviors. Finally, review what you learned. The positive information is something you want to keep reinforcing because this is how your brain gains control over social anxiety and learns that anxiety is not dangerous.

CASE EXAMPLE

Here's what Dave learned after the exposure:

How was the outcome different than what you expected? What surprised you?

I successfully shared an opinion during the meeting. While it was hard, and maybe my words weren't as eloquent, nothing bad happened. I didn't lose my train of thought. In fact, someone agreed with me during the meeting, and other people nodded their heads when I was speaking.

Did you engage in safety behaviors?

I dropped the avoidance behavior of being quiet in the meeting. I also worked on lightening up and not being so serious, which made me come across as more confident.

What did you learn from this exposure?

The experiment helped me see that I am capable of communicating well even in stressful situations. I redefined my initial belief to, "I get anxious sometimes and that's okay. I can still get my points across and make a positive impression on others."

Over time, doing these experiments helped Dave feel more confident. He worked on different experiments for all of his beliefs. He kept a journal of what he had learned from the various experiments.

Now, answer the following questions with your results:

How was the outcome different than what you expected? What surprised you?

_____

_____

Did you engage in safety behaviors?

_____

_____

What did you learn from this exposure?

_____

_____

Repeating the same exposure or doing a new one

It's important to keep repeating exposures and doing new ones. The more you repeat old exposures and do new ones and vary the conditions of how and where you do your exposures, the more you will improve.

TIP

Make copies of the Exposure Worksheet in Chapter 11 to keep repeating exposures.

Ending Negative Patterns at Work

Several unhelpful thinking and behavioral patterns at work can come from social anxiety. These are patterns you want to catch and see if you can respond to them differently. The following sections outline how these patterns come up for Dave. As you read these descriptions, see if any of these apply to you and think about how you could change them.

Comparing yourself to others

Making frequent social comparisons to others at work leads to self-criticism and not feeling good enough. For example, Dave looks at the achievements of others and finds himself lacking. He thinks he is not as knowledgeable, impressive, or as confident as others. When you compare your social rank and abilities with those of others, it results in social anxiety if you think you are not on par with them. Dave learned by changing his thinking that he was equal to his peers and others.

Being overly self-critical

When you have a strong inner critic, you can tear yourself apart with negative observations and labels. For example, Dave focuses on his flaws and does not acknowledge his accomplishments. This is called having a negative mental filter. Over time, Dave kept a diary of his accomplishments and recognized that he was not socially flawed or incapable of doing his job.

Dwelling afterward

Dwelling on a work interaction afterward is also known as rumination. When you ruminate, you worry and beat yourself up about how you came across to others. Dave ruminates in the evening about what he could have done differently and what others in his company may be thinking about him. This causes him to have high anxiety at home and difficulty relaxing and sleeping. He decided to find relaxing activities to do in the evenings to keep his mind busy and to redirect his mind when it floated to what he thought were negative experiences during the day.

Catastrophizing

Dave tells himself he does not have an executive presence and will not be promoted. Dave worries that all of his successes could go away and that he might be laid off or fired and then he would not be able to support his family. Dave realized that he was catastrophizing. He started to practice evaluating whether his thoughts were realistic and then imagining different possibilities and assigning probabilities. Then he set the unrealistic worries aside.

Overworking

If you don't feel good about yourself, you may overwork to compensate for your fear of not being good enough. Dave was working 50 hours a week, which didn't include the time he took to answer emails in the evenings and weekends. He was getting so tired that some days he was having trouble keeping his eyes open during meetings, further exacerbating his fears about how he was coming across in meetings, one of his core worries. As he realized that overworking was actually backfiring and causing him to become unproductive, he cut back on his work hours and shut down his computer by dinner time. He learned that he was more productive and efficient when he worked fewer hours.

Chapter **19**

Children with Social Anxiety

K nowing that your child experiences social anxiety can be emotionally painful. You feel for them when they struggle to make friends, speak up in class, or are left out of groups. Social anxiety can impact their social development in many ways. Some of the problems associated with social anxiety disorder in children include poor school performance, low confidence in social situations, trouble developing and maintaining friendships, depression, and alcohol or drug use.

In any given year, about 7 percent of children receive a formal diagnosis of social anxiety disorder, and an equal number of girls and boys experience it. Social anxiety disorder usually begins between the ages of 11 and 19, although it can start earlier. A child may develop social anxiety suddenly after a stressful or embarrassing experience or slowly over time. A strong correlation exists between bullying and the development of social anxiety. Many times, social anxiety runs in families either genetically or by role modeling if the child's parent experiences anxiety, is overprotective, doesn't let the child develop independence, or is overly critical.

In this chapter, you find out how social anxiety impacts children and how to help your child if they struggle with it. The goal of this chapter is to help you guide your child to reframe their fearful thinking and face their fears by applying the steps first outlined in Chapters 10 and 11 in a more kid-friendly way.

TECHNICAL STUFF

Throughout this chapter, when I use the terms *children* or *kids,* I am referring to all children from ages 5 to 19. I use the terms *teens* or *teenagers* to refer to children between the ages of 13 and 19. Most of what's in this chapter applies to all age groups; however, you as a parent will be more involved the younger your child.

Signs Your Child May Have Social Anxiety

Social anxiety in children can manifest in several ways. You may notice that your child feels self-conscious, fears being judged, avoids certain situations, criticizes themself, worries about social interactions, mind reads what others think of them, or has thoughts that jump to the worst-case scenario.

You may not think of tantrums and anger as part of social anxiety, but it often is. A young child with social anxiety may cry or have temper tantrums more often than is typical for their age. An older child may show irritation or anger more than expected. Whether it's a tantrum, crying, screaming, anger, or irritation, it can all reflect that the fear center in the child's brain has been activated. Fight-flight-freeze are all part of a fear response.

HOW SOCIAL ANXIETY IS DIFFERENT FROM SHYNESS

In children, social anxiety disorder and shyness are different but can look the same to outsiders. When a child is shy, they are sometimes said to be "slow to warm up." Their shyness typically goes down after they adjust to being in a situation or begin to feel comfortable around a new person. Shyness does not typically cause significant distress to the child or impair their daily functioning. Shyness involves less fear of judgment and criticism than social anxiety.

Social anxiety, on the other hand, is present before, during, and after social situations. Kids with social anxiety have excessive worry, fear, or nervousness that can significantly impact their emotional well-being and daily life. Kids experiencing social anxiety usually try to avoid social settings altogether. Fear of what other kids will think of them is greater than their desire or need to be involved.

Here are common ways social anxiety may show up in children:

>> **Psychologically:** You may notice your child engaging in negative self-talk. They may say things like "I'm socially awkward," "I'm stupid," "No one likes me," "I'm ugly," "Everyone thinks I am weird," "I'll look like an idiot," "If everyone does not like me, then there must be something wrong with me."

>> **Behaviorally:** You may notice your child avoiding social interactions, refusing to go to school, having difficulty making friends, being alone too often, speaking in class or social situations, having difficulty making eye contact, avoiding eating at school, changing in the locker room or using the restroom, to name just a few.

>> **Physically:** When socially anxious, your child may experience blushing, headaches, dizziness, trembling, shaking, lightheadedness, sweatiness, stomachaches, nausea, cramps, vomiting, or muscle and body aches.

Table 19-1 outlines some common signs your child may have social anxiety at different developmental stages. Note that there's some overlap between these stages and that these issues can come up at just about any age. The signs of social anxiety are endless, so if you do not see your child's behavior in this chart, it could still be a sign of social anxiety.

TABLE 19-1   Common Signs of Social Anxiety in Children

Elementary School	Junior High and High School	College Students
Being fearful in the classroom	Feeling pressure to fit in with peers	Worrying about being on their own in college
Having trouble making friends	Comparing themself to others on social media	Having trouble making friends in college
Being clingy or scared to separate from you	Avoiding parties and sports	Having difficulty living with roommates in college
Not wanting to go to school	Sitting alone at lunch or being a loner	Avoiding joining social groups in college
Difficulty with making eye contact	Falling behind academically	
Avoiding birthday parties and sleepovers	Worrying about appearance	
Avoiding raising their hand in class	Having difficulty talking to teachers	
Having difficulty talking to unfamiliar people	Avoiding raising their hand in class	
Not talking at all	Resisting group projects or presentations	
	Avoiding ordering in a restaurant	
	Not wanting to text or talk on the phone	
	Excessive sick days	

WARNING

It's important to teach your child to recognize bullying and to intervene as soon as possible. Many factors contribute to social anxiety, but research shows that bullying is highly correlated with social anxiety. Bullying can range from obvious and visible behaviors like punching or hitting to subtle behaviors that only the victim and participants are aware of. The four most common types of bullying are physical, verbal, relational, and cyberbullying. It is important to sit down with your child and educate them about the types of bullying and what to do if they see it happen to others or are experiencing it themselves, such as telling you or a teacher.

BEING A "GOOD ENOUGH" PARENT

The concept of being a "good enough" parent is important to remember. Don't expect to be a perfect parent. This is unrealistic. Being empathic and responsive to your child's needs most of the time, not all the time, is a realistic goal. Healthy parenting balances validation, guidance, and support while allowing children to explore and navigate the environment.

Some parenting styles can influence the development of social anxiety in children. You are likely a good parent — or you would not be reading this book — but you may be overanxious or overprotective, which can interfere with the development of your child's autonomy. Being too critical, demanding, or punitive can create a strong inner critic in your child. If you notice some of these parenting styles in yourself, you can work on them and improve.

REMEMBER

Managing your social anxiety is critical for you and your child, as your anxiety can have an impact on your child. For example, if you have trouble with socializing, your child will have fewer opportunities to learn social skills. Your social anxiety can also impact your child if you engage in social situations with a lot of anxiety or if you try to avoid them altogether, such as parent-teacher conferences, hosting birthday parties, attending your child's sports games, and interacting with other parents. If you struggle with social anxiety, it is important to work through your fears with the steps in this book so you can teach by example.

Recognizing Safety Behaviors in Children

As first defined in Chapter 2, *safety behaviors* are actions people take to reduce anxiety. They may make them feel safe in the short term, but such behaviors reinforce social anxiety in the long term and keep it going. Children have many safety behaviors. Some common safety behaviors of kids include:

- ❯❯ Avoiding social situations or events

- ❯❯ Sitting in the back of the classroom

- ❯❯ Being quiet or not talking

- ❯❯ Not making eye contact or speaking at a low level

- ❯❯ Wearing baggy clothes

- ❯❯ Wearing headphones when in public

- ❯❯ Looking at their phone to look busy and prevent other kids from talking to them

- ❯❯ Sitting alone at lunch and recess

- ❯❯ Not raising their hand in class

- ❯❯ Asking you to do things for them

Be on the lookout for the safety behaviors your child may do.

Helping Your Child with Social Anxiety

In this section, you discover how to help your child overcome social anxiety while looking at an example of a hypothetical child who experiences social anxiety at school and around her peers.

CASE
EXAMPLE

Meet Allie. Allie is a 12-year-old girl entering the seventh grade. She was shy and slow to warm up when she was younger, but her shyness has evolved into social anxiety. She now experiences excessive worry, fear, and nervousness around other kids and adults. She has been trying to avoid social activities altogether. Allie has a fear of what other kids think of her and feels socially awkward due to her social anxiety. She doesn't think she fits in, although she does have one close friend at school who happens to be her neighbor and someone she's known since the third grade when Allie's family moved from out of state. She compares herself to other kids and thinks they are better than her because she thinks they wear nicer clothes and are prettier than she is. When Allie is interacting with other kids, she experiences physical symptoms of anxiety like shakiness, blushing, and a fast heartbeat, and she stumbles over her words. She tries to avoid too much social interaction because she worries that others can see her symptoms and will make fun of her.

Allie is on the cusp of being a teenager. She is still clingy with her mom, but at other times, she wants to be independent. Her mother is worried that Allie is beginning to avoid social interactions and socially isolate herself too much. Her mother has some social anxiety herself, but she tries to push through it. Allie's dad wants Allie to be successful but can be critical instead of validating. Her mom wants to help Allie overcome her social anxiety.

Identifying your child's thinking traps

The first step in helping Allie overcome her social anxiety is to identify her thinking traps and then work to reframe her negative self-talk.

REMEMBER

A *thinking trap* is an unhelpful pattern of thought that causes your child to have unpleasant emotions and view situations more negatively than they are. *Self-talk* is the voice inside your child's mind and how they talk to themself. Self-talk is important because it affects how your child thinks and feels about themself and others. Self-talk also drives behavior. Healthy self-talk contributes to your child's self-esteem and confidence when facing challenges. See Chapters 7 and 10 for more about thinking traps and self-talk.

Just like adults, children with social anxiety have many thinking traps. Thinking traps usually develop in childhood and can become entrenched by their teen years. When your child's mind gets stuck in a negative way of thinking that doesn't make sense or isn't based on facts, they're probably caught in a thinking trap. They may not even be aware of their thinking traps, and they probably fall into the same traps again and again.

Chapter 7 defines several types of thinking traps, many of which you may also see in your child. Table 19-2 outlines a few that are common in children.

TABLE 19-2 **Thinking Traps Common in Children**

Thinking Trap	What It Is	Example
Catastrophizing: Making a mountain out of a molehill	Thinking of the worst case with a downward spiral	If I say the wrong thing, kids will make fun of me, and I won't have any friends.
Emotional reasoning: I feel it, so it is true	Using your feelings as evidence of the truth	I feel nervous, so this means I'm awkward.
Fortune-telling: Looking through a crystal ball	Predicting things will turn out badly	No one is going to talk to me at the party, so I may as well not go.
Labeling: Calling yourself names	Using a negative word to describe yourself or another person	I'm stupid. I'm a loser. I'm ugly.
Mind reading: Being a psychic	Assuming you know what others are thinking	They think I am weird.
Shining the spotlight: All eyes are on me	Assuming others are paying more attention to you than they really are	People can see I'm anxious.

TIP

Understanding your child's thinking traps can be helpful because it lets you see some common patterns and why your child says or does the things they do. It is helpful for your child to learn about thinking traps so that they can spot them when they show up.

TIP

Listening to and watching your child can help you guess what their thinking traps may be. Review the list of thinking traps in Table 19-2 with them and then ask them which ones they believe they have. Thinking about the things your child says or does, what do you believe their thinking traps are? Write them down in Table 19-3.

TABLE 19-3 **Your Child's Thinking Traps**

Possible Thinking Traps	What Your Child Says	What Your Child Does

Reframing your child's fearful self-talk

As discussed in Chapter 10, you can change negative self-talk in several ways, and many of those ideas also apply to children. While the steps outlined in Chapter 10 are helpful for both adults and children to change their self-talk, implementing them formally with your child may be more challenging. In this section, you discover kid-friendly strategies you can use with your child.

REMEMBER

The goal of reframing your child's self-talk is to help your child learn that their fearful thoughts are not completely true. For the thoughts that have some validity, you can help them reframe those thoughts with thinking that is more compassionate, accepting, logical, and motivating.

CASE EXAMPLE

Allie's mom talked to Allie about what made Allie feel nervous. They discussed some of her fearful thoughts and came up with some ways Allie could talk to herself differently. Here is one example of a situation Allie and her mom worked on:

Situation: Allie is invited to a birthday party.

Feelings: Anxious, scared, sad, worried.

Fearful thoughts: Other kids think I'm a loser. No one likes me. People will be mean to me if I go. They won't care if I go or not anyway.

Thinking traps: Mind reading, labeling, fortune-telling.

Allie's mom used the reframing skills outlined in Chapter 10 to help Allie change her fearful thinking into CALM thinking, as illustrated in Table 19-4.

TABLE 19-4 Allie's CALM Thinking

Compassionate: What can you say to yourself that's gentler and kinder?	It's normal to feel scared when someone gets invited to a birthday party. Everyone wants to be liked.
Accepting: What part is true about yourself or the situation, and can you accept in a nonjudgmental way?	I don't have a lot of friends, and sometimes I feel like no one likes me.
Logical: What thinking traps do you notice? What can you say to yourself that's more realistic or helpful?	I think I may be mind reading again. No one has ever called me a loser, so thoughts like these may be in my imagination when I get scared.
Motivating: What can you remind yourself of that can inspire you to meet your goals?	If I go to the party, I'll be facing my fears. I will feel good about myself afterward, and my mom will be proud of me.

Sit down with your child and discuss what they think when they are faced with something that makes them nervous. Work with your child on a specific fearful thought and come up with a few ideas of what they can tell themselves instead. Help them see the pattern in their thinking by identifying the thinking trap in the thought.

Situation: _____

Feelings: _____

Fearful thoughts: _____

Thinking traps: _____

Now, use the reframing skill to fill in Table 19-5 with thoughts that are compassionate, accepting, logical, and motivating.

TABLE 19-5 **Reframing Your Child's Fearful Thinking**

Compassionate: What can your child say to themselves that's gentler and kinder?	
Accepting: What part is true about your child or the situation and can they accept in a nonjudgmental way?	
Logical: What thinking traps do you notice? What can your child say to themselves that's more realistic or helpful?	
Motivating: What can you remind your child of that can inspire them to change?	

Guiding Your Child to Face Their Fears

Sometimes, it's better to dip a toe in the pool than avoid it altogether. It may feel cold at first, but the water may feel refreshing after the initial shock wears off. This is how exposure therapy feels. As your child does exposures, there will be some initial discomfort. By embracing their anxiety and learning that what they thought would happen did not come true or that they can handle anxiety even if it does come true, they will have an easier time managing their social anxiety.

REMEMBER

You don't necessarily need to follow a formal process with your child to help them face their fears unless you think it would be more helpful to work with your child in a methodical way. Instead, in this section, you find out how to simplify the steps outlined in Chapter 11 for facing and overcoming social anxiety fears and how to communicate them to your child.

Following are the general steps to help your child face their fears:

1. Sit with your child and create a target list of things to work on.

2. Identify the safety behaviors you think your child should stop.

3. Create a realistic and achievable fear ladder with your child.

4. Slowly help your child experiment with facing their fears by doing an exposure.

5. Ask your child what their worry is before the exposure and debrief after the exposure about what actually happened and what they learned.

6. Repeat the same exposure or do a new one.

Creating a target list

The first step in helping your child face their fears is to sit down with your child and review a list of actions that may cause them anxiety.

CASE EXAMPLE

Allie's mom created a list of actions that seemed scary to her. She had Allie rate each action based on whether it would be hard, medium, or easy for her to do. With her mom's help, Allie came up with a few things that made her nervous, including talking to other kids at school, having sleepovers, inviting someone to her house, and raising her hand in class.

Use the following list to help determine what actions may seem difficult or scary for your child and whether it would be hard, medium, or easy for them to do. Label each item as H, M, or E. You'll use these ratings when you create your child's fear ladder in the next section. Use the blank lines at the end to fill in your own actions that may not be listed here.

Common Situations Children with Social Anxiety Find Difficult

___ Talking with other kids

___ Coming up with something to say after the conversation has started

___ Meeting the friends of your friends

___ Having a play date

___ Inviting someone to your house

___ Having a sleepover

___ Texting or calling someone

___ Going to school

___ Attending a party, dance, or other school activity

___ Raising your hand in class

___ Speaking to adults such as a teacher, principal, or school nurse

___ Acting, singing, dancing, or playing a sport

___ Eating, drinking, or writing in front of others

___ Making a speech or presentation to your class

___ Taking a test

___ Using the bathroom at school or public places

___ Working with a group on a project

___ Having a panic attack in public

___ _____

___ _____

Identifying safety behaviors to stop

REMEMBER

Safety behaviors are things your child does to reduce anxiety when they are in an uncomfortable situation that causes social anxiety. Their safety behaviors could include outright avoidance, or it may be subtle behaviors that make them feel safer like asking for reassurance, speaking softly, or avoiding eye contact. Safety behaviors can make exposures backfire because your child may not learn that their fears don't come true or that they can cope with their social anxiety.

CASE EXAMPLE

Allie's mom looked at the list of safety behaviors in the earlier section, "Recognizing Safety Behaviors in Children," and identified several that Allie had to overcome, including avoidance, speaking too softly, and not making eye contact to be sure she was fully engaging in the exposure.

Look back at the list earlier in this chapter to identify some safety behaviors your child needs to eliminate or reduce to make sure they are fully engaging in the exposure. You may be aware of others not included in the list.

Your child's avoidance and other safety behaviors:

_____

_____

_____

Building a fear ladder

The next step is to build a fear ladder for one of the items identified in the target list your child wants to work on. Allie and her mom decided to work on talking to other kids at school. They created a fear ladder with some things she could do before she talked to one of her classmates.

CASE EXAMPLE

Table 19-6 outlines the fear ladder Allie and her mom created to help Allie work on her fear of talking to one of her classmates. Each item is listed from the easiest for her to do to the hardest.

Allie's goal: Talk to one of her classmates.

TABLE 19-6 **Allie's Fear Ladder**

Level of Difficulty	Anxiety Rating	Situation
Hardest	10	Talking to a classmate during recess
	8–9	Talking to one of my classmates who sits next to me
		Saying hi to someone at school
Moderate	6–7	Talking to a kid in my neighborhood
	4-5	Practicing talking to my friend, who I've known for a while
Easiest	2-3	Practicing talking with my mom pretending she's a classmate

Now, create a fear ladder in Table 19-7 with your child.

Your child's goal:_____

TABLE 19-7 ## Your Child's Fear Ladder

Level of Difficulty	Anxiety Rating	Situation
Hardest	10	
	8–9	
Moderate	6–7	
	4–5	
Easiest	2–3	

TIP

Alternatively, if working on a fear ladder systematically isn't a fit for you and your child, you can take some things off your target list and come up with ideas for exposures. Sometimes having a list with a variety of things to do can be a good first step before working on a specific goal. For example, Allie and her mom made another exposure list of actions that were not directly related to talking to someone at school. These activities can help lessen her social anxiety before attempting to talk to someone at school.

Other ways to work on exposures:

>> Call the library and ask if a specific book is available.

>> Order food at a fast food restaurant.

>> Text your aunt or uncle.

>> Ask someone at the mall what time it is.

>> Say hi to someone on a walk with your mom.

>> Talk to a checkout person at the grocery store

>> Return an item to a store.

>> Hang out with a neighbor.

Engaging in exposures

An important part of making exposures work is to first discuss with your child what they are scared of happening. Then, debrief on what they learned afterward.

CASE EXAMPLE

Allie and her mom decided that Allie would experiment saying hi to someone at school and seeing what Allie could learn from this exposure.

> **Exposure:** Saying hi to someone at school.
>
> **Safety behaviors to reduce or eliminate:** Avoidance, speaking too softly, not making eye contact.
>
> **Worries before the exposure:** They will think I am weird. It'll be scary and I might not be able to do it.
>
> **Learnings after the exposure:** I said hi to someone at school, they smiled and said hi back to me. It wasn't as scary as I thought, and I think the other girl might like me and want to be friends.

Now, pick a goal from the target list you created with your child and see if you and your child can come up with baby steps toward accomplishing it.

> **Exposure:** What exposure does your child want to experiment with?
>
> _____
>
> _____
>
> **Safety behaviors:** What does your child need to eliminate or reduce?
>
> _____
>
> _____
>
> **Worries before the exposure:** What is your child scared of?
>
> _____
>
> _____

Learnings after the exposure: What happened and what did your child learn?

_____

_____

Debriefing after the exposure

In debriefing after the exposures, think about what you and your child did and what you learned. Ask your child how the outcome was different than what they expected and whether there were any surprises. Evaluate how well they did with letting go of safety behaviors. The most important part is to summarize what they learned. You want their exposures to keep reinforcing what went well. This is how your child's mind learns to deal with their social anxiety and that the feelings they have before and during exposures are not dangerous.

CASE EXAMPLE

Here's what Allie and her mom learned after the exposure:

How was the outcome different than what you and your child expected? What surprised you and them?

Allie and her mom were surprised Allie did the exposure without too much resistance. Allie said hi to someone at school and the other child said hi back.

Did your child engage in safety behaviors?

Allie said softly and made a little eye contact. Allie and her mom agreed they would work on this more in the next exposure.

What did your child learn from this exposure?

Allie learned that it was hard at first to go out of her comfort zone, but it got easier with practice.

Now, answer the following questions based on your child's exposure:

How was the outcome different than what you and your child expected? What surprised you and them?

_____

_____

Did your child engage in safety behaviors?

_____

_____

What did you and your child learn from this exposure?

_____

_____

Repeating the same exposure or doing a new one

It's important that your child keeps repeating exposures and doing new ones so that they will become more comfortable in those situations. In Allie's case, she wasn't quite ready to talk to anyone at school, so she and her mom decided that Allie would say hi to someone else the next day.

What will your child try next? Will you repeat the same exposure or try a new one?

Resisting the Urge to Accommodate Your Child's Social Anxiety

A parental accommodation is something you do to try to alleviate your child's anxiety or stress. It's critical to reduce the number of times you accommodate your child's social anxiety and help them face stressful life situations. Partnering with your child on new things they can do to face their fears can help them develop the skills to more effectively face life challenges. This promotes long-term persistence, resilience, and confidence.

It's hard to reduce your urge to accommodate your child when you see them struggling. Your child may have intense reactions when you try to reduce accommodations. They may cry, have angry outbursts, or even display aggressive behavior. This may make you feel like a bad parent, especially if they are telling you that you are.

Following are examples of parental accommodations:

>> Letting your child avoid social activities or cancel events

>> Doing things for your child, such as ordering off a menu for them

>> Calling or texting people for your child

>> Letting them stay home from school

>> Calling the school and asking for too many accommodations

TIP

The main accommodation to try to eliminate is allowing your child to avoid situations. If you do make accommodations, make it an exception and communicate that clearly to your child. Also, you can gradually help them reduce safety behaviors and accommodations as they start doing exposures.

Providing Support as Your Child Faces Their Fears

As a parent, you can still provide helpful support for your child without accommodating. For example:

>> Discuss their social anxiety openly with them.

>> Validate and show empathy for their feelings.

>> Have realistic expectations.

>> Teach your child how to reframe negative thoughts.

>> Work on friendship skills with your child.

>> Help your child face their fears by breaking actions down into baby steps.

>> Know when to push and when to slow down.

>> Be a cheerleader for your child and praise them for their efforts.

TIP

To help your child work on their social anxiety, they have to be open to your input. Often, this is easier with younger children and can be more difficult with preteens and teens who tend to think they know it all. It can be even harder if your relationship is strained. So before commenting, develop some goodwill by doing something fun with your child or making them a special meal first. Then, they may be open to hearing what you have to say.

The Part
of Tens

Discover that even famous people have social anxiety, including fear of public speaking, imposter syndrome, agoraphobia, and more.

Explore some common social anxiety habits to break and what to do instead.

Chapter **20**

Ten Famous People with Social Anxiety

t can be hard to imagine that a celebrity who is adored by millions of fans and appears to be living a perfect life could be struggling with social anxiety. You may be wondering how someone whose job is to be in the media spotlight could have anxiety in social situations. Believe it or not, celebrities are people, too. Many famous people also have a fear of judgment and worry about what people think of them because all eyes really are on them. Like you, they know what it's like to panic, worry, or avoid social situations.

Over the past several years, more and more celebrities have spoken up about their battles with social anxiety. By opening up, celebrities are helping to end the stigma around social anxiety and prove that you can be extremely successful in spite of it. In this chapter, you discover ten celebrities you probably never knew have social anxiety, fear of public speaking, imposter syndrome, agoraphobia, and more.

Adele

Adele is one of the world's best-selling musical artists, with sales of over 120 million records worldwide. She is famous for megahits like "Rolling in the Deep" and "Someone Like You." Would you imagine that someone who has received 16 Grammy Awards, an Academy Award, a Primetime Emmy Award, and a Golden Globe Award could have social anxiety?

Adele has publicly revealed that she suffers from severe anxiety attacks that make it hard to perform in front of large audiences. She told *Rolling Stone* magazine in 2011 that she's scared of large audiences and has anxiety attacks a lot. "Once in Brussels, I projectile-vomited on someone," she said.

Adele also said that she has drawn some strength from Beyoncé, another award-winning performer. "I was about to meet Beyoncé, and I had a full-blown anxiety attack," she said. "Then she popped in looking gorgeous and said, 'You're amazing! When I listen to you, I feel like I'm listening to God.'" When Adele later found herself on a balcony, crying hysterically, she asked herself, "What would Sasha Fierce [Beyoncé's alter ego] do?" Adele pulls out a combination of Sasha Fierce and her own alter ego, Sasha Carter, whenever she needs to give herself a shot of confidence.

Barbra Streisand

Barbra Streisand is an EGOT, one of the only 19 performers in the world who has won Emmy, Grammy, Oscar, and Tony awards. Getting to EGOT status is the "grand slam" of show business. Yet even EGOTs have social anxiety.

Barbra avoided giving live performances for nearly three decades due to forgetting her lyrics at a concert in New York's Central Park in 1969. She did not return to performing until the early 1990s. In an interview with Diane Sawyer for CBS News in 2005, Barbra said, "I didn't sing and charge people for 27 years because of that night . . . I was like, 'God, I don't know. What if I forget the words again?'"

Barbra also told Sawyer about her fear of receiving negative reviews. When she got a negative review, her mind hung onto it. She took in the negative information, but the positive information bounced off her mind because it did not fit her self-perception. This is an example of the negative mental filter thinking trap described in Chapter 7. "You know, I can't remember my good reviews. I remember negative ones. They stay in my mind," she said.

In an interview with Oprah Winfrey in 2006, Barbra talked about using medication to help with her social anxiety: "One reason I can perform now is that they have pills for stage fright. I wish somebody had told me about these pills years ago."

Donny Osmond

Donny Osmond was one of the biggest heartthrobs of the 1970s. He was a pinup for teenagers across America. He and his sister performed weekly on the *Donny & Marie* show, where they performed their hit songs "Puppy Love," "Go Away Little Girl," and "A Little Bit Country."

In the public eye from age eight, Donny experienced the pressure of performing and being constantly judged. He eventually developed social anxiety disorder and panic disorder in his preteen years. His underlying worries were the pressure to be perfect and the fear of judgment. In a 2000 interview on CBS's *48 Hours,* Donny explained that there were times when if he had the choice of going out onto stage or dying, he would have chosen death. He was that afraid of making a mistake.

With the help of his therapist, Donny did three days of intensive cognitive restructuring and exposure therapy. Donny said, "I know when I walk out there, I'm not going to give the best performance. I'll make a mistake. I'll trip. I'll do something stupid. But it's okay; you pick up and just move on."

To help others with social anxiety and reduce the shame and isolation of the disorder, Donny has been an honorary director of the Anxiety and Depression Association of America (ADAA) since 2004.

Ed Sheeran

Ed Sheeran is one of the most popular singer-songwriters today with hit songs like "Bad Habits," "Eyes Closed," "Shape of You," and more. Ed is one of the world's bestselling music artists having sold over 150 million records worldwide, yet he too is afflicted with social anxiety.

Ed has come out as living with "crippling social anxiety" and struggling when meeting large groups of people. In a 2019 interview with iHeartRadio, Ed described the issue as "ironic" because he plays to large audiences on tour. He said the contradiction makes him feel "claustrophobic" because he does not like being around too many people. Ed said he has no problem having a conversation. He said, "It's just when people film me . . . and just stare at me. It makes me feel weird because it makes me feel like I'm not human."

Eva Longoria

Eva Longoria is an actress, model, director, producer, and businessperson. In addition to starring in movies and soap operas, she became a household name playing the character of Gabrielle Solis in the comedy-drama *Desperate Housewives*. More recently, she has been hosting her own show called *Eva Longoria: Searching for Mexico*.

In an interview with E! News in 2023, Eva revealed her ongoing struggle with social anxiety and imposter syndrome. She said that when she gets ready for the red carpet, she always has to "mentally prepare for a very long night. I get social anxiety. I have so many friends in the business, but I still go, 'There's going to be big stars there.' There's still that anxiety of, 'Do I belong?'"

Julia Roberts

Julia Roberts is one of the top actresses in the acting field. She won an Oscar for Best Actress and was also nominated many times for Oscars for her acting performances. According to The Stuttering Foundation, Julia and her brother, Eric, both struggled with stuttering. The foundation said this highlights the heredity/genetic link in stuttering.

Julia has not spoken out much about her stuttering and how it led to a fear of public speaking. HuffPost reported in 2015 that in interviews, Julia has confided that she overcame her stuttering problem through speech therapy and that achieving fluid speech helped her gain confidence as a public speaker.

HuffPost also reported that Julia's role as a professor of public speaking in the 2011 movie *Larry Crowne* brought her back to her own struggles with fluid speech. She said she was terrified of the teaching scenes. "All these faces looking up at me, thinking, What is she going to teach us? I needed to find my composure. It was very hard — it was terrible, in fact."

Kim Basinger

Kim Basinger is famous for her many movie roles, including playing a Bond girl in *Never Say Never Again* and films such as *The Natural* and *9½ Weeks*. Kim has won an Academy Award for her work in *L.A. Confidential* and has a star on the Hollywood Walk of Fame. Would you think someone like Kim Basinger could possibly have social anxiety?

Kim discussed her social anxiety, panic attacks, and agoraphobia in a 1991 episode of HBO's *America Undercover* series called

"Panic: A Film About Coping." She said, "When I came to Hollywood, I could wear a bikini, but I was in misery because people were looking at me. So I wore baggy clothes and watched other girls get the big parts and awards. I used to go home and play piano and scream at night to let out my frustrations."

Kim was so withdrawn as a child that her parents had her tested for autism. Growing up, her worst fear was reading aloud in class, to the point that teachers believed she was having a nervous breakdown. She would lie and make up excuses at school so she could be sent home. When Kim accepted her Oscar for her role in LA Confidential, she struggled to find her words despite rehearsing her speech for days.

Kim's battle with social anxiety eventually developed into agoraphobia. In 2022, in her first interview in 14 years with Red Table Talk, Kim opened up about her struggle with agoraphobia. Kim said she wouldn't leave the house and would no longer go out to dinner. She credits her daughter for being "a great teacher and a great healer." This shows the importance of social support to help heal anxiety.

Naomi Osaka

Naomi Osaka is a professional tennis player and was ranked number one in singles by the Women's Tennis Association. She is a four-time Grand Slam singles champion and has won more titles than you can imagine. Naomi made headlines in 2021 when she withdrew from the French Open due to her struggles with depression and social anxiety and her decision to prioritize her mental health. With a misunderstanding of social anxiety, the French Open had the gall to fine her $15,000 and threatened more.

In a May 31, 2021, post on X (formerly Twitter), Naomi said she had "suffered long bouts of depression since the U.S. Open in 2018 and had a really hard time coping with that. . . . anyone that has seen me at tournaments will notice that I'm often wearing headphones as that helps dull my social anxiety." She also noted that her social anxiety is particularly bad when speaking to crowds at press conferences and that she is not a natural public speaker. She says gets really nervous and finds it difficult to always be engaging.

Shonda Rhimes

Shonda Rhimes is an award-winning writer and television producer with a career that spans over 20 years. Her hit series include *Grey's Anatomy, Scandal, How To Get Away With Murder,* and the Netflix hit *Bridgerton.* Shonda's social anxiety was so disabling that it kept her from enjoying crucial moments of her life. For example, when interviewed by Oprah Winfrey, her fear that she would make a mistake prevented her from remembering much of what took place. I am sure you can relate to this one!

In her 2015 memoir, *Shonda Rhimes: My Year of Saying Yes to Everything,* she wrote about how her social anxiety was so overwhelming that she would always say no to events or speaking engagements. When she realized that her first instinct was to say no, she decided to start saying yes to more things.

You can think of her experiment with saying yes as a form of exposure therapy. Shondra forced herself to do the things she feared. Shonda said shortly after her experiments of saying yes, she gave the commencement address at her alma mater. She said it was terrifying, but she did it. And once she pushed through, it became easier and she actually started to enjoy herself.

Warren Buffett

Warren Buffet is the one of the world's greatest investors. Now in his 90s, he has a net worth in the hundreds of billions of dollars yet he suffered from public-speaking anxiety as a young man. Warren has publicly shared his journey to overcoming public speaking anxiety in a 2017 HBO documentary titled *Becoming Warren Buffett* that chronicled his life as well as in numerous books and essays.

Until the age of 20, Warren had a fear of public speaking. He said just the thought of it made him physically ill and caused him to throw up. Warren said he worked through his fears by attending a Dale Carnegie course. When the course was over, Warren started teaching as a professor. He said he knew that if he didn't speak in front of people quickly, he would lapse right back to where he started. Warren said if you have a fear of associating with people, you have to go out there and do it, even if it's painful. Warren still proudly shows off his Dale Carnegie public-speaking certificate, which he received on January 13, 1952.

Chapter **21**

Ten Social Anxiety Habits to Break

When you have social anxiety, it is important not to get into bad habits like avoidance, reassurance-seeking, practicing ineffective self-talk, or people-pleasing. While these behaviors may provide short-term relief, they do not help you overcome social anxiety. In this chapter, you explore some common social anxiety habits to break and what to do instead.

Avoiding Your Fears

Avoidance is the number one behavior that perpetuates social anxiety. You may engage in complete avoidance of social inter-actions and situations. But it's more common to have partial avoidance by engaging in safety behaviors to help you cope with your uncomfortable feelings. However, avoidance doesn't help reduce social anxiety over the long term because you never learn that what you are thinking about the situation may not in fact be true or that you can handle social situations if your fear does happen.

TIP

Ways to stop avoiding your fears:

>> Come up with something you want to do and create a plan that includes baby steps to help you accomplish it.

>> Use motivating self-talk to help you approach your fears.

>> Celebrate success after every small accomplishment.

Asking for Reassurance

You are reassurance-seeking when you ask others what they think, hoping they will tell you that things are okay. You may have an excessive reliance on others for comfort and support. With social anxiety, you may be uncertain about how you acted in a social interaction and ask someone else for their opinion about what you said or did. You may spend excessive time asking friends or family how you look before engaging in a social situation. You get temporary relief, but you can never really take it in or learn to handle your feelings of social anxiety on your own. We all need social support, and reassurance is part of that. It's only a problem when you become too dependent on reassurance from others.

TIP

Ways to stop asking for unnecessary reassurance:

>> Learn to soothe your own emotions.

>> Get comfortable with uncertainty.

>> Ask yourself whether the answer is within you already.

>> If you must ask for reassurance, make sure it's only once.

Using Empty Mantras

A mantra is a few words or phrases you say to yourself to make yourself feel more confident. On an old episode of the sketch comedy show *Saturday Night Live*, the character Stuart Smalley told himself, "I'm good enough, I'm smart enough, and doggone it, people like me." While it makes sense to say kind things to yourself, there needs to be substance behind the words. When you say things you don't actually believe, your mantra can backfire, and you may find you're actually telling yourself the opposite in disguise.

TIP

Ways to stop using empty mantras:

>> Find positives that are true, believable, and have depth.

>> Use the CALM thinking skills to develop self-talk that is compassionate, accepting, logical, and motivating.

>> Don't repeat affirmations mindlessly.

Drinking Too Much Alcohol

A strong correlation exists between alcohol abuse and social anxiety. Alcohol can reduce feelings of social anxiety in the short run, but it may increase anxiety, irritability, and depression as the effects of the alcohol wear off. In addition, you may end up doing things you regret when you are under the influence and ruminate the next day about having acted foolishly.

TIP

Ways to stop drinking too much when you feel anxious at social events:

>> Commit to limit alcohol to just one or two drinks.

>> Hold a glass of sparkling water to keep your hands busy.

>> Challenge yourself to try not to drink at all and face your social fears.

Hiding Your Anxiety

You may fear people noticing your social anxiety so much that you try to hide it. You may believe that people would look down on you if they knew you had social anxiety. As a result, you may try to hide any signs of anxiety from being visible to others. You may try to hide such signs of anxiety as sweating, having a shaky voice, or blushing by doing things to compensate for these reactions or avoiding situations where these reactions could happen.

TIP

Ways to stop hiding your anxiety:

>> Recognize that people are probably not focusing on you as much as you think they are.

>> Design an experiment where you allow yourself to have anxiety symptoms and see if people notice.

>> Shift your focus away from what people might be thinking and focus on what you want from the interaction. Ironically, you may have fewer bodily sensations when you focus outward.

Pretending to Be Confident

Fake it 'til you make it may work for socially confident people, but this tactic seldom works with social anxiety. In fact, "faking it" could even make you feel worse. You may be told to just act as if you aren't shy, nervous, or anxious. If you could do this, you'd already be doing it.

TIP

Ways to stop pretending to be confident:

>> Acknowledge your feelings of social anxiety to yourself and possibly to others.

>> Be accepting of who you are and be okay with not being the most outgoing person.

>> Don't feel pressure to be someone you aren't.

Keeping People at a Distance

If you have social anxiety or an avoidant personality, you are not anti-social. You generally want to have friends and a social life. If you are an introvert, you may not desire a lot of friends or to go partying too often, but you want close relationships. However, you may keep people at a distance or entirely avoid people to keep yourself safe because social situations are stressful for you.

TIP

Ways to stop keeping people at a distance:

>> Accept invitations to do things with people.

>> Take small steps to build connections.

>> Find friends and acquaintances through hobbies and interests.

Trying to Be Perfect

Social anxiety can increase feelings of perfectionism because its root cause is a fear of judgment or disapproval. Excessive self-consciousness can drive perfectionism. As a perfectionist, you constantly try to prove your worth to yourself and others. You have unrealistically high standards, you focus on results instead of the journey, and you motivate yourself with harsh language. You become afraid of making mistakes and can't forgive yourself for even honest mistakes. You may set unrealistically high standards for social interactions and become self-critical when you can't meet them. These behaviors can lead you to become demotivated and avoid doing things or interacting socially because trying to achieve your standards is exhausting.

TIP

Ways to stop trying to be perfect:

>> Set realistic goals for your social performance.

>> Allow yourself to make mistakes and learn from them.

>> Focus on the bigger picture and avoid all-or-nothing thinking.

Being Passive

When you are passive, you may hide your feelings from others and not speak up when it is appropriate to do so. You may not take action and instead let things happen to you. You may avoid clearly expressing your views or speak quietly or apologetically. Being passive can result from your social anxiety and worry about what others will think of you if you share your opinions or speak up for your needs.

TIP

Ways to stop being passive:

>> Practice giving your opinion.

>> Pay attention to what you are feeling, thinking, and wanting.

>> Ask for things you want or need.

>> Be aware of your language and practice speaking assertively.

Being a People Pleaser

As a people pleaser, you have a strong urge to please others, even at your own expense. You may alter your personality around others and not have a strong sense of self. The root cause of people pleasing is insecurity and low self-esteem. You may be perceived as one of the nicest people around because you are helpful and kind, which increases your self-worth. However, you may end up with imposter syndrome because you are in per-formance mode for others, and you don't feel authentic.

TIP

Ways to stop trying to be a people pleaser:

>> Try to figure out your own interests and passions.

>> Don't be afraid to say no, and remember that you don't always have to be "nice."

>> Recognize that rejection is a normal part of life.

Index

D

dating anxiety
  changing mindset
    self-talk, 266–267
    thinking traps, 264–265
  exposure therapy for
    debriefing after, 273–274
    during exposures, 273
    fear ladder, 270–271
    overview, 267–268
    pre-exposure plan, 272–273
    repeating exposures, 275
    safety behaviors, 269–270
    target list, 268–269
  identifying anxiety inducing situations, 263
  negative patterns linked to
    avoidance, 275
    catastrophizing, 276
    inner critic, 275–276
    rumination, 276
  overview, 261–263
  thinking traps, 127–128
DBT (dialectical behavior therapy), 217, 236
decatastrophizing
  creating distance from your thoughts, 172
  by imagined coping, 170–171
  noticing strengths, 173
  perspective-taking, 171–172
  by rating possible outcomes, 169–170
deep breathing, 229–230
defectiveness schema, 46–47
demanding critic, 163
depression, 30–32
derealization, 73
Diagnostic and Statistical Manual of Mental Disorders, Fifth Edition (DSM-5), 24, 27–28, 247
dialectical behavior therapy (DBT), 217, 236
diary
  of exposures, 189
  as tool to reinforce positive self-talk, 173
diet, healthy, 228–229
distancing yourself from others, 331. *See also* avoidance

distraction, using to avoid feelings, 87
downward arrow technique, identifying core beliefs, 136–138
DSM-5 (*Diagnostic and Statistical Manual of Mental Disorders, Fifth Edition*), 24, 27–28, 247
Dweck, Carol S., 149

E

eating well, 228–229
EISS (External and Internal Shame Scale), 103
email, writing, 61–62
embracing your social anxiety
  acceptance
    defined, 216
    giving up vs., 216–217
    overview, 215
    strategies for, 217
  loving-kindness meditation, 221–222
  mindfulness
    formal, 219
    informal, 218–219
    meditation vs., 218, 220
    overview, 217–218
  self-compassion, 220
  values
    identifying, 211–214
    values list, 215
emotional constriction schema, 47–48
emotional deprivation schema, 48–49
emotional needs
  autonomy, 41
  competence, 41–42
  freedom of expression, 42–43
  limits and self-control, 42
  secure attachment, 40–41
  spontaneity and play, 43
emotional reasoning, 116–117
engaged life, 196–197
esteem needs, 39
excessive checking, 87–88
executive presence, 281
exercise, 227–228

About the Author

Laura Johnson, LMFT, LPCC, is a specialist in cognitive behavior therapy for social anxiety. She's worked extensively with adults and children with social anxiety, avoidant personality, and selective mutism along with other anxiety disorders. Laura's approach focuses on positive, strength-based counseling. She has a passion for her work as a cognitive behavior therapist and schema therapist to help her clients make lasting changes in their lives.

Laura is one of the few therapists who is both a Certified Cognitive Therapist with the Academy of Cognitive Therapy and an Advanced Certified Schema Therapist with the International Society of Schema Therapy. Laura has been a long-standing clinic member of the National Social Anxiety Center. She has a bachelor's degree from the University of Miami and a master's degrees from both Santa Clara University and Columbia University.

Dedication

This book is dedicated to my husband and two daughters. Thank you for allowing me to have the time to write this book and for your love and support throughout the process.

Author's Acknowledgments

I'd like to thank my editors, who have spent numerous hours reading my book chapters and providing me with feedback. Great thanks to Katharine Dvorak at Wiley for being my primary editor. A big shout out to Katy Manetta at Belmont Psychological Services in Long Beach, California, for her technical input on social anxiety. I'd also like to recognize Tara Cutland Green of Schema Therapy Associates in the United Kingdom for providing technical input on the schemas. I am indebted to Jennifer Yee at Wiley for discovering me and asking me to write this book. This couldn't have become a true *For Dummies* book without my cats and dogs sitting with me while I was writing.

Publisher's Acknowledgments

Senior Editor: Jennifer Yee

Senior Managing Editor:
Kristie Pyles

Project Editor: Katharine Dvorak

Technical Editor:
Katy Manetta, PhD

Production Editor:
SaiKarthick Kumarasamy

Cover Image:
© gece33/Getty Images

Take dummies with you everywhere you go!

Whether you are excited about e-books, want more from the web, must have your mobile apps, or are swept up in social media, dummies makes everything easier.

Find us online!

dummies.com

Leverage the power

Dummies is the global leader in the reference category and one of the most trusted and highly regarded brands in the world. No longer just focused on books, customers now have access to the dummies content they need in the format they want. Together we'll craft a solution that engages your customers, stands out from the competition, and helps you meet your goals.

Advertising & Sponsorships

Connect with an engaged audience on a powerful multimedia site, and position your message alongside expert how-to content. Dummies.com is a one-stop shop for free, online information and know-how curated by a team of experts.

- Targeted ads
- Video
- Email Marketing
- Microsites
- Sweepstakes sponsorship

20 **MILLION** PAGE VIEWS EVERY SINGLE MONTH

15 MILLION **UNIQUE** VISITORS PER MONTH

43% OF ALL VISITORS ACCESS THE SITE VIA THEIR MOBILE DEVICES

700,000 NEWSLETTE SUBSCRIPTIO TO THE INBOXES OF

300,000 UNIQUE INDIVIDUALS EVERY WEEK

# of dummies

Custom Publishing

Reach a global audience in any language by creating a solution that will differentiate you from competitors, amplify your message, and encourage customers to make a buying decision.

- Apps
- Books
- eBooks
- Video
- Audio
- Webinars

Brand Licensing & Content

Leverage the strength of the world's most popular reference brand to reach new audiences and channels of distribution.

For more information, visit **dummies.com/biz**

PERSONAL ENRICHMENT

9781119187790	9781119179030	9781119293354	9781119293347	9781119310068	9781119235606
USA $26.00	USA $21.99	USA $24.99	USA $22.99	USA $22.99	USA $24.99
CAN $31.99	CAN $25.99	CAN $29.99	CAN $27.99	CAN $27.99	CAN $29.99
UK £19.99	UK £16.99	UK £17.99	UK £16.99	UK £16.99	UK £17.99

9781119251163	9781119235491	9781119279952	9781119283133	9781119287117	9781119130246
USA $24.99	USA $26.99	USA $24.99	USA $24.99	USA $24.99	USA $22.99
CAN $29.99	CAN $31.99	CAN $29.99	CAN $29.99	CAN $29.99	CAN $27.99
UK £17.99	UK £19.99	UK £17.99	UK £17.99	UK £16.99	UK £16.99

PROFESSIONAL DEVELOPMENT

9781119311041	9781119255796	9781119293439	9781119281467	9781119280651	9781119251132	9781119311056
USA $24.99	USA $39.99	USA $26.99	USA $26.99	USA $29.99	USA $24.99	USA $34.00
CAN $29.99	CAN $47.99	CAN $31.99	CAN $31.99	CAN $35.99	CAN $29.99	CAN $41.99
UK £17.99	UK £27.99	UK £19.99	UK £19.99	UK £21.99	UK £17.99	UK £24.99

9781119181705	9781119263593	9781119257769	9781119293477	9781119265313	9781119239314	9781119293323
USA $29.99	USA $26.99	USA $29.99	USA $26.99	USA $24.99	USA $29.99	USA $29.99
CAN $35.99	CAN $31.99	CAN $35.99	CAN $31.99	CAN $29.99	CAN $35.99	CAN $35.99
UK £21.99	UK £19.99	UK £21.99	UK £19.99	UK £17.99	UK £21.99	UK £21.99

dummies
A Wiley Brand